The Horse

The Horse

A Miscellany of Equine Knowledge

Julie Whitaker
with **Ian Whitelaw**

THOMAS DUNNE BOOKS
St. Martin's Press ⌘ New York

To Amelia and Gabriel

THOMAS DUNNE BOOKS.

An imprint of St. Martin's Press.

www.thomasdunnebooks.com
www.stmartins.com

ISBN 10: 0-312-37108-X
ISBN 13: 978-312-37108-1

A CIP catalog record for this book is available
from the Library of Congress

First U.S. Edition: May 2007

This book was conceived, designed, and produced by
Ivy Press
The Old Candlemakers
West Street
Lewes, East Sussex
BN7 2NZ, U.K.
www.ivy-group.co.uk

Creative Director Peter Bridgewater
Publisher Jason Hook
Editorial Director Caroline Earle
Art Director Sarah Howerd
Senior Project Editor Stephanie Evans
Project Designer Joanna Clinch
Designer Ginny Zeal
Illustrators David Ashby, Ivan Hissey, John Woodcock
Picture Researcher Shelley Noronha

Printed in Thailand

Contents

B ORN INTO A non-horsey family, I seem to have been stricken by horse fever at a very early age. In my youth, all I cared about were horse toys, horse pictures, and, before long, horse books. I have learned a great deal from a large variety of horse books over my long life with horses, and I have often written about how important I consider reading and studying to be for riders and horse enthusiasts from every discipline.

Foreword

One book I didn't have in my childhood horse library was a proper miscellany, and how I would have loved the present one! Although the concept of a miscellany—a mixture of various things—sounds slightly old fashioned, the form of the present volume perfectly suits its content, enabling it to be both wonderfully broad in scope, yet concise and succinct. It strikes a neat balance between illustration and text, and is both factually informative and entertaining to read. This makes for an ideal browsing book that can be as readily dipped into or consulted as read from cover to cover. It will suggest many new avenues for the average horse-oriented reader to explore, for, after all, you cannot know what areas you may wish to learn more about until you know that they exist.

That is why a miscellany such as this comes as such a pleasant surprise in this era of intensive specialization. It can serve as an excellent starting point for many readers, providing both an historical and a geographical perspective for the whole range of equestrian activities, and showing where the horse fits and has fitted into the scheme of things through the ages. In other

words, it provides an admirable overview of the varied content within its purview. This is important, coming at a time when many horse people may know a great deal about their own particular discipline, activity, or area of interest, but have very little general knowledge of horses.

There is another aspect to this. The horse culture is very democratic, but it is also quite particular. One can enter it through many different portals, but if you fail to acquire its language—a good horse vocabulary and a wide frame of reference—some people will never be able to take you seriously. Having a broad general knowledge of horses will enable you to "talk horse" with horse people from any discipline and of every generation.

The electronic revolution has certainly changed the basic character of the horseman's information-retrieval mechanism. Today's plethora of how-to books on every conceivable form of equestrian training, riding, driving, and competition must compete with the extensive instructional material that has become available in magazines, on video tape or DVDs, and on the Internet, which has become an inexhaustible resource. None of these can provide,

Foreword

however, the instant accessibility that a book collection affords.

For all of the reasons touched upon above, I strongly urge horse enthusiasts of every age and every persuasion to supplement their horse activities by creating and cultivating a substantial horse-book library and trust that they will find a place in it for a good miscellany or two. Because the subject of horses in all its ramifications has become so vast, the task of putting together a valid and useful miscellany based on horses has become an especially daunting one. Horse enthusiasts should be grateful that the co-authors of the present compendium have taken on and executed this challenge with such energy, skill, and judgment. I am confident that the product of their labors will find a place on the shelves of horse devotees of many different generations and equestrian interests, who will derive both edification and pleasure from perusing it. I can only hope that they enjoy traversing the following pages as much as I have done.

WILLIAM STEINKRAUS

The Origins of the Horse

The earliest member of the horse family, the enchantingly named "dawn horse," or "Eohippus," dates back to the Eocene period, 55 million years ago. From that time right up to the present, we are fortunate to have an almost complete record of the evolution of the horse and its near relatives. Indeed, the fossil evidence of the *Equidae* is so good that scientists have been able to piece together a more accurate picture of the evolutionary lineage of the horse than of any other mammal.

The Early Discoveries

American paleontologist Othniel Charles Marsh (1831–1899) made an important series of *Equidae* fossil finds in the latter half of the nineteenth century. Indeed, so complete and vital were his finds that they helped to establish Charles Darwin's theory of evolution by means of natural selection. Until that time, there had been no empirical evidence to support Darwin's theory that animals evolved in response to a changing environment— as expounded in his *Origin of the Species by Means of Natural Selection* (1859)—and Darwin's work had not been widely accepted.

Importance of the Toe Bones

Marsh, the first professor of paleontology in the USA and only the second in the world, discovered many of his important fossils in Nebraska, Wyoming, and in the Dakotas. By looking primarily at the metacarpal, or toe, bones of his finds, Marsh determined a clear line of equine descent. The earlier specimens had four digits: metacarpals II through V. He discovered that the later the specimen, the shorter the metacarpal bones II, IV, and V, and the greater the weight borne by the third metacarpal. Marsh studied the bones of modern horses and found remnants of II and IV along the cannon bone of each leg. Examination of the forearms, legs, and teeth also supported Marsh's theory of horse evolution. The more recent the skeleton, the stronger the horse's forearms and legs, which presumably developed in response to the horse becoming faster and larger.

The Equidae Family

Horses and other equids— including zebras and asses— belong to the Order *Perissodactyla*, a name derived from Greek, meaning "odd-numbered finger or toe." Perissodactyls are odd-toed ungulates—hoofed mammals—that bear their weight on a central toe, a group that also includes tapirs and rhinos. Members of this order are herbivores, have mobile upper lips, and share a similar tooth structure designed for chewing plant material. The perissodactyls originated in the late Paleocene (65–56 million years ago) less than 10 million years after the demise of the dinosaurs.

Evolution of the Teeth

The teeth demonstrated a progression from browsing teeth to those of a grazing animal. Marsh's fossils supported Darwin's idea of natural selection and the survival of the fittest, showing that larger and faster horses were better able to survive than their smaller three- or four-toed ancestors. Marsh's equine fossil collection gave considerable impetus to Darwin's theories, which were soon being taken seriously by the scientific world and the general public alike.

Evolution of the Hoof

The first horses were browsers that lived in swampy-forest conditions. They had four toes on their front feet,

Foot of Eohippus
Eohippus had four toes on its front legs, three on the hind limbs, which were supported by a thick pad, similar to that of a dog.

Foot of Mesohippus
The number of toes on the forelimbs is now reduced to three, and the central toe— the third metacarpal—is more prominent than the outer toes.

Foot of Merychippus
At up to 36 inches (90 centimeters) in height, Merychippus was much larger than its ancestors. The middle toe increasingly bears more weight, and the outer toes are clearly becoming vestigial.

Foot of Pliohippus
As the first single-hoofed horse, Pliohippus was the prototype of the modern horse. The horse's weight is now completely borne by the middle toe.

Foot of Equus, the modern horse
The cannon bone is longer and stronger and there is no external sign of the vestigial toes. Side ligaments prevent the hoof from twisting.

which prevented them sinking in the soft earth. Over millions of years, grasslands began to replace the primeval forests, the equid diet shifted to grasses, and the horse became a grazing mammal. This new, more open, environment put a premium on speed, and over time the horse developed longer limbs with fewer toes that enabled it to move quickly over a large area in search of pasture and also to avoid predators.

Did You Know?

Foals are occasionally born with three toes, each equipped with hooves. This phenomenon is known as a phylogenetic atavism, an evolutionary throwback involving the reappearance of primitive characteristics.

Hyracotherium

Hyracotherium—also known as "Eohippus," or the "dawn horse"—is the earliest known member of the horse family, first appearing some 55 million years ago. A nearly complete skeleton of this little equid was found in 1867 in Eocene rock formations in Wyoming. This first horse is believed to have thrived over a large area of North America, and remains have also been found in Europe and Asia. *Hyracotherium* was a forest-dwelling herbivore that browsed on fruit, soft leaves, and plant shoots.

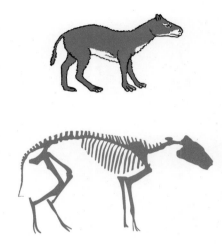

Hyracotherium is the earliest known equine, living some 55 million years ago.

A Dog-like Horse

Hyracotherium has been described as looking more like a small dog than a horse, with a relatively short head and neck, an arched back, and a long tail. *Hyracotherium*'s brain was small, with especially poorly developed frontal lobes. It stood between ten and 17 inches (25 and 45 centimeters) high at the shoulders, averaged two feet (60 centimeters) in length, and weighed approximately 12 pounds (5.5 kilograms). The limbs showed an early adaptation to speed, being long relative to its body. The major limb bones were unfused, leaving them flexible and able to rotate. There were four toes on the front feet and three on the hind, and the feet were padded. Each toe terminated in a small "hoof" rather than a claw.

This primitive horse possessed 44 low-crowned teeth typical of an omnivorous browser: three incisors, one canine, four premolars, and three "grinding molars" located on each side of the jaw.

The Eocene Equids

The Eocene equids survived largely unchanged for about 20 million years. The most notable evolutionary changes occurred in the teeth, as evident in the fossil remains of *Orohippus* and *Epihippus*, close relatives of *Hyracotherium*. As the environment changed, there was less fruit and foliage available, and these early horses began to develop better grinding teeth to cope with the tougher plant material that now made up the bulk of their diet.

Mesohippus and Miohippus

A recognizably different form of equid emerged in the early Oligocene, about 34 million years ago. *Mesohippus*, meaning "middle horse," was larger than its Eocene ancestors, measuring 24 inches (60 centimeters) at the shoulder. Its face, snout, and neck were longer, and its back less arched. The *Mesohippus* brain was significantly

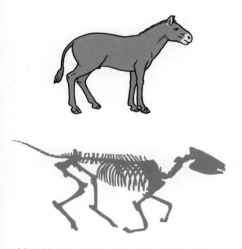

Mesohippus, *which evolved some 34 million years ago, was less dog-like in appearance than* Hyracotherium.

During the early Oligocene epoch, a split occurred in the *Mesohippus* population, with one group evolving into the *Miohippus* genus. It is believed that this genus coexisted with *Mesohippus* for around 4 million years, but over time came to replace *Mesohippus. Miohippus* was larger than *Mesohippus* and had a longer skull. The upper cheek teeth showed a variable extra crest, a characteristic feature of later equids. The ankle joint also differed from that of *Mesohippus*.

Mesohippus became extinct in the mid Oligocene (28 to 25 million years ago) while *Miohippus* evolved into two major groups in the early Miocene.

larger and distinctly equine. Each side of the jaw had six grinding "cheek teeth" with a single premolar in front, similar to the modern horse. *Mesohippus* had longer, slimmer legs, better suited to escaping predators. The less swampy environment meant that *Mesohippus* no longer needed as many toes to prevent it sinking in soft mud, and the front limbs only had three toes on each foot, although the three hind toes remained. The middle toe was now more prominent and capable of bearing more weight.

Miohippus *evolved from* Mesohippus. *It was larger and had a longer skull than* Mesohippus.

Did You Know?

Although the 1867 fossil find in Wyoming is the first complete specimen of Eohippus, remains of the little dawn horse had, in fact, been found in Europe some 20 years earlier by an English paleontologist, Richard Owen (1804–92). Owen incorrectly identified his partial specimen as belonging to Hyrax, *a genus of rabbit-like mammals, and named it* Hyracotherium, *or "hyrax-like beast." Although this find was eventually identified as belonging to the* Equidae, *scientific decorum dictates that* Hyracotherium, *as the first published name, remains the official title of the animal, and Eohippus is considered a synonym, hence it is written without italics.*

The Miocene Equids

The early Miocene (24 million years ago) heralded a rapid diversification of equine species, and the horse began to split into at least two main evolutionary lines. There is also evidence of a line of pygmy horses, which included the *Archeohippus*. However, these horses did not survive long and played no further part in the ancestry of the modern horse. One very successful line, the anchitheres, were three-toed browsers that spread into the Old World and thrived for tens of millions of years. Genera include *Anchitherium*, *Hypohippus*, and *Megahippus*. The third line evolved to become efficient grassland grazers. This line included *Kalobatippus*, *Parahippus*, and, most notably, *Merychippus*.

Merychippus

Merychippus evolved on the North American plains in the mid Miocene, some 17 million years ago. It probably moved in herds and was a forerunner to the grazing horse of today. At around ten hands high (40 inches; 102 centimeters), *Merychippus* was the largest equine yet, and it looked distinctly more like a modern-day horse. It also had a much larger brain than its equid predecessors, making it more intelligent. *Merychippus* had stronger and wider molars, capable of chewing on the strong plains grasses. It still had three toes, but increasingly the weight was supported by an enlarged single hoof on the central metacarpal, so that the horse moved on tiptoe. The legs were elongated, the ulna and radius in the forearm were fused, so eliminating leg rotation, and the fibula was reduced in length. These changes made *Merychippus* capable of swift movement over hard ground.

The Miocene equid Merychippus *was more "horsey" in appearance than its predecessors.*

Evolution of Equus

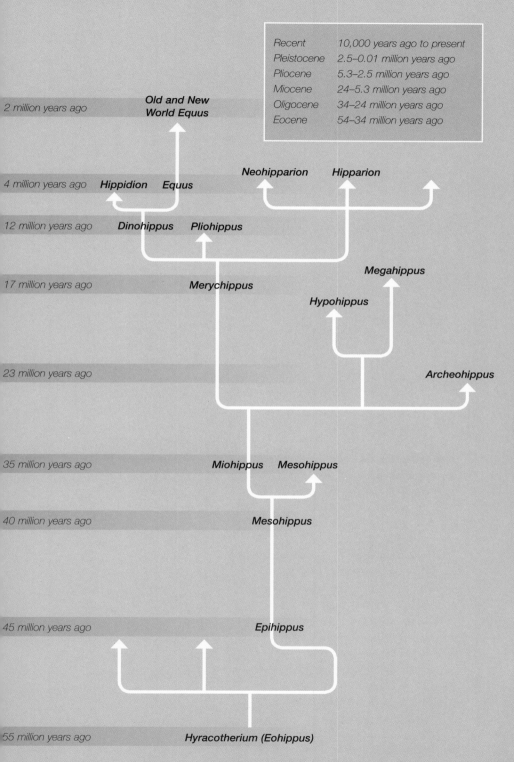

Recent	10,000 years ago to present
Pleistocene	2.5–0.01 million years ago
Pliocene	5.3–2.5 million years ago
Miocene	24–5.3 million years ago
Oligocene	34–24 million years ago
Eocene	54–34 million years ago

2 million years ago — Old and New World Equus

4 million years ago — Hippidion Equus Neohipparion Hipparion

12 million years ago — Dinohippus Pliohippus

17 million years ago — Merychippus

Megahippus

Hypohippus

23 million years ago — Archeohippus

35 million years ago — Miohippus Mesohippus

40 million years ago — Mesohippus

45 million years ago — Epihippus

55 million years ago — Hyracotherium (Eohippus)

17

Diversification of the Horse Family

Often referred to as the "Merychippine Radiation," the Miocene saw a burst of evolutionary activity that resulted in more species and genera of the horse family than ever before or since. Three new major horse groups are believed to have developed from the different varieties of *Merychippus*—hipparions, protohippines, and "true equines."

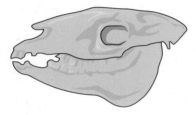

Merychippus *had the appearance of the horse as we know it. It had a long face and high-crowned cheek teeth. It is the first known horse grazer.*

The Hipparions and Protohippines

The hipparions were the size of a small pony. They had three-toed hooves, but the outer toes did not touch the ground. They developed large and elaborate facial fossae—depressions in the facial bones. The hipparions were the most different from *Merychippus*, and recent research suggests that they may be an ancestor of the zebra and the donkey rather than the horse. The protohippines include *Protohippus* and *Calippus*, and they were much smaller animals than the other two equid groups. The true equines probably arose out of the later merychippine species, such as *M. carrizoensis*. These merychippines were large and had small side toes. It is thought that they gave rise to at least two groups of one-toed horses.

Pliohippus

Pliohippus, which appeared around 12 million years ago, in the mid Miocene, was once believed to be the ancestor of the modern horse because of its many anatomical similarities. It had long slender legs, designed for speed, and is considered the first true monodactyl—one-toed animal—in evolutionary history. It did, in fact, have the remnants of outside toes, but these were visible only as callused stubs. Certain anatomical differences, however, such as its strongly curved teeth and deep facial fossae, suggest that it is an evolutionary sideline to *Equus* that probably gave rise to *Astrohippus*, another one-toed horse.

Did You Know?

Some 8,000 years ago, the horse became extinct on the North American continent. No one knows for sure why this occurred, although it may have been the result of severe changes in climate. For the first time in millions of years, there were no equids in the New World. The horse was reintroduced to the Americas by the Spanish conquistadores in the sixteenth century, when Hernando Cortez landed in Mexico.

Dinohippus

Researchers now believe that the most likely candidate for the ancestor of the modern horse is *Dinohippus*. The earliest known species are *D. spectans*, *D. interpolatus*, and *D. leidyanus*. *Dinohippus* had less curved teeth and smaller facial fossae than *Pliohippus*. A later specimen, *D. mexicanus*, showed even straighter teeth and even smaller fossae. In the late Pliocene, *Dinohippus* was the most common horse in North America, and it is almost certain that this equid evolved into *Equus* approximately four million years ago.

Tapirs—along with rhinoceroses, the other odd-toed ungulates—are the closest living relatives of the horse.

Fossil remains of Dinohippus *reveal closer similarities to the skull of the modern horse than any previous equids, making* Dinohippus *a likely ancestor to* Equus.

Equus

The first members of the *Equus* genera were the size of a medium pony (around 13.2 hands). They displayed high-crowned, straight grazing teeth, a rigid spine, long neck, long legs, fused leg bones, long nose, flexible muzzle, and a deep jaw—all traits found in the modern horse. Fossil evidence suggests that they diversified into four different groups, comprising at least 12 species. These species coexisted with other one-toed horses, such as *Astrohippus*, as well as the hipparions and protohippines.

The Spread of Equus

The late Pliocene saw the spread of the *Equus* genus from North America over the land bridges to Asia, South America, Europe, and Africa. In Africa, evolution led to the modern zebras, while Asia, the Middle East, and North Africa saw the emergence of onagers and asses.

Before the last ice age, land bridges connected North America with other parts of the world, and allowed the spread of the equine species.

Environmental Adaptation

Later in the fossil record, the remains of four distinct horse groups are found. The exact lines of descent that link them to the ancestors that left North America are unclear, but they evidently adapted to the environments in which they lived. The four types are: the Forest Horse, the Asiatic Wild Horse, the Tarpan, and the Tundra Horse.

The Forest Horse

The Forest Horse—*Equus ferus silvaticus*, also known as the Diluvial—was heavily built, stood 15 hands high, and had a thick, coarse coat. Its sturdy legs and large feet made it suitable for the marshy terrain of Northern Europe.

The Asiatic Wild Horse

Also known as the Przewalski (*see pp. 24–25*), the Asiatic Wild Horse is the only one of the four primitive types to have survived into the modern age. The Asiatic Wild Horse lived on the steppes of Europe and Central Asia.

The Tarpan

Scientifically known as *Equus caballus gmelini*, the Tarpan survived on the Eastern European steppes until the

The Tarpan was a dun-colored horse, more lightly built than the Forest Horse.

> **Did You Know?**
>
> *Although it became extinct in the nineteenth century, the Tarpan has been back-bred to life! Using selected Konik and Huçal stock, breeders have bred a horse resembling the original wild horse.*

nineteenth century, although by then it had crossbred with domestic stock. The Tarpan was dun in color, with black points.

The Tundra Horse

Remains of the Tundra Horse have been discovered in the valley of Yana, in northeast Siberia. The Tundra Horse may be an ancestor of the Yakut, a small pony of the same area, but otherwise is not thought to have had much influence on the development of the modern breeds.

The Four Basic Horse Types

Some leading experts in equine history believe that four basic types—two pony and two horse—evolved from these primitive horses. This theory was first proposed by four horse prehistorians—J.G. Speed of Edinburgh, E. Skorkowski of Cracow, F. Ebhardt of Stuttgart, and R. d'Andrade from Portugal. According to this theory, the pony types were more suited to a wet, cold climate, and were able to hide from their natural enemies in swampy, forested areas. The horse types were better suited to outrunning predators in more open habitats, and to surviving in drier, warmer conditions.

The Four Types of Horse

Pony Type 1

Pony Type 1 lived in the forest areas of northwest Europe and developed a resistance to the wet and cold conditions of that region. It had the look of the archetypal modern pony and stood between 12 and 12.2 hands. The Exmoor Pony, a native British breed, is one of the nearest modern equivalents.

Pony Type 2

Pony Type 2 inhabited the taiga region of northern Eurasia, and was well adapted to the cold and frosty climate. Standing between 14 and 14.2 hands, Pony Type 2 was a larger animal than Type 1 and it was also more heavily built. Its modern equivalents include the Highland Pony and the Norwegian Fjord Pony.

Horse Type 3

Horse Type 3 was a horse of the desert, and it inhabited the steppes of Central Asia. It could withstand both heat and drought. At around 14.3 hands, it was the tallest of the four types. Type 3 was thin-skinned and sinewy in appearance, with a long, narrow body, long neck, and long ears. The Akhal-Teke of the Turkmenistan desert is probably the closest modern equivalent.

Horse Type 4

Although measuring only 12 hands, Type 4 is considered a horse because of its body proportions. It was the most beautiful of the four types, delicate and finely boned, with a refined head. Its profile was slightly concave. The mane and tail were fine and silky, and the tail was set high. It lived in Central Asia and was well adapted to hot conditions. Its modern equivalent can be found in the Caspian.

Relatives of the Modern Horse

The donkey, the Asiatic and Asian wild asses, and the zebra family are all members of the *Equidae*. Unlike the horse, however, which originated in North America and migrated to the Old World, these three family members all evolved in the Old World.

The donkey is a member of the Equus *genus.*

The Donkey or Domestic Ass

The donkey, *Equus asinus*, is commonly believed to have originated from the Nubian Wild Ass, *Equus africanus*, a medium-sized donkey with a gray-and-white coat, stripes on its back and legs, and a tall, upright mane with a black tip.

Donkeys range in height from the miniature Mediterranean, at under 36 inches (91 centimeters), to the Mammoth Jack at 14 hands and above. The average domesticated donkey is around 10 hands high. Although gray-dun is perhaps the most familiar coloring of the donkey, they also come in brown, bay, black, light-faced roan, sorrel, albino-white, few-spot white, and spotted colors. Donkeys typically have a dorsal strip running down the back, and shoulder crosses. Light points on the muzzle, belly, around the eye, and on the inner leg are common, and the ears usually have dark points. The ears are proportionally longer than a horse's.

The donkey lacks a true wither, making its back much straighter than that of the horse. The mane is short and stands upright, and there is no forelock. The donkey's tail is cow-like, with a tufted end. The hooves are small and narrow. The donkey is vocally distinct from the horse. It has a brassy bray, the characteristic "hee-haw" sound.

The Asiatic Ass

The scientific term for this group of equines is "hemionid," meaning "half-ass." It is also known as the onager, from the Greek word for "ass." The onager is found in Mongolia, northern Iran, Tibet, India, and Pakistan. It is able to survive for long periods without water, which makes it well adapted to the desert regions of these countries.

Did You Know?

Now the symbol of the Democratic Party in the USA, the donkey first became associated with the party during the 1828 US presidential election, when the opponents of Andrew Jackson labeled him a "jackass." Jackson turned the insult to his advantage by using the donkey on his campaign posters.

The onager is larger than an average domesticated donkey, standing between 12 and 13.2 hands and measuring about six and a half feet (just over two meters) long. The color varies depending on the season— reddish-brown in summer, yellowish-brown in the winter. The underside is paler. They have a black stripe bordered in white that extends down the middle of the back, but no cross or shoulder stripe.

The onager has been domesticated, and the ancient Sumerians used it to pull their chariots. Of the six subspecies, one is extinct and two are endangered.

The Zebra

The open, grassy plains of eastern and southern Africa are home to the three surviving species of zebra: Grevy's zebra (*Equus grevyi*), the mountain zebra (*E. zebra*), and the plains zebra (*E. burchelli*). The quagga (*E. quagga*) died out in the nineteenth century. At 13.2 hands, Grevy's zebra is the largest of the species.

The Mongolian Kulan, one species of onager, is capable of speeds of over 40 mph (60 km/h)—faster than a Thoroughbred.

Each species has its own variety of striping. The coat of a plains zebra has broad stripes, especially towards its hindquarters, while the Grevy's zebra has narrow, closely spaced stripes that cover most of the body, right down to the hooves. The mountain zebra typically has narrower stripes on its body than its rump, while the extinct quagga had very little striping at all, some being almost stripeless.

Zebras have a noisy distinctive barking whinny, more akin to that of the donkey than the horse.

Zebras are social animals, living in herds of one dominant male, mares, offspring, and groups of bachelor males. They can be migratory or sedentary, depending on food availability.

The stripes of a zebra's coat are broader on the rump than elsewhere on its body.

Did You Know?

No two zebras have the same striped pattern, and each coat is as unique as your fingerprints.

The Last Wild Horse

The Asiatic wild horse, also known as the Przewalski, is the only truly wild horse still in existence today. Its traditional habitat is the Mongolian steppes. It is a very hardy animal and can survive in arduous conditions in Central Asia, where temperatures range from 104 degrees Fahrenheit in summer down to 49 degrees below freezing in winter (between 40 degrees and minus 45 degrees Centigrade).

The Przewalski is stockily built, standing between 12 and 14 hands high, with a heavy skull and jaw and a thick neck. It is beige-brown or dun in color, with black, often striped,

The Przewalski is a small dun-colored horse with black mane, tail, and legs.

lower legs. It typically has an eel-stripe running down its back, often with a shoulder cross. The mane is upright and does not fall to one side, unlike most horses, and there is no forelock. The tail is donkey-like, with short dock hairs and longer hairs further down the tail. The mane and tail hairs are black in color and harsh in texture.

Przewalski are social animals, living in groups consisting of four to eight mares and their offspring led by one stallion. They display aggressive behavior and may be migratory. Young stallions form bachelor groups until they are mature and dominant enough to form their own harems.

The Mongolian name for Przewalski is *Takhi*, meaning "spirit." The horse is an important part of Mongolian life, and the *Takhi* is the national symbol. Unlike the domesticated horse, which has 64 chromosomes, the Przewalski has 66. If the Przewalski is bred with a domesticated horse, the resulting offspring has 65 chromosomes.

Discovery

The Przewalski—pronounced "shuh-vall-ski"—owes its name to Nikolai Przewalski, a colonel in the Russian Imperial Army and one of the greatest explorers of the time. In 1879, he came across a group of wild horses on the edge of the Gobi Desert in an area known as Tachin Schah, "The Mountains of the Yellow Horse." The local Kirghiz hunters gave Colonel Przewalski a horse's skull and hide, which he presented to I.S. Poliakov, the conservator at the Zoological Museum of the Academy of Sciences in St. Petersburg. In 1881, Poliakov published a scientific description of the horse, naming it *Equus przewalskii* after the colonel.

The Prehistoric Wild Horse

Some 20,000 years ago, flourishing populations of wild horses roamed across Asia and Europe, from China to France and Spain. However, the end of the last ice age greatly diminished their habitat, as wood and forest replaced steppe. Human pressure, too, greatly affected the wild horse population, firstly by hunting, then, as the human population grew, more land was turned over to agriculture and domesticated livestock, and the wild horses were pushed into increasingly marginal lands. By the late nineteenth century, the wild horse had more or less disappeared completely from Europe and Przewalski's horse was restricted to the edge of the Gobi Desert in northern China and southern Mongolia.

Extinction in the Wild

The desire of zoologists, collectors, and zoos to obtain specimens of the rare "new" wild horse may have hastened its demise in the wild. Many adult horses were killed in the effort to capture foals, which were not as swift or elusive as the older horses. Sadly, only a few dozen of the foals survived the long and perilous journey to Europe and North America. By the outbreak of World War II in 1939, the captive world population of Przewalski was reduced to just 31 horses, of which only 12 actually bred. In 1947, a final mare was caught in Mongolia, and she became the founder of the present population.

The last Przewalski herds became extinct in the wild in the late 1960s, perhaps the victims of hunting.

Breeding Program

Fortunately, the Przewalski species has been preserved, owing to a successful captive-breeding program, and it is estimated that there are now around 1,500 pure Przewalski in captivity. Zoo-bred herds have recently been reintroduced into the wild, and the fierce little Asiatic wild horse is once again roaming the Mongolian steppes.

Captive-born Przewalski horses have been reintroduced to the Asian steppes.

The Horse
in History

Without the majestic horse, the whole chronicle of human history would be a much less glorious one. Mighty empires would never have flourished, decisive battles would not have been fought, and the world's great religions could not have spread as they did. In the words of author John Trotwood Moore (1858–1929): "Wherever Man has left his footprint in the long ascent from barbarism to civilization, we find the hoofprint of a horse beside it."

The Hunted Horse

Evidence of early contact between horse and human comes from prehistoric cave paintings that date from about 15000 BCE. The horses that appear in these paintings bear some resemblance to the Przewalski horse, with a large head and erect mane. These paintings give us an insight into the nature of the relationship between primitive humans and the natural world, and show that the horse was an important source of food. Cave paintings from Lascaux and Pech-Merle in France and Altamira in Spain depict the horse as a prey animal, and huge quantities of horse bones have been found at some of the European caves, including Lascaux.

found the bones of around 10,000 horses that had been chased off a cliff by Cro-Magnon hunters.

The horse may originally have been domesticated for its meat.

The Vogelherd Horse

The oldest animal carving ever found is of a horse. It dates back some 31,000 years and was found in the Vogelherd cave in southern Germany. Measuring approximately two inches (five centimeters) long, it is made from mammoth tusk and has clearly been worn smooth by constant handling. Archeologists believe that the small sculpture may have been carried by a prehistoric hunter as a good-luck charm in his search for food.

There are many prehistoric cave paintings from Europe depicting the horse.

Early humans lacked the means to slay animals at a distance and had to use guile instead. A herd would either be chased into a natural dead end and the horses clubbed or speared to death, or the herd would be driven over a cliff, causing them to fall to their deaths. Evidence of this latter method has been found at the Rock of Solutré in France, where archeologists have

This ivory figurine from the Vogelherd cave is over 30,000 years old.

Domestication

The dog is the most likely candidate for the first animal to be domesticated. Archeological evidence suggests hunter-gatherers were using the dog's unique hunting skills as early as 15000 BCE. Goats, sheep, pigs, oxen, and poultry were also tamed long before the horse. Why or how the horse became domesticated must remain the subject of conjecture, but it is highly likely the first herds were kept for meat.

The Horse as a Draft Animal

The Near East was home to the first settled populations, and farmers began using the ox as a draft animal from early in the fourth millennium BCE. By 3000 BCE, vehicles with disk-like wheels were being pulled by equids—either onagers or asses. The Standard of Ur, dating from around 2500 BCE, from southern Mesopotamia—modern Iraq—depicts a four-wheeled wagon being drawn by four equids controlled by a nose-ring. The wagon driver is holding a rein from the nose ring in one hand and a whip in the other. Because of its superior speed, the horse soon became the favored harness animal.

The First Riders

The discovery of equine remains in Dereivka on the Ukrainian steppes suggests that the horse may have been sufficiently tamed to be ridden approximately 6,000 years ago. Horse teeth from this excavation show signs of bit wear, and two pieces of antler bone that have holes bored in them may have served as cheek pieces for a primitive bridle. The peoples of the steppes were nomadic and left no written or other material records, so little is known of these first "riders." However, the archeological evidence at Dereivka suggests that the horse may have been ridden first, and not originally used to pull wheeled vehicles as was previously thought.

Archeological evidence from Dereivka in Ukraine suggests that there were horseback riders possibly as early as 4000 BCE.

The Chariot Peoples

The first chariots had solid wheels, and were probably used more for transport than warfare. However, the invention of the spoked wheel in Mesopotamia in the mid second millennium BCE transformed the chariot into a lightweight vehicle suitable for military use. The development of the chariot had a far-reaching effect on the civilizations of the ancient world, increasing mobility and enabling the exploitation of the fertile plains around the Tigris and Euphrates. The earliest known fully developed chariots come from the chariot burials of the Andronovo Timber-Grave sites of the Sintashta-Petrovka culture in modern Russia and Kazakhstan, which date from around 2000 BCE. It was from the chariot peoples of Asia Minor that use of the chariot spread into Persia, India, and Upper Egypt.

The introduction of the spoked wheel transformed the use of the chariot.

Both the chariot and the horse itself were introduced to Egypt some time around 1600 BCE by the Hyksos, a nomadic people from Central Asia. Tomb paintings from Egypt, as well as six chariots found in Tutankhamun's tomb, show how important the chariot was to the ancient Egyptians.

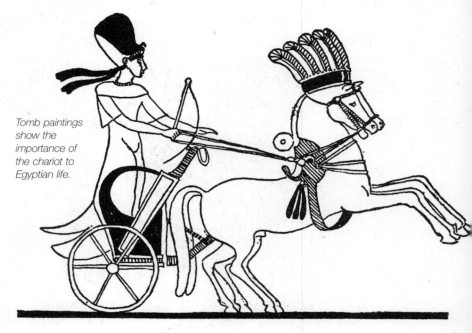

Tomb paintings show the importance of the chariot to Egyptian life.

The Assyrians used mounted horsemen in battle.

The Hittites from Asia Minor were great charioteers. They were also one of Egypt's most formidable enemies, and many great conflicts took place between the two empires, culminating in the greatest chariot battle in history, at Kadesh in Syria, in c. 1274 BCE. The Hittite army sent into battle more than 2,500 chariots as well as 17,000 foot soldiers, and overwhelmed the forces of King Ramesses II of Egypt.

The Babylonians and Assyrians came to power after the Hittites, and their art also shows the use of the chariot in hunting and for warfare, although the horse did not play such a large part in their histories.

The Kikkuli Text

The first known book on training horses, *The Kikkuli Text*, appeared around 1345 BCE. It was written by Kikkuli the Mittanian, horsemaster to the Hittite King Suppiluliuma. The text was written in cuneiform on four clay tablets.

Before the reign of King Suppiluliuma, horses played only a minor role in Hittite society. The king, however, recognized their value in warfare and bought a large number of Arabian horses to be trained by Kikkuli. The *Kikkuli Text* details a seven-month training schedule designed to achieve maximum fitness with minimum injury. Kikkuli advised "interval training," which involved alternating short, fast bursts of intensive training with slow, easy activity and periods of rest, similar to that recommended for modern athletes. He also counseled long periods of leading the horses at the trot, canter, and gallop rather than subjecting them to the additional weight and stress of a rider. He goes into fine detail about the general care and feeding of horses.

Did You Know?

In 1991, Ann Nyland, a doctoral student at the University of New England, Australia, replicated the Kikkuli training and feeding schedule on ten Arabian horses. The horses' levels of fitness were tested before and after the seven-month program. Results showed that the horses were significantly fitter after the program, and that they had remained well throughout their training.

The Persian Empire

The great Assyrian empire finally came to an end early in the sixth century BCE, defeated by a coalition of enemy forces that included the Babylonians and the Medes. The Babylonians established their rule in the "Fertile Crescent" of the Middle East, but fell less than 70 years later to the Persian cavalry forces led by Cyrus the Great (550–530 BCE). The reign of Cyrus saw the establishment of a great Persian empire that became the dominant force in Asia for the next two centuries. The Persian cavalry was a highly trained and successful military machine, and it was instrumental in the spread of Persian rule.

The horse was a powerful status symbol in Persia. Any nobleman of worth would always be seen in public on horseback, and aristocratic boys were taught to ride from the age of six years. Although there were many different breeds of horse, the mount of choice was the magnificent Nisean horse. Standing at 15 hands high, the Nisean was a larger animal than previous riding stock, and was powerfully built. Images of this magnificent horse adorn the castle walls at Persepolis, the Persian ceremonial capital built during the reign of Darius I (521–486 BCE).

Did You Know?

The Persians were the first people to recognize the value of the horse as a means of communication. According to Greek historians Herodotus and Xenophon, the first postal service came into existence in the sixth century BCE during the reign of Cyrus the Great. Post houses were established a day's riding distance apart.

> " The armored Persian horsemen and their death-dealing chariots were invincible. No man dared face them. "
>
> HERODOTUS, GREEK HISTORIAN (484–430 BCE)

Nisean horses formed part of the tribute given to the Persian king at Persepolis.

The Scythians and Parthians

In the early sixth century, the Scythians, a nomadic tribal people from the Russian steppes, invaded the northern borders of the Near East. The Scythians occupied part of what is now modern Iran for around 40 years. They were skilled riders, and possessed many horses. They left no written records, but archeologists have discovered artifacts from this period that reveal the importance of the horse in their culture.

The Parthians most likely emerged from one of the tribes of the Scythian confederation. They established a kingdom that stretched from Mesopotamia to the Hindu Kush, and which lasted from c. 250 BCE to 226 CE. They, too, owe their military success to their mastery of the horse.

Parthian archers, in particular, were skilled horsemen. They would gallop away from their enemies in simulated flight, then suddenly turn their bodies round and fire arrows over the horse's tail at their surprised pursuers.

An archer firing the infamous "Parthian shot" at his enemy.

The Pazyryk Tombs

In 1929, archeologists discovered a series of frozen *kurgans*, or tombs, in Pazyryk, in the mountainous Altai region of western Siberia. Dating from the Scythian-Sakae period—between the sixth and fourth centuries BCE— these tombs contained over 5,000 items as well as the bodies of humans and animals, all perfectly preserved by the ice. Among the remains is an arthritic middle-aged mare, about 13 hands high. She wore richly adorned

tack, including a "reindeer mask," the skull of a reindeer with large antlers. The significance of this is unclear, but it is probable that the reindeer played a significant role in the early history of these people and may have come to be revered by them. Certainly, petroglyphs from that time commonly depict men riding on "antlered horses."

The reindeer was central to the early history of the Scythian people.

The Horse in Ancient Greece

Wealthy, artistic, and cultured, ancient Greeks nonetheless needed an efficient cavalry in order to quell both neighbors and internal divisions. The mountainous terrain of Greece limited the use of the chariot in warfare, but the horses of the early period of Greek civilization were too small to be ridden. Nowhere is there a better description of the role played by the horse-drawn chariot than the *Iliad*. Composed somewhere around 800 BCE by Homer, the *Iliad* is an epic account of the Trojan War:

Did You Know?

Chariot racing was introduced at the 25th Olympiad in 680 BCE. Four-horsed chariots competed against each other, and the owner of the winning chariot, not the driver, was proclaimed champion. The Olympic champion received a wreath made from a branch of the sacred olive tree. The games were held in honor of Zeus, the father of the gods.

“Chariots were being smashed in all directions, and many a man came tumbling down from his own car to fall beneath the wheels of that of Patroclus, whose immortal steeds … sprang over the trench at a bound as they sped onward.”

HOMER, *THE ILIAD*, BOOK XVI

Because of his understanding of the horse, the Greek soldier and historian Xenophon is called the "Father of Classical Equitation."

The Art of Horsemanship

Xenophon (c. 430–355 BCE) was a Greek historian, philosopher, and solider. He joined the 10,000-strong mercenary army of the Persian prince Cyrus the Younger and was also in the service of the Spartan government. Xenophon wrote prolifically on the horse and its role in life. *The Art of Horsemanship* is the oldest surviving manual on the riding horse. This great work details how to select, care for, and train a horse. To get the best performance from a horse, Xenophon advised that horse and rider should build up a relationship of mutual trust, one that is based on non-abusive actions.

Xenophon was also a highly experienced soldier, and his work *The Cavalry Commander* reveals his understanding of the skills necessary for military success.

"The one great precept and practice in using a horse is this—never deal with him when you are in a fit of passion. When your horse shies at an object and is unwilling to go up to it, he should be shown that there is nothing fearful in it, least of all to a courageous horse like him; but if this fails, touch the object yourself that seems so dreadful to him, and lead him up to it with gentleness. Compulsion and blows inspire only the more fear; and when horses are at all hurt at such times, they think what they shied at is the cause of the hurt."

EXCERPT FROM *THE ART OF HORSEMANSHIP*

Bucephalus was said to have cost 13 talents, an extraordinary sum, since a talent was the equivalent of 56 pounds of gold or silver.

Alexander and Bucephalus

Alexander the Great (356–323 BCE), the king of Macedonia, was one the greatest military commanders in history. By the time of his death, he had led his army over 12,000 miles and conquered most of the known world, extending the Greek Empire into Egypt and India.

The horse played a large part in the Greek military campaigns, and it is fitting that such a heroic leader as Alexander should have had an equally legendary horse. Bucephalus, Alexander's mount for his great campaigns against the Persians, is perhaps the most famous horse of all time. Bucephalus is described as being a large, black horse with a star on his forehead, a walleye, and of the "best Thessalonian strain." The name Bucephalus means "ox-head," which some sources say referred to the mark of the ox's head on his haunch. Others say that it was because of his large, bull-like head.

According to ancient Greek sources, notably the writings of Plutarch and Pliny the Elder, the horse was offered for sale by Philonicus the Thessalian to Alexander's father, King Philip II. Although magnificent in stature, the horse proved so wild and vicious that none of Philip's attendants could mount him. As the horse was about to be led away unsold, the 12-year-old Alexander said, "What an excellent horse do they lose for want of address and boldness to manage him!" Alexander asked to ride the horse, and promised to pay the price of the animal should he fail. Phillip was said to be annoyed at his young son's arrogance but agreed to let him try. Alexander, spotting that the horse was scared of its own shadow, turned the horse to face the sun and, after calming him, mounted the horse and galloped him around. The stunned Phillip said to the young boy, "O my son, look thee out a kingdom equal to and worthy of thyself, for Macedon is too little for thee."

Alexander and Bucephalus are one of the most famous equestrian partnerships in history.

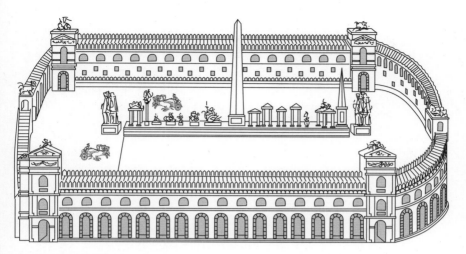

The Death of Bucephalus

Alexander rode Bucephalus into many battles, the last of which was the Battle of Hydaspes in June 326 BCE, in which Alexander defeated the Indian King Porus. The grand old horse, said to have been some 30 years old, died of wounds inflicted in that battle. The horse was honored with a state funeral, and Alexander founded a new city, Bucephala, now close to modern-day Jhelum in Pakistan, in his memory.

The Circus Maximus

The ancient Romans loved chariot racing, and the greatest Roman hippodrome was the Circus Maximus in Rome. It was founded by Tarquinius Priscus, the fifth king of Rome, in the early sixth century BCE. At first it was little more than a marshy field, but through the centuries improvements turned it into a magnificent stadium, a U-shaped arena measuring some 2,000 by 600 feet (610 by 190 meters), and holding more than a quarter of a million people. A long barrier, called the "*spina*," ran down the middle of the track, and seven large wooden "eggs" were placed on the spina to mark the completion of

The Circus Maximus was a magnificent arena used for chariot racing.

each lap. (The Empress Agrippa later added seven bronze dolphins for the same purpose.)

The *currus quadrigae*, or "quadriga"—a type of chariot pulled by four horses—had a yoked pair in the middle and two outside horses attached only by a trace. The speed, sharp turns, and inevitable collisions in the races resulted in horrific injuries for both horses and charioteers. The best charioteers, however, could win fabulous prize money and some became immensely wealthy.

The quadriga was a racing chariot pulled by four horses.

The Horse in Ancient Mythology

The ancient Greeks and Romans had a rich pantheon of gods and goddesses, and many temples were dedicated to their worship. The horse appears frequently in the legends of these civilizations, usually as a noble, powerful, and graceful creature.

Poseidon

Poseidon was one of the most important gods for the Greeks. His chariot was drawn by a hippocamp, a seahorse-like creature with the head and forelegs of a horse and the body of a fish. Horses were often offered as a sacrifice to Poseidon, especially by sailors. Their form of sacrifice always involved drowning, in deference to Poseidon's role as god of the sea.

There are many myths concerning Poseidon's amorous adventures, two of which resulted in the birth of a horse. One story tells how Poseidon tried to seduce his sister Demeter. In an effort to escape the attentions of her brother, the goddess transformed herself into a mare. (Demeter is often depicted with a mare's head.) However, Poseidon deceived the goddess by taking the form of a stallion. Their union resulted in the fabulous horse, Arion.

On another occasion, the gorgon Medusa was the object of Poseidon's lust. When young, Medusa was a

Poseidon is best known as god of the sea, but he was also the god of horses, and his chariot is pulled through the ocean waves by a hippocamp, a creature that is half-fish, half-horse.

Pegasus was a wild, winged horse ridden by Bellerophon.

beautiful priestess at the temple of Athena, goddess of wisdom. However, she outraged the goddess by having relations with Poseidon at the temple. In revenge, Athena turned the gorgon's hair into living snakes. Medusa was the only gorgon to be mortal, and she was eventually killed by the hero Perseus, son of Zeus and Danae. He cut off her head and gave it to Athena, who wore it on her shield. The winged horse Pegasus sprang from her dead body.

Pegasus

Pegasus was a beautiful winged horse, the son of the gorgon Medusa and Poseidon. He was often associated with the Muses, the Greek goddesses who preside over the arts and sciences, and who inspire others to great works. The thundering of his hooves on Mount Helicon caused the sacred spring of Hippocrene, from which the Muses drank their inspiration, to gush forth. Pegasus was tamed by the Corinthian hero Bellerophon, who used a golden bridle given to him by Athena.

Bellerophon killed the monster Chimera while riding on Pegasus. He also tried to reach Mount Olympus, home of the gods, on Pegasus, but an angry Zeus sent a horsefly to bite Pegasus and the horse threw his rider off his back. Thereafter, Pegasus lived on Mount Olympus and carried thunderbolts and lightning for Zeus. He is also seen as a constellation in the night sky.

Epona

Epona was a Celtic goddess of horses, donkeys, and mules—the name comes from the Gaulish word for horse—"*epos*." She accompanied the soul on its final journey to the lands of the dead. The Romans adopted her into their pantheon, and the cult of Epona became widespread throughout the Roman Empire. She is depicted sitting side-saddle on a horse, lying on a horse, or sitting on a throne surrounded by two or more horses or foals. One of her attributes is the cornucopia, the horn of plenty, which suggests that she may also have been a goddess of fertility.

The Centaurs

The centaurs were creatures with the head and torso of a human above the body of a horse. In Greek mythology it is told that Ixion had planned to seduce Hera, the wife of Zeus, but Zeus deceived Ixion by fashioning a cloud into Hera's form. The centaurs were the result of that union and became known as Ixionidae. Centaurs were known for their wild, bestial behavior. One exception was the wise and kind Chiron, the tutor of Greek heroes Jason and Achilles.

The Horse in China

The horse was first domesticated in China around 5,000 years ago during the Lungshan period. From this time onward, the horse played a vital part in the survival and expansion of the Chinese Empire. Sophisticated wheeled chariots were in use by the time of the Shang Dynasty— c. 1450–1100 BCE—and archeological evidence from that period shows that these chariots, together with the horses that pulled them, were entombed with their owners so that

The horse is one of the 12 signs of the Chinese zodiac. People born in the Year of the Horse are said to be hardworking, popular, and independent.

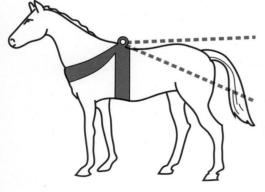

Unlike the throat-and-girth system (top), the Chinese breast-strap harnessing system (bottom) allowed the horse to use its natural strength and power effectively.

they could accompany them on their journey to the next life.

The greatest threat to the Chinese people came from the Huns, the marauding nomadic tribes to the north and west. Chariots proved no use against these fearsome invaders, and the Chinese were forced to use mounted soldiers to defend themselves.

Great Inventions

When humans first began utilizing the horse as a draft animal, they looked to the yoke system in use for the ox. However, the physiology of the horse is quite different. To account for this, a throat-and-girth harnessing system was devised, but it severely restricted the horse's breathing and limited the weight that a horse could pull. The Chinese invented the breast-strap harnessing system, which allowed the horse to breathe freely and increased its pulling power.

The second significant equine contribution of the Chinese was the invention of the stirrup. This was as vital as the breast-strap harness, as it greatly improved the stability of the mounted rider. At first, there was only one stirrup, and it was used as a mounting aid. The first evidence of paired stirrups appears in a tomb from the Jin Dynasty, dated to around 322 CE.

The Heavenly Horses

The Chinese recognized that the nomad invaders had superior horses, and so began a selective-breeding program to upgrade their own animals. This program accelerated during the reign of the Emperor Wudi (157–87 BCE).

The great Chinese explorer, Zhang Qian, discovered a new breed of horse among the Dayuan people of the Ferghana Basin in Central Asia. Zhang Qian returned home and told the Emperor about the superb breed of "blood-sweating" horses that he had discovered. The Emperor desperately wanted some of these horses and he sent a large amount of gold with an expeditionary force to obtain some stock. However, the Dayuan people declined to sell any horses and stole his gold. Refusing to be defeated, Wudi sent an expedition of 60,000 soldiers and 30,000 horses. This large force overcame the resistance of the Dayuans and obtained ten "elite" horses and 3,000 of lesser quality. Only 1,000 horses survived the journey home. Wudi believed that the Dayuan horses were a very special breed and called them "Celestial" or "Heavenly Horses." They were probably ancestors of the modern Akhal-teke desert horse (*see Plate 9*).

The Celestial Horses of Imperial China were bred for speed and endurance.

Did You Know?

The Emperor Wudi believed that the "blood-sweating" exhibited by the Dayuan horses proved that the horses belonged to a divine race, touched by heaven. However, recent research has attributed the blood-sweating to a more earthly cause, namely a parasite. Modern horses of the Ferghana region also sweat blood, and it was originally thought that this was caused by blood bursting through their thin skins during strenuous exercise. Scientists have now discovered that it is caused by a subcutaneous parasite found in rivers. At a certain period in its lifecycle the parasite breaks through the skin, and this is the cause of the bleeding.

The Spread of Islam

During the seventh and eighth centuries, Muslim culture and the religion of Islam spread from the Arabian Peninsula westward across North Africa and then north into Spain. Comprising Arabs and North African Berbers, the invading Muslim army brought into Europe the Arabian horse and the Barb—the small, swift, light horses of the desert. These horses were to have a profound effect on almost all the breeds we know today.

The Arabian Horse

This is probably the oldest pure breed of horse. Arabian horses (*see Plate 8*) were being selectively bred by the tribal Bedouin people of the Arabian Peninsula before the time of Muhammad, but there are also carved reliefs from Mesopotamia and Ancient Egypt that depict war horses with the Arab's distinctive dished facial profile and the

The Arabian horse has a very fine, elegant head and often holds its tail erect.

tail held high. Careful breeding resulted in a spirited horse that was eminently suited to desert conditions and to warfare—fast, hardy, and intelligent, able to survive in hot, dry conditions, and possessing great endurance.

These same qualities were eagerly embraced by Europe, and Arabian bloodlines are to be found in the ancestry of several breeds, including the Thoroughbred, the Appaloosa, the American Quarter Horse, the Morgan, and the Percheron. The strength of the Arabian genetic constitution is such that it has left a determining mark on all of these breeds and many others besides.

The Barb

Another relatively small desert horse, the North African Barb has also been an important contributor to the riding

66 The horse is God's gift to mankind. 99

ARABIAN PROVERB

horses of Europe and North America, and especially to the Spanish horse, the modern Andalusian. Quite unlike the Arabian in many ways, the modern Barb undoubtedly has some Arabian blood, but its own genetic stock is so strong that it has retained its convex facial profile and holds its tail low.

East Meets West

The northward progress of Islam was halted in southern France at the Battle of Tours—also known as the Battle of Poitiers—in 731 CE, and it was a clash of two different styles of army. The Muslim horsemen traveled light on their small, agile horses, and this had enabled them to advance the spread of Islam so rapidly. Their style in battle was to ride high in the saddle, with short stirrups, able to wield a sword or shoot a bow from this position. However, the cavalry developed and

organized by Charles Martell, a military genius and the effective ruler of the Frankish kingdom, was heavier and more organized, and the horsemen rode deep in the saddle with long stirrups and the feet well forward, giving them great stability. Under the leadership of Charles' grandson, Charlemagne, the European Christian cavalry played a pivotal role in pushing the Muslim army southward again.

The Best of Both

The contrast between the swift and agile Muslim mounts and the solid and somewhat ponderous Frankish horses led the Christians to introduce Barb bloodlines into their own studs, and there is evidence that the Limousin charger of medieval Europe was descended in large part from the Barb. The influence of the North African steeds can be seen in the wild white horses of the Camargue in southern France (*see Plate 11*) and also in the wild Mustangs of North America. Barbary, or Berber, horses were being imported into the English royal studs by the fourteenth century.

Frankish horsemen rode with long stirrups.

The Knight on Horseback

The successes of Charlemagne's cavalry against the Moorish forces in northern Spain and his founding of the Holy Roman Empire in 800 CE did much to establish the image of the chivalrous Christian knight on horseback. The next 200 years saw the creation of a permanent military class of armed and mounted soldiers, both independent "freelance" knights whose services were for hire and landholding members of the nobility who owed military service to an overlord.

When William, Duke of Normandy, invaded England in 1066, the army that he brought across from France may have included a cavalry of as many as 3,000 knights and horses. William was only able to raise such a large number by promising them the spoils of war in the form of land, and this is largely how the Anglo-Saxon landowners came to be replaced by the Norman aristocracy.

Toward the end of the eleventh century, when the law of primogeniture was introduced and only the first-born son could inherit tenure of the land, a class of landless knights developed in

The medieval warhorse was built strongly to take the weight of a heavily armored knight.

Europe, and it was largely these young warriors who made up the great orders of Christian knighthood, at once both religious and military.

In 1095, Pope Urban II urged good Christians to take up arms and set forth on a military pilgrimage to the Holy Lands to wrest Jerusalem from

As the Bayeaux Tapestry reveals, many horses took part in the Battle of Hastings in 1066.

the control of the Seljuk Turks, and it was at this time that the Knights Templar, Knights Hospitallers, Teutonic Knights, and other orders came into being. Epitomized in the legends of King Arthur, the knights were expected to uphold the chivalric values of honor, valor, generosity, compassion, and loyalty.

Warhorses at this time were being bred for greater size and strength, not only to bear the weight of an armored knight but also to lend greater impetus to the knight's lance in battle and to resist the impact of the enemy. Between the twelfth and fifteenth centuries, the tournament became the training ground for young knights, and they would travel throughout Europe to compete against each other for fame, glory, and rich rewards.

The hero El Cid and his horse Babieca helped end Islamic rule in Spain.

Did You Know?

Legend has it that the devil once visited a blacksmith named Dunstan, asking to have his cloven hooves shod. Dunstan caused the devil so much pain, applying red-hot shoes and driving the nails deep into the devil's feet, that he begged for mercy and agreed never to visit a home where a horseshoe hangs. Traditionally, the shoe is hung with the tips pointing upward so the luck won't pour out. Dunstan later became the Archbishop of Canterbury (960–988 CE) and was made a saint after his death.

El Cid

Possessing the ideal qualities of the chivalrous Christian knight, Rodrigo Diaz led the Reconquista movement that was to oust the last of the Islamic dynasties from Spain. His leadership and military conquests earned him the title of "El Cid," "The Lord," but his white Andalusian horse Babieca was almost as famous. A twelfth-century epic poem recounts that Rodrigo's godfather, a Carthusian monk, gave him the pick of any horse from an Andalusian herd. Disgusted at his godson's choice—a young and unremarkable stallion—the monk exclaimed *"Babieca!"*—meaning "stupid." This became the horse's name, but he proved to have all the virtues of a perfect warhorse. Legend has it that at the end of their illustrious career, El Cid's body was strapped upright in his saddle and Babieca was sent out into battle by the warrior's wife, who knew his troops would suffer defeat if they were aware of his death.

The Mongol Hordes

No army has ever used the horse more effectively or more ruthlessly than the Mongols of the thirteenth and fourteenth centuries. Initially, they were one of many tribal confederations that inhabited the desert and steppe lands to the north of China but, under the leadership of Genghis Khan, the Mongols united all the tribes and ultimately dominated the largest contiguous empire the world has ever known. The horse was a central element in their success.

Following the establishment of Great Mongolia in 1206, the Mongolian cavalry—every soldier in the Mongolian army was mounted—set out to subdue the neighboring tribes. The soldiers'

Genghis Khan (c.1162-1227), the formidable founder of the Mongol Empire.

weaponry included the battle axe, scimitar, lance, and powerful recurved bow. Initially the purpose was to secure the trading routes on which prosperity was founded, but the scope soon widened into empire building. At times numbering almost quarter of a million soldiers, the army quickly earned a terrifying reputation for its speed, high

The Mongol Empire was founded on the skill of its horsemen and the strength of its horses.

degree of organization, and the ruthless destruction that it wreaked. Entire cities were destroyed and their populations slaughtered, except for the artisans and potential warriors who might be of use to the Mongols. Looted treasure from these exploits was sent back to the homeland as the horde extended Mongol control in all directions. This policy of wholesale devastation meant that the Mongols left few enemies behind them, and increased the likelihood that the cities ahead would surrender more readily, becoming vassals to the Mongol emperor.

The army carried some food supplies, but largely lived off the land and by plundering. Each horseman had several steeds, and a herd of additional horses followed the army. At first these were the small, hardy Mongolian ponies, but as the army moved further afield it captured and used other breeds. Being able to change mounts meant that the army could move swiftly, and the herd provided mare's milk and fresh meat—for the Mongols were far from sentimental about their animals. When they were on the move, the soldiers also supplemented their diet by taking blood from the horses and thickening it over a fire.

Successive khans expanded the empire until, at its greatest, it stretched from the Pacific coast in the east to the borders of the Holy Roman Empire in the west, encompassing China, northern India, Afghanistan, Turkey, Russia, Poland, and Hungary. Genghis' successors included Kublai Khan and Tamerlane, whose reputation for ruthlessness exceeded even that of the Mongols' first khan.

> ### Did You Know?
>
> *The Mongols were also known as the Tatars. When traveling long distances, food supplies would be carried in the form of slabs of meat laid under the saddle. The meat would become tenderized by the weight of the rider and to some degree preserved by the horse's sweat. This meat was often eaten raw, and this "delicacy" was taken up in Europe as steak tartare—raw ground beef with chopped onion and raw egg. In its cooked form it became known as Hamburg steak in Germany, and eventually as hamburger in the USA.*

Tamerlane (c. 1336–1405) was a cruel leader, responsible for the massacres of thousands.

The Spanish Conquistadores

Following the expulsion of the Moors from the Iberian Peninsula in 1492, the Spanish turned their attention to the discovery of new lands. The fifteenth and sixteenth centuries saw a wave of explorations, culminating in the discovery and conquest of the Americas. The Spanish conquistadores—from the Spanish for "conqueror"—were inspired by the tales of El Dorado, the city of gold, and pursued their quest for wealth with ruthless determination. They committed great acts of savagery against the native peoples of America, and totally wiped out the great civilizations of the continent.

That the conquistadores succeeded in subjugating the natives with a relatively small force was down, in part, to their use of the horse. Until the arrival of the conquistadores, the horse had been extinct in the Americas for over 8,000 years, and the native peoples had never seen an animal of its kind.

The New World

The first horses to arrive in the New World came with Christopher Columbus on his second voyage from Spain to the Americas. Columbus brought 35 horses to the Caribbean island of Hispaniola—now Haiti and the Dominican Republic—in 1493, and horse-breeding ranches were set up on the island. Within a few years, the horse had became established on the neighboring islands of Puerto Rico, Cuba, and Jamaica, providing animals for subsequent expeditions to the Americas.

The Spanish conquistadores reintroduced the horse to the Americas.

Did You Know?

Hernando Cortez had a black stallion called El Morzillo, which he rode on his expedition to Honduras. Unfortunately, the stallion's foot became badly infected from a large splinter, and Cortez was forced to leave El Morzillo behind with a native chief at Peten-Itza Lake. The Indians treated El Morzillo like a god, and gave him offerings of chickens and fruit. Whether the horse died from this inadequate diet or from the wound is not known, but after his death the Indians worshipped El Morzillo as Tziminchac, the Mayan god of thunder and lightning.

Hernando Cortez

In 1519, Hernando Cortez (1484–1547) and his band of mercenary soldiers landed in Mexico to crush the great Aztec civilization, ostensibly in the name of God, but more likely in the search for personal riches. As well as a force of some 500 Spanish soldiers and 200 native Indians, Cortez brought 16 horses with him. Although few in number, the horse had a profound influence on the outcome of the expedition. To the Americans, they appeared as a monstrous apparition. Bernal Díaz del Castillo, who chronicled

Did You Know?

A chestnut mare gave birth to a foal on board Cortez's ship, but the colt escaped from the Spaniards during the march to Mexico City. Legend has it that the young stallion ran free with deer for some years before enticing away a mare from a herd brought by subsequent conquistadores.

> " Next to God, we owed the victory to the horses, for they struck terror into the natives who, naturally, had never seen the like of these armored beasts before. "

HERNANDO CORTEZ, IN A LETTER TO CHARLES V OF SPAIN

the expedition, wrote, "The natives had not seen horses up to this time and thought that the horse and rider were all one animal."

Although the Aztecs were in awe of the fearsome-looking horses, they fought bravely against the Spanish cavalry, which had been augmented by more mounted soldiers sent by the Spanish crown, and they killed many of the animals. On one occasion, the Indians took away the body of a slain horse and kept its mangled remains as a trophy. Despite these losses, the use of the horse in battle gave the Spaniards a great advantage over the more numerous Aztecs, and Mexico City fell to the conquistadores in 1521.

Cortez and El Morzillo—when the Spanish first arrived, some Native American peoples thought horse and rider were one creature.

The uniform of the Polish hussars featured giant feathered "wings."

A New Type of Cavalry

The cavalry that made its mark in France and Spain and in the Crusades—armored knights on relatively large horses, seated deep in the saddle and overpowering the enemy through the impetus of their attack—remained an essential element in the armies of Europe for several centuries, but the Hundred Years' War (1337–1453) heralded a change. The French knights, probably the largest and best-trained cavalry in Europe at the time, suffered terrible losses under the onslaught of arrows from the English longbow, which could pierce armor and decimate a cavalry charge before the knights were close enough to use their weapons.

Birth of the Hussars

After the defeat of the Serbian heavy horse by the light cavalry of the Ottomans in the Battle of Kosovo in 1389, the Serbs regrouped in Croatia, and a new form of European cavalry came into being, possibly taking on board lessons learned from both the Ottomans and the Mongols. Hussars, as these light horsemen were known, became highly trained fighting units in Hungary in the second half of the fifteenth century. They rode with short stirrups, leaning well forward in the saddle with knees bent. They carried light arms, such as the lance and sword, and were able to move quickly in unison in battle.

Colorful Heroes

In the early sixteenth century, many hussars moved to other parts of Europe, taking their training with them

> **Did You Know?**
>
> *In the sixteenth and seventeenth centuries, the uniform of the Polish armored cavalry, or "Hussaria," included giant feathered wings attached to the back of the armor or to the saddle. The sight of winged horsemen attacking at a full gallop struck terror into the enemy, and Hussaria wings are still featured in the insignia of the Polish Air Force and Armored Divisions.*

and leading to the creation of hussar units in the armies of many countries. While in Hungary and Poland-Lithuania, the hussars took up armor and returned to a heavier form of cavalry, Western Europe integrated the light hussars into the cavalry alongside its heavy horse. The heavier cavalry still had a role in breaking through enemy lines, but the dashing hussars relied on their horses' speed and agility, and were ideal for reconnaissance, raids on artillery positions, and harrying retreating enemy forces.

The colorful uniforms of many regiments harked back to their Hungarian origins, and the hussars of the eighteenth and nineteenth centuries were regarded as the elite of the cavalry. In Russian, French, and English literature, the hussar is frequently portrayed as a hard-fighting, hard-playing rascal with a penchant for good wine and the fair sex.

The Charge of the Light Brigade
The Charge of the Light Brigade during the Crimean War (see Plate 6) still stands as the greatest cavalry tragedy of all time. Acting on orders received, Lord Cardigan commanded his brigade of hussars, dragoons, and lancers

to advance up a valley that had Russian artillery positions at its head and along both sides. The result was total carnage.

The Horse and Artillery
From the sixteenth century onward, the introduction of firearms was to influence the role of the cavalry. In the first place, the horses were vulnerable to musket and rifle fire, and, secondly, firearms that were light enough to be carried, aimed, and fired on horseback did not have the accuracy or the range of the infantryman's long-barreled weapon. Horses nonetheless continued to play a significant part in battles throughout the eighteenth and nineteenth centuries. For example, horse-drawn light artillery was deployed to great effect in the Battle of Waterloo, although many cavalry horses lost their lives in attacks on infantry positions.

Hussars were notable for their flamboyant uniforms and "devil-may-care" attitude.

Napoleon and Marengo

The French Emperor Napoleon (1769–1821) rode many different horses during his campaigns, but his favorite mount was Marengo, a white Arab stallion. Marengo was six years old in 1799 when he was captured from the Turks after the Battle of Aboukir Bay and taken to France. Napoleon named him after his victorious battle against the Austrians at Marengo (1800). This horse is said to have carried Napoleon at the battles of Austerlitz (1805), Jena (1806), Wagram (1809), and Waterloo (1815). He was also involved in the ill-fated Russian campaign in 1812, in which the 19-year-old horse walked an amazing 3,000 miles (4,830 kilometers) to Moscow and back.

Marengo passed into British hands after Napoleon's defeat at Waterloo, when he was bought by General J.J. Angerstein, who took him to England. The horse was first exhibited at the Waterloo Rooms in London's Pall Mall for the fee of one shilling, before being put out to stud in Cambridgeshire. Although he sired two colts and one filly, he wasn't considered a suitable stud, and he was eventually retired to Suffolk where he stayed until his death in 1832 at the age of 38. The skeleton of this famous horse was preserved and later given to the Royal United Services Institute. It is now on display, minus one hoof, at the National Army Museum in Chelsea. The missing hoof was made into a snuff box on the instructions of General Angerstein, who presented it to the officers of the Brigade of Guards. It is still in use at the Wellington Barracks.

Marengo was just 14.1 hands high—big enough for the diminutive French emperor.

Did You Know?

Napoleon may have spent a great deal of time in the saddle, but his equestrian skills did not impress everyone. His valet Constant wrote, "The Emperor mounted a horse without grace … and I believe that he would not have always been very sturdy on the horse if we had not taken so much care to give him only horses perfectly trained."

A comrade of the emperor, Ernst Otto Odeleben, was similarly unimpressed, "Napoleon rode like a butcher … whilst galloping, his body rolled backward and forward and sideways, according to the speed of his horse."

Wellington on Copenhagen, the Thoroughbred turned warhorse.

The Duke of Wellington and Copenhagen

Waterloo produced another heroic horse, Copenhagen, the chestnut charger ridden by Arthur Wellesley, later the first Duke of Wellington.

Copenhagen was a Thoroughbred, just over 15 hands high. His sire was Meteor, who came second in the Epsom Derby, and his dam was Lady Catherine, General Grosvenor's mount at the Siege of Copenhagen. Copenhagen started life on the race tracks, but only had one win in 13 starts. His racing career curtailed, Copenhagen was sent to Spain during the Peninsula War, where he was purchased by the Duke of Wellington.

At the Battle of Waterloo—June 18, 1815—the Duke of Wellington rode Copenhagen from dawn to dusk, galloping all over the battlefield. At the end of the day, historic records recall that the horse still had sufficient energy to lash out at his master as he dismounted, missing him by inches.

Although never unduly sentimental about his horse, the Duke appreciated Copenhagen, saying, "There may have been many faster horses, no doubt many handsomer, but for bottom and endurance I never saw his fellow." The horse received a hero's welcome when he returned to England.

Copenhagen died, deaf and blind, in 1838 at the age of 28 years, and was given a funeral with full military honors. He is buried at Stratfield Saye, the Hampshire country estate awarded to the Duke of Wellington by the British government as a reward for his military services. Copenhagen's headstone bears the epitaph written for him by the English poet R.E. Egerton Warburton: "God's humbler instrument, though meaner clay, should share the glory of that glorious day."

The American Warhorse

The US Cavalry played a significant part on both sides in the American Civil War, and in the battles against the Plains Indians that broke out in the succeeding years. Among the thousands of steeds, several stand out and have found their places as legends in American history.

General Robert E. Lee

"If I was an artist like you, I would draw a true picture of Traveller; representing his fine proportions, muscular figure, deep chest, short back, strong haunches, flat legs, small head, broad forehead, delicate ears, quick eye, small feet, and black mane and tail." So wrote Robert Lee of the gray horse that accompanied him throughout the Civil War. Traveller served him well: strong, calm, and "bomb-proof" in the turmoil of battle, although on one occasion the horse spooked and caused Lee to break both his hands.

At Lee's funeral, in 1870, Traveller followed the hearse with the General's boots reversed in the stirrups. When

Did You Know?

By tradition, the doors of Traveller's old stable on Washington and Lee University campus are left open to allow his spirit to roam free.

General Robert E. Lee on Traveller.

> " Hurrah, hurrah for Sheridan! Hurrah, hurrah for horse and man! "

"SHERIDAN'S RIDE," THOMAS READ (1822–1872)

the horse died the following year from tetanus, he was buried at Washington and Lee University. He was later disinterred and his skeleton displayed, but in 1971 his remains were reburied close to the Lee family crypt.

In 1862, Union general Philip Henry Sheridan was given a 16-hand black gelding by one of his fellow officers. Named after the skirmish at Rienzi, Mississippi, the horse, which stood far taller than the General himself, carried him through the Civil War.

In September 1864, his men suffered a surprise attack while Sheridan was away in nearby Winchester. Hearing the sound of artillery fire from some 20 miles away, Sheridan rode hell for leather to Cedar Creek and was able to rally his men and disable the enemy forces. The escapade was immortalized in "Sheridan's Ride," a poem by Thomas Buchanan Read

Did You Know?

The McClellan saddle was introduced in 1859, and almost half a million of them were made before the end of the Civil War. George Brinton McClellan based the design on the Hungarian saddle used in the Crimean War, and McClellan saddles remained standard issue until the start of World War II. They are still used by US mounted police units.

that was to bring fame to both Sheridan and his horse—now renamed Winchester to commemorate the event. The poem was used as part of the Republicans' campaign efforts and may even have played a role in Abraham Lincoln's election victory.

Did You Know?

When he died in 1878, Winchester was stuffed and placed in the US First Army Museum in New York City. Saved from a fire at the museum in 1922, he was taken, with an army escort, to the Smithsonian, where he remains on display at the National Museum of American History, Behring Center.

Lieutenant Colonel Custer

Having made a name for himself as a cavalry commander in the Civil War, Lieutenant Colonel George Armstrong Custer is best remembered for his misguided attack on a camp of Sioux and Cheyenne on the banks of the Little Big Horn River, when he grossly underestimated their numbers. The defeat of the 7th Cavalry, one of the worst of the Indian Wars, cost the lives of 258 soldiers, including Custer, as well as that of his favorite horse, Vic.

World War I

Many hundreds of thousands of horses died on active duty during World War I (1914–1918). The killing fields of Flanders tested the bravery of both man and horse to the extreme, and both rose admirably to the occasion. The horses faced shelling and machine-gun fire as well as the hardships of the mud and cold on a daily basis, but rarely had to be driven by force into the danger area.

Horses acted as the backbone of the support lines, carrying food, supplies, and munitions. They also pulled gun carriages, wagons, and ambulances. Conditions on the European battlefields were hellish, and there was often little in the way of food or water for the horses. Throughout this terrible time, man and horse worked tirelessly together, and many memoirs from this period lament the passing of a soldier's horse. The soldier's deep affection for his animal comrade is nowhere better reflected than in Fortunino Matania's illustration, *Goodbye Old Man*, which shows a gun driver stopping to bid farewell to a fatally injured horse.

The cavalry did not play a significant role on the Western Front, hampered by the mud and barbed-wire barricades. However, the Palestine Campaign of 1917–1918 was another matter. Led by General Sir Edmund Allenby, the British army in Egypt had the task of expelling the Ottoman Turks from the Sinai-Palestine peninsula. One of the definitive battles in this campaign was the Battle of Beersheba.

> " I believe that every soldier who has anything to do with horse or mule has come to love them for what they are and the grand work they have done and are doing in and out of the death zones. "
>
> CAPTAIN SIDNEY GALTREY, 1918.

The light draft horse and the mule formed the "forgotten army," without which the battle on the Western Front would have been virtually impossible.

After the end of World War I, the horses that had served so bravely in the campaign in Palestine were sold to a life of extreme hardship in Egypt. In 1930, Dorothy Brooke, the wife of Sir Geoffrey Brooke, who had commanded the Cavalry Brigade in Egypt, traveled to Cairo and witnessed the plight of thousands of ex-cavalry horses on the streets. On her return to England, she wrote to the Morning Post *newspaper appealing for funds to help save them. The public responded generously, and she was able to buy back some of the warhorses, and in 1934 established the Old War Horse Memorial Hospital to provide free veterinary help for all the working horses and donkeys of Cairo.*

Goodbye Old Man *by Fortunino Matania. The original painting was commissioned in 1916 by The Blue Cross to raise money to relieve the suffering of warhorses in Europe.*

The Battle of Beersheba

Often referred to as "the last successful cavalry charge in history," the Battle of Beersheba took place on October 31, 1917. The aim of the offensive was to break the Turkish defensive line that stretched from Gaza to Beersheba, some 30 miles (50 kilometers) inland. Dwindling water supplies dictated that the wells at Beersheba be taken with some urgency.

The Australian 4th Light Horse Brigade, under Brigadier-General William Grant, was assembled for the task, mounted on Australian Stock Horses (*see Plate 23*). The brigade command knew that their only chance of success lay in speed and surprise. The order to charge was made, and the cavalry charged at a full gallop for four miles (6.5 kilometers) toward the Turkish trenches. The speed of the attack took the enemy completely by surprise, and the 4th Light Horse Brigade quickly overran the trenches and secured the surrender of the Turks. The Australians lost only 31 men in the attack. The brigade's victory at Beersheba was an outstanding achievement, one that is still celebrated in Australia today.

The Horse
at Work

There's a Yiddish proverb that says, "The wagon rests in winter, the sleigh in summer, the horse never." This was certainly true in the eighteenth and nineteenth centuries, when the horse played a central role in the new technologies fostered by the Agricultural and Industrial Revolutions. The horse was an essential part of both rural and urban life in Europe and North America, and fulfilled a role as both a pack and a draft animal well into the twentieth century.

The Agricultural Revolution

Although the horse had been used as a draft animal as early as the second millennium BCE, most agricultural work up to the eighteenth century was still carried out by a team of oxen. In the 1800s, the revolution in agricultural technology created a need for a larger and stronger type of draft animal to pull the new equipment, leading to the development of the heavy agricultural horse.

The Agricultural Revolution began in Britain with the introduction of crop rotation and the development of several innovative agricultural tools. In 1731, Jethro Tull (1674–1741) came up with an idea for a new type of seed drill. Farmers had previously sown their fields by hand, a time-consuming and wasteful activity. Tull's seed drill was a horse-drawn wheeled vehicle that sowed the seed at a controlled rate in straight lines. Other notable inventions included Jethro Tull's horse hoe and the Arbuthnot plow (1771).

With the introduction of these new farming tools, the role of the ox as draft animal became largely obsolete.

> **Did You Know?**
>
> *According to the* Guinness World Records, *the tallest horse in the world was a Shire gelding named Mammoth. The mighty horse was born in 1846 in Bedfordshire, England, measured 21.2½ hh (86½ in), and weighed an estimated 3,000 lb (1,360 kg).*

The horse has played an essential and versatile role in agricultural life for many centuries.

The horse could work faster and in heavier soil conditions, and it became an essential part of rural life in the eighteenth and nineteenth centuries.

The Draft Horse

The draft horse developed from the heavy European breeds of warhorse. They are at least 16 hands high, and weigh 1,600 pounds (725 kilograms) or more. Modern breeds include the Belgians, Clydesdales, Percherons, Shire, and Suffolk Punches (*see Plates 19, 20, 21*).

Agriculture in North America

North America during the 1800s was a land of rapid expansion, and the horse played a prime role in the exploration and settlement of virgin lands.

In 1834, Cyrus Hall McCormick (1809–1884) patented the mechanical reaper, the forerunner of the modern combine harvester. This machine could do the work of 30 men, and did much to change the face of American agriculture. Before 1790, the size of an average American farm was approximately 100 acres (40.5 hectares), 60 years later it had more than doubled.

The McCormick reaper and other new equipment—steel plows, double-width harrows, seed drills, mowers, and others—greatly increased

The Amish use teams of powerful but placid draft horses to work the fields.

the need for heavy draft horses, and the first of these were brought from Europe in the late 1830s. During the subsequent seven decades, more than 27,000 of these muscular animals were imported.

Amish Society

The Amish are an Anabaptist Christian sect that live primarily in Indiana, Pennsylvania, and Ohio. The rules of Amish life are dictated by the *Ordnung*—"order" in German—and they are designed to ensure that members of the community live a simple life devoted to God, family, and the community. According to the *Ordnung*, modern technology, including the car and electricity, should be avoided whenever possible, as these promote sloth, envy, and vanity. The horse, therefore, still plays a central role in everyday Amish society, and is used for both farming and transport. The Amish do not ride on horseback but prefer to travel in a distinctive horse-drawn buggy, usually pulled by Standardbreds and other lighter breeds. For working the fields, the Amish use draft horses, commonly Belgians or Percherons.

Pit ponies carried mining equipment through miles of underground tunnels.

Horse Power to Horsepower

If the story of agriculture features the horse in a leading role, so does the development of industrial society around the world. Nowhere is this more so than in Great Britain, where the Industrial Revolution had its roots.

Down the Mine

From the earliest days of large-scale industrial mining in Britain, it fell to the horse and the pony to provide the pulling power. In simple tunnel mines, ponies were used to carry baskets of coal from the face. As the demand for coal rose sharply during the Industrial Revolution, and mines were dug ever deeper, larger horses were employed

to turn the winding gear that lifted men and coal up the shafts. More and more ponies spent their lives underground, transporting men, equipment, and the mined coal through the endless miles of tunnels, and the numbers increased greatly after 1842, when legislation prohibited women and children from working in the mines. A small wagon could be pulled over a smooth surface, and with the introduction of rails in the mines, a single pony was able to pull several wagons at once.

The working conditions, for both men and animals, were severe, but the Coal Mines Regulation Act of 1887 brought the animals some protection, and their lives began to improve. The number of ponies in the mines reached a peak in 1913, when government figures show there were some 72,000 four-legged employees. However, mechanized coal-cutting equipment eventually produced coal faster than pit ponies could remove it, so powered wagons and then conveyor belts were introduced, and by the 1970s just a few hundred ponies remained.

The mining companies used ponies underground to haul coal wagons.

Did You Know?

The principal breeds used underground in Britain were Welsh ponies, the stocky Dales ponies of Yorkshire, and the small but sturdy Shetland ponies, which average 10.2 hh, and originated in the Shetland Islands off the north coast of Scotland. Shetlands also worked in the mines of the eastern USA.

Industrial Workers

The coal that the ponies hauled fueled the Industrial Revolution, but industry itself needed the power the horse provided—at least for a while. Newly invented mechanical means of production, especially in the cotton mills, held the key to an incredible increase in productivity, but only if the power was available to drive the machines. Where there was no water to drive a wheel, the horse was the obvious alternative to power a treadmill or turn a gin—an abbreviation of "horse engine"—that drove shafts, belt pulleys, and gears to operate the factory. Horses were also used to drive pumps, saws, drills, mill wheels, and even the machinery that bored out cannons at London's Woolwich Arsenal. However, the horse's brush with industry was short lived. Factory machines soon needed more power than horses or water wheels could provide, and the steam engine took over from the late eighteenth century onward, accelerating the "progress" that was to sweep the world.

Did You Know?

James Watt was so confident of the efficiency of his steam engine that he agreed to sell his engines in return for a royalty of one-third of the savings in coal over the Newcomen steam engines that they replaced. However, in the case of customers who were using horses he needed a different way to calculate the royalty, and to do this he invented the unit of "horsepower," which has been in use to define the power of an engine ever since.

The heavy draft horse was a vital element in the development of the new industrial age.

Commercial and Public Transport

Throughout the eighteenth and nineteenth centuries there was a growing need to transport raw materials, finished goods, and people, quickly and efficiently, and the horse, again, provided part of the answer.

By Road ...

The general road system throughout England in the seventeenth century was in poor shape. Toll roads were better maintained, but in general the haulage of heavy goods, using wide carts and teams of horses, was slow and difficult. Lighter goods made better progress, being carried by light horse-drawn carts or pack horses.

... Rail ...

In Britain the system of rails that helped the ponies to drag coal from the mines were soon extended to take the coal on its onward journey.

The first railroads were wooden wagonways along which horses pulled the coal to nearby waterways to be loaded into boats or barges. In the late 1760s, companies began to strengthen the surfaces of the rails with cast iron plates. The improved rails made the horse's task so much easier that it could haul a load 20 times heavier than on the rough unsurfaced roadways.

... and Water

Water transport was a vital link in industrial Britain, as boats could carry vastly greater quantities than a wagon, and with far less effort. Navigable rivers were of limited use, and so the

The horses that pulled the canal barges were called "boaters."

canal system was born, starting in the 1760s. Beside the canal ran a level towpath, along which the heavy horse plodded, towing a barge that might carry in excess of 20 tons of coal or other raw materials. This means of transport was so efficient that it quickly cut the cost of coal by more than half, and horse-drawn barges were still economically viable into the 1950s.

The Omnibus and the Streetcar

Within cities in the USA, the early 1800s saw the development of true public transport: the omnibus or 'bus. These horse-drawn vehicles traveled a regular local route, picking up and dropping off passengers at predetermined points. Taking advantage of the developing railroad technology, these soon evolved into the more efficient streetcar lines, allowing horses to pull greater numbers of passengers along a network of smooth iron rails that ran along the city streets, first in Baltimore (1828), then in New York (1832), and, within 50 years, in cities the length and breadth of the country.

Safe, smooth, and economical, this horse-powered system had its drawbacks, however. Individual horses could only work a few hours a day, and each company needed several horses to run each car.

In the late 1800s, the equine workforce probably numbered more than 250,000 animals, which required considerable stabling, grooming, and feeding, and created copious amounts of manure for the companies to deal with. There was also the issue of health, and when equine flu hit the horse population in the winter of 1872 it brought public transport to a standstill. In their search for alternatives, the streetcar companies tried steam and then cable systems, but it was the electric tram that finally won the day, putting the horses out of business by the end of the century.

Did You Know?

Horse-powered ferries, using a horizontal treadmill to drive the paddle wheels, were a relatively common sight on North American waters throughout the nineteenth century. There are no surviving examples, but the remains of a horse-propelled boat were discovered in 1983 on the bed of Lake Champlain near Burlington, Vermont, with all its propulsion machinery intact.

Heavy horses were used by the railroad companies for shunting work.

Coaching

The coach was an enclosed four-wheeled vehicle drawn by four or six horses. It was first produced in Europe during the Middle Ages, but the road conditions at that time made it a less than comfortable means of transport, and travel was more commonly undertaken on horseback. In the eighteenth century, however, a number of design improvements were made to the coach, and these, together with the development of better roads, made coach travel more popular. In 1785, the London-to-Edinburgh, Scotland, coach route was established, a 400-mile (643-kilometer) journey that took between ten and 12 days. That same year, the New York City-to-Albany stagecoach route opened.

Coaches would travel between 12 and 18 hours a day, and cover anything from 25 to 40 miles (40–64 kilometers). Typically, the coach carried between eight and 14 passengers, some traveled on the outside of the coach, sitting with the driver, while the more fortunate—and wealthy!—passengers traveled inside. Coach horses were bred for strength and speed, and new breeds included the Cleveland Bay (*see Plate 17*).

Coach travel became a popular mode of transport in the eighteenth century.

The Coaching Inn

The traditional British pub owes its existence to the age of coaching. Coaching inns were established at approximately seven-mile (11.25-kilometer) intervals to provide stabling for horses and refreshments for passengers and coach drivers. Although they no longer provide stabling facilities, many of the inns from this period survive as public houses.

Highwaymen

Robbery was one of the greatest hazards faced by the eighteenth-century coach passenger. Coaches were commonly held up by a masked pistol-wielding highwayman on a horse, who demanded valuables from the coach's occupants. One of the most notorious highwaymen in England was Dick Turpin (1706–1739), who rode a Thoroughbred horse called Black Bess. The mare herself had been acquired during a robbery. Legend has it that Dick Turpin once rode Black Bess 150 miles (241 kilometers) from London to York in 15 hours while fleeing from justice. Dick Turpin was eventually hanged on the gallows for horse rustling.

Privately Owned Vehicles

During the eighteenth century, the privately owned horse-drawn vehicle began to enjoy popularity with the aristocracy. Many were of a sporty nature, including the Phaeton. There were many different types of Phaeton, but they all had four very large wheels, were lightly sprung, and were capable of relatively fast speeds. The Spider Phaeton was named for its delicate body, and it was usually drawn by a

The armed highwayman was a constant threat to the coach passenger.

pair of horses. It originated in the USA in the 1860s, but also enjoyed great popularity in Europe toward the end of the century. Although designed to be driven by the owner, the Spider Phaeton had a seat at the rear for a groom.

There were also a number of privately driven carts, which were originally used as sporting vehicles. The Dog Cart had a ventilated compartment, and was used to carry fox hounds to the hunt. There was also a Cocking Cart, used to transport fighting cocks. These carts eventually lost their sporting intention and developed into pleasure carts.

Did You Know?

The term "Phaeton" has a classical origin. According to Greek legend, Phaethon, the son of the sun-god Helios, drove the Chariot of the Sun so recklessly that Zeus struck down the youth with a lightning bolt.

The Pony Express

The Pony Express was founded in 1860 by William H. Russell, William B. Waddell, and Alexander Majors to provide a system of communication between the Midwest and California. Before then all mail went by stagecoach and took several months to reach its destination. The Pony Express greatly reduced mail delivery times.

The Pony Express carried mail between St. Joseph, Missouri, and Sacramento, California, traversing the states of Kansas, Nebraska, Colorado, Wyoming, Utah, and Nevada on the way. The journey was 1,966 miles (3,154 kilometers) long, and the route was fraught with danger. Riders faced the constant danger of Indian attacks, treacherous terrain, and severe weather.

The service began on April 3, 1860, with riders leaving simultaneously from St. Joseph and Sacramento. The very first trip to Sacramento took just nine days and 23 hours.

More than 180 men rode for the Pony Express. Their youngest rider, Charlie Miller, was only 11 years old. They rode 24 hours a day, through all weathers, for a monthly pay of $100. One rider would cover between 75 and 100 miles (120–160 kilometers) before

Did You Know?

The fastest ride in Pony Express history took seven days and 17 hours, and involved a very important item of mail—the riders were carrying President Lincoln's Inaugural Address.

Although short-lived, the Pony Express is one of the enduring legends of the American West.

"WANTED. Young, skinny, wiry fellows. Not over 18. Must be expert riders. Willing to risk death daily. Orphans preferred."

PONY EXPRESS RECRUITING ADVERTISEMENT

> "Our coach was a swinging and swaying cage of the most sumptuous description—an imposing cradle on wheels ... drawn by six handsome horses ...."

MARK TWAIN (1835–1910) IN
ROUGHING IT (1872)

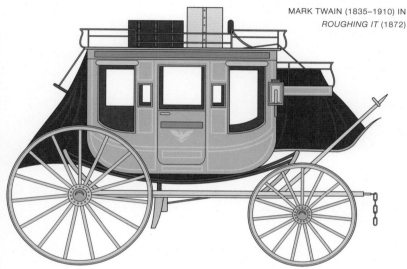

The Wells Fargo stagecoaches were made by the Abbot-Downing company of Concord, New Hampshire.

another took his place, but horses were changed every ten miles (16 kilometers) or so. There were between 400 and 500 horses in service, including Mustangs, Morgans, and Thoroughbreds. In its 18-month history, approximately 35,000 pieces of mail were carried over more than 650,000 miles, and only one sack of mail ever went missing. The company closed in October 1861 because of financial losses and the completion of the Pacific Telegraph line.

Wells Fargo Overland Stagecoach

In 1852, Henry Wells and William Fargo opened the first office of the Wells Fargo & Co. in California. It served the banking interests of the West, and soon earned a reputation for honest dealing. As well as banking services, the company offered express delivery of gold and other valuables by any means available—steamship, railroad, and stagecoach. At first, Wells Fargo & Co. used privately owned stage companies for their deliveries, but in 1866 the company united all the existing Western stagecoach lines, and began the operation of the Wells Fargo Overland Stagecoach line.

Between 1866 and 1869, all the major routes east of the Missouri River were served by a six-horse Wells Fargo stagecoach. Armed outriders rode shotgun in hostile Indian country and also protected the coaches from "road agents" who would hold up the coaches to rob passengers of their valuables and hijack payroll strongboxes.

The city horse had a tough life, and was often severely ill-treated.

The City Horse

In the nineteenth century, thousands of horses were employed in the cities of North America and Europe. They were used to pull a variety of vehicles, from fancy aristocratic carriages to fire engines, and from funeral hearses to brewery wagons. The lot of the working horse was hard, and the animals were often beaten and abused to the point of death.

Fire departments used horses to pull their trucks to the scene of a fire.

Horse-Drawn Fire Engines

The New York Fire Department first began using horses in 1832, and by 1906 nearly 1,500 horses were employed to pull the fire trucks. When the fire alarm sounded, horses would be moved into position underneath suspended harnesses. These would then be lowered onto their backs and secured. The entire operation took less than two minutes.

The Funeral Horse

The wealthy members of society took their last journey in an ornate horse-drawn funeral hearse. The traditional hearse was a black, glass-sided carriage, decorated with gold and silver gilt. The hearse was pulled by six black horses, commonly Friesians (*see Plate 14*), each one adorned with a large black ostrich-feather plume.

The caparisoned horse is the riderless horse that follows the casket in a funeral procession. Traditionally, the empty boots of the deceased are put in a reversed position in the stirrups. This tradition is believed to have originated in the time of Genghis Khan, when a horse was sacrificed to honor a dead warrior. In the USA, any officer ranked Colonel or above in the Army or Marine Corps is honored with a caparisoned horse at his funeral, including the President as the nation's military Commander-in-Chief. The most famous caparisoned horse was Black Jack, who took part in the military funeral processions of three US presidents: John F. Kennedy (1963), Herbert Hoover (1964), and Lyndon B. Johnson (1973).

Black Beauty

Anna Sewell's novel *Black Beauty* was first published in 1877, and it has remained in print ever since. The book is narrated by the horse Black Beauty, and tells the story of his life and the hardships and cruelty that he and his friends, Ginger and Merrylegs, have to endure. Sewell wrote the book in an effort to seek more humane treatment for the nineteenth-century working horse, in particular the abolition of the bearing rein, a form of restraint used to keep a horse's head erect as it pulled a carriage. The bearing rein is vividly described by Black Beauty in the book:

… we had a steep hill to go up. Then I began to understand what I had heard of. Of course I wanted to put my head forward and take the carriage up with a will, as we had been used to do: but no, I had to pull with my head up now, and that took all the spirit out of me, and the strain came on my back and legs … Day by day, hole by hole our bearing reins were shortened, and instead of looking forward with pleasure to having my harness put on as I used to do, I began to dread it.

The book had a profound effect on the lot of the working horse, and led to the abolition of the bearing rein.

The novel Black Beauty *led to an improvement in the life of the carriage horse.*

The modern police horse sometimes needs to wear protective riot gear.

The Police Horse

The police horse is a common sight in many cities around the world, used to patrol streets, direct traffic, control crowds, and suppress riots. No particular breed is used, although a police horse must have the necessary calm temperament to tolerate heavy traffic conditions and jostling crowds. A police horse must undergo intensive training to teach it to stay calm despite being subjected to frightening noises, smoke bombs, and missiles.

The Royal Canadian Mounted Police

Dressed in a distinctive uniform and armed with a reputation for always "getting his man," the Canadian "Mountie" is probably the most famous mounted policeman in the world. The

Royal Canadian Mounted Police force was created in 1873 by Sir John A. Macdonald, the first Prime Minister of Canada, as a temporary body to bring law and order to the frontier regions. Originally known as the Northwest Mounted Police, the Royal Canadian Mounted Police (RCMP) became the official police force of Canada in 1920. Until 1966, all RCMP recruits had to undergo equestrian training, but officers must now apply specifically to be part of the mounted unit.

The Canadian Mountie wears a distinctive red coat and broad-brimmed hat.

Did You Know?

Established in 1758, the London Bow Street Horse Patrol is the oldest known mounted police unit in the world.

The Ceremonial Horse

Many countries still have mounted regiments that fulfill a purely ceremonial role. On state occasions these regiments provide a colorful display of pomp and ceremony that bears little resemblance to the role of the cavalry on the bloody battlefields of yesteryear.

The Household Cavalry

The Household Cavalry is a mounted unit of the British Army, consisting of the Life Guards and the Blues and Royals—formerly the Royal Horse Guards and the 1st Royal Dragoons. It is responsible for guarding and escorting the British monarch at ceremonial occasions, including Trooping of the Colour and during state visits by foreign leaders.

The horses used by the squadrons of the Household Cavalry are black, although of no particular breed. The drum horse used by the Household Cavalry is much heavier in build, and is usually piebald or skewbald in color. As well as a rider, the drum horse has to carry two large kettle drums weighing 44 pounds (20 kilograms) each. A drum horse is controlled by reins attached to its rider's feet.

The US 1st Cavalry Division

Despite the mechanization of the US Cavalry, its history and traditions are maintained by the Horse Cavalry Detachment, based at Fort Hood, Texas, whose mission is to serve as a link to America's military past, to aid the US Army's recruiting efforts across the country, and to represent the 1st Cavalry Division in military and civic ceremonies, parades, and demonstrations.

The displays of ceremonial regiments bear little resemblance to the role of the cavalry at war.

The Structure of the Horse

Several specific evolutionary features make the horse a most remarkable creature. The exceptional development of its long lower leg and foot bones, together with the powerful tendons and musculature of the upper legs and torso, enable the horse to maintain high speeds over a considerable distance. Both forelegs and back legs are angled under the body to give the animal great stability and enable it to stay absolutely level while running—for which riders should be grateful.

This chapter looks at every aspect of the horse's anatomy to give a complete physical picture of this unique animal.

Points of the Horse

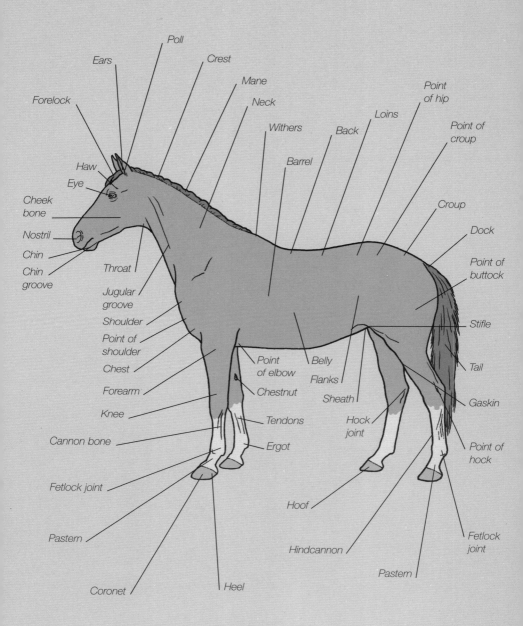

Poll
Ears
Crest
Mane
Neck
Forelock
Withers
Barrel
Back
Loins
Point of hip
Point of croup
Haw
Eye
Cheek bone
Croup
Nostril
Dock
Chin
Point of buttock
Chin groove
Throat
Jugular groove
Shoulder
Point of shoulder
Stifle
Chest
Point of elbow
Belly
Flanks
Tail
Forearm
Chestnut
Sheath
Gaskin
Knee
Tendons
Hock joint
Point of hock
Cannon bone
Ergot
Fetlock joint
Pastern
Hoof
Fetlock joint
Hindcannon
Coronet
Heel
Pastern

Physical Terminology

Some of the terms used to describe the points of the horse are unique to the equine world and can cause confusion to the novice. In order to understand the conformation of the horse and to discuss any physical problems or illnesses with your veterinarian or farrier, a working knowledge of these terms is essential.

Back The area that extends between the withers and the loins.

Barrel The "body" of the horse. The curve of the barrel is formed by the ribs.

Cannon bone The lower leg, below the knee of the foreleg and hock of the hind leg.

Chestnut The horny growths found on the inside of the legs.

Coronet The area of soft tissue just above the hoof; connects the hoof to the pastern.

Crest The convex line formed by the upper part of the horse's neck; extends from the poll to the withers.

Croup The area from the highest point of the hindquarters to the top of the tail.

Dock The flesh-and-bone part of the tail. A docked tail has been cut back to this point.

Ergot The horny growth found behind the fetlock joint.

Fetlock The narrow sloping area just above the hoof.

Forelock The tuft of hair that falls between the ears onto the forehead.

Flank The slightly indented area behind the barrel, where the hind legs and the stomach of the horse meet.

Gaskin The upper hind leg, between the hock and the stifle.

Hock The joint between the gaskin and cannon bone; corresponds to the human ankle.

Loins The area where the back ends.

Muzzle The part of the face that includes the chin,the mouth, and the nostrils.

Mane The long, coarse hair growing from the crest of the neck.

Pastern The angled part of the horse's lower leg, just above the hoof and below the fetlock.

Poll The highest point of the horse, the spot between the ears where the cranium meets the vertebrae.

Stifle The area located at the front of the hind leg, below the point of the hip.

Withers The highest point of a horse's shoulder, between the neck and the back. The height of a horse is measured at this point.

Conformation

The conformation of a horse refers to the way a horse's body parts are put together—its skeletal frame and muscular structure. Horses with "good" conformation are more likely to remain sound; those with poor conformation tend to put undue stress and strain on the limbs, which predisposes them to lameness. Conformational standards vary according to the breed and the type of work for which the horse has been bought, but the following characteristics give an indication of the ideal form.

Head

The head should be well proportioned with the rest of the body. A head that is too large or too small will affect the balance of a horse. The face should be straight and taper to a small muzzle with wide nostrils. The forehead should be flat and broad. Clear, generous eyes, set wide part, are desirable. The jaw should be balanced, and the teeth should meet in a neat bite. Horses with jaw deformities, such as an underbite, will have dental problems or difficulties in eating.

Neck

The neck should have a slight arch and be of a good length. It should meet the shoulders at a 45-degree angle, and there should be a slight dip in front of the withers. A high-arched, or "swan," neck—where the head meets the neck at an acute angle—may cause respiratory problems.

Body

The withers should be prominent enough to keep a saddle in place. The chest should be deep and muscular, with well-sprung ribs to allow for good respiratory and digestive capacity. The horse should have a strong, well-muscled back and loin that is not too long. Long-backed horses tend to be weaker. The hindquarters should be muscular and strong, and there should be a gradual slope from the croup to the dock.

Genders

Foal *A baby horse.*

Filly *A female horse or pony under the age of four years.*

Colt *A male horse or pony under the age of four years.*

Mare *A female horse over the age of four years.*

Gelding *A castrated male horse or pony.*

Stallion *An uncastrated male horse, also known as "entire."*

Conformation of the Horse

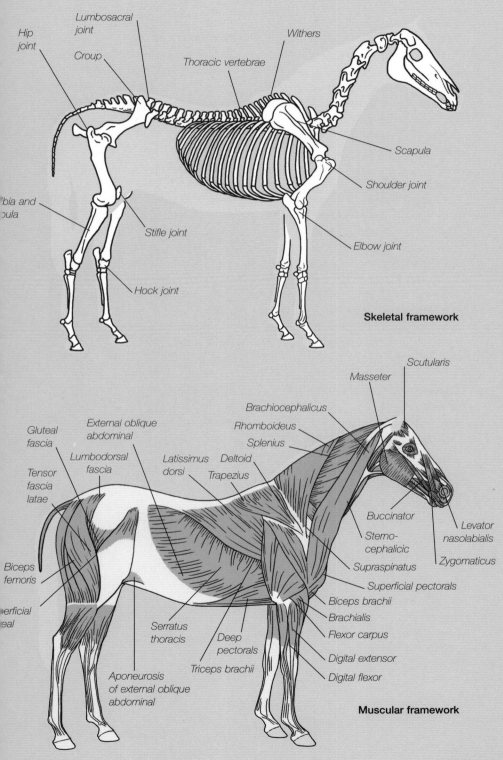

Skeletal framework

Hip joint

Lumbosacral joint

Croup

Thoracic vertebrae

Withers

Scapula

Shoulder joint

Elbow joint

bia and ula

Stifle joint

Hock joint

Muscular framework

Gluteal fascia

External oblique abdominal

Lumbodorsal fascia

Latissimus dorsi

Deltoid

Trapezius

Splenius

Rhomboideus

Brachiocephalicus

Masseter

Scutularis

Buccinator

Levator nasolabialis

Zygomaticus

Sterno-cephalicic

Supraspinatus

Superficial pectorals

Biceps brachii

Brachialis

Flexor carpus

Digital extensor

Digital flexor

Tensor fascia latae

Biceps femoris

erficial eal

Serratus thoracis

Deep pectorals

Triceps brachii

Aponeurosis of external oblique abdominal

The Limbs

The leg bones should be flat, clean, and free of swelling. When the horse is standing square, the weight should be distributed evenly on all four legs. When a horse is trotting, the hind legs should travel in the same path as the front. This is known as "tracking up."

The Forelegs

The legs should be strong and straight, and the width between the feet should match that between the forearms at the chest. The knees should be flat at the front. When the legs are viewed from the front, a straight line from the point of the shoulder should divide the legs into equal halves. From the side, there should be a straight line through the forearm, knee, cannon bone, fetlock, and the bulb of the heel.

Conformational Faults of the Forelegs

Base narrow A horse with a wide chest will often have legs that tend to slope inward.

Base wide In narrow-chested horses there is often a greater distance between the feet than between the limbs at the chest.

Pigeon toe (toe in) In this case, the toes point inward. The whole limb may turn inward or the deviation may occur lower down, for example at the fetlock. Pigeon toes may cause the horse to "paddle," or swing outward, as it moves.

Remedial horseshoes can help to correct some conformational faults.

Splay foot (toe out) In this instance, the feet turn outward. Again, it may occur high up. This conformational fault may cause the horse to swing his foot inward, an action known as "winging," causing damage to the opposite leg.

The Hind Legs

When viewed from behind, there should be a straight line through the point of the buttock down the center of the leg. From the side, the line should pass from the point of the buttock, down the cannon bone, and touch the ground just behind the heel. The hocks should be clean cut, large, and deep.

Conformational Faults of the Hind Legs

Cow hocks A horse with cow hocks has legs that are base narrow to the hocks and then base wide from the hocks to the feet. This causes additional stress on the hock joint, and may also cause bone spavin (*see p. 298*).

Sickle hocks A sickle-hocked horse stands with its legs placed too far forward. This is because there is too much angle in the hock. This is a serious conformational fault that causes severe stress on the hock joint.

Conformational Faults of the Limbs

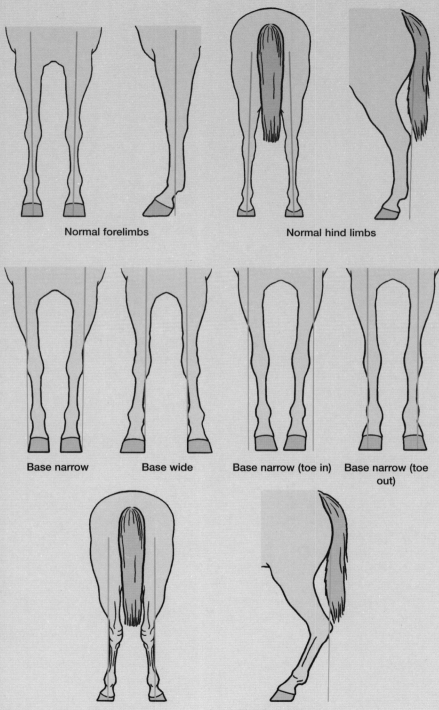

Normal forelimbs

Normal hind limbs

Base narrow

Base wide

Base narrow (toe in)

Base narrow (toe out)

Cow hocks

Sickle hocks

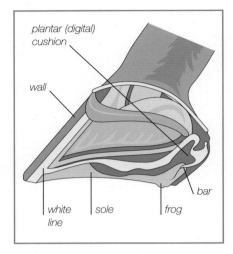

plantar (digital) cushion

wall

bar

white line

sole

frog

The walls, bars, and frog are the weight-bearing structures of the foot.

The Foot

The foot bears the weight of the horse, and well-shaped feet are essential if the horse is to remain sound. The feet pairs should be of the same size and shape. Hooves should be round and wide at the heel, with a thick wall. The sole should be slightly concave—the hind soles more so than the front. A perpendicular line from the center of the heel, through the frog to the toe, should divide the hoof into equal halves.

Conformational Faults of the Foot

A horse with poor leg conformation will typically have poor foot conformation, as the hoof will usually land unevenly on the ground, putting additional strain and wear on one part of the foot.

Flat feet The soles of the foot are not as concave as they should be. This often causes bruising. A horse will also tend to land on his heels to avoid pressure on the soles. Remedial shoeing will help. A farrier can fit a shoe with a shock-absorbent pad to ease the pressure.

Contracted feet The foot is smaller and narrower than it should be, especially at the heels. The frog, which acts as a shock absorber, will shrivel. Contracted feet can be caused by poor shoeing or by leaving the shoes on for too long. Navicular disease (*see p. 300*) also causes the heels to contract.

Clubfoot With a clubfoot, the angle of the hoof to the ground is much steeper than normal, making the foot more upright. The toe is typically shorter than normal and the heel is typically longer than normal. Clubfoot may be an inherited condition or it may be caused by injury or poor shoeing.

Dropped sole A dropped sole is usually the result of laminitis (*see p. 302*). The sole will drop below the level of the walls and will bruise easily.

Thin walls and soles This is an inherited condition that predisposes the horse to lameness.

Did You Know?

According to the Guinness World Records, *the world's smallest living horse is a miniature sorrel-brown mare belonging to Kay and Paul Goessling of St. Louis, Missouri. The tiny horse measures just 17½ in (44.5 cm), or just over 4.1 hh.*

Measuring a Horse

The height of a horse is measured in hands (abbreviated to hh). One hand is defined as four inches or 10.2 centimeters. This somewhat odd form of measurement originates from the ancient practice of measuring a horse with the width of the palm and closed thumb. It is very important that a horse or pony be measured accurately, as many equestrian competitions have height restrictions.

Nowadays, a measuring stick is used to determine the height of a horse. The horse should be stood on level ground and must stand "square." The measurement is taken from the top of the withers to the ground. A horse that measures 16 hands high is 64 inches (163.2 centimeters) from the ground to the top of the withers. If a horse measures 65 inches, this is written as 16.1 hh and expressed as "sixteen-one," a hand being divided into four one-inch (2.5-centimeter) increments.

Did You Know?

A pony is classified as 14.2 hh or lower. Anything over this height is classified as a horse.

A horse is measured from the top of the withers to the ground.

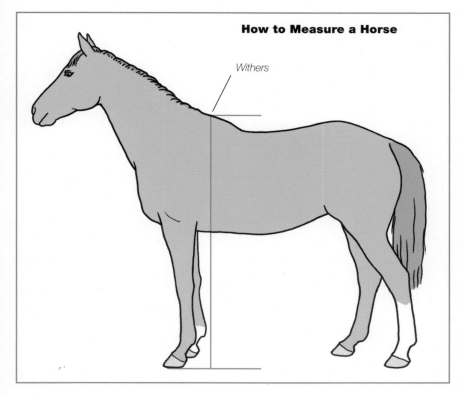

How to Measure a Horse

Withers

Equine Dentition

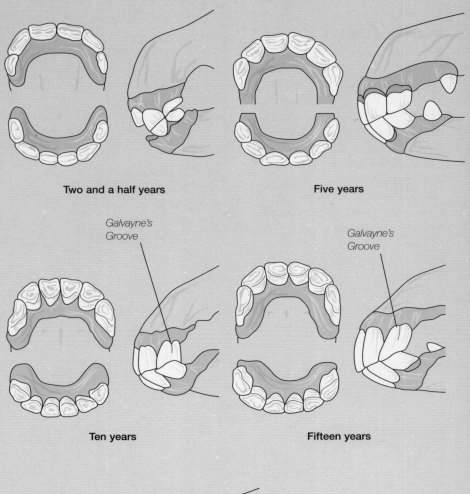

Two and a half years

Five years

Galvayne's Groove

Ten years

Galvayne's Groove

Fifteen years

Galvayne's Groove

Twenty years

From the Horse's Mouth

Unless a horse has official registration papers, the best method of assessing its age is from the teeth. Although it isn't a foolproof method, looking at the growth, wear, and angle of a horse's teeth will give a fair indication of the age of the animal.

A foal is born toothless, but the first incisors will appear eight to ten days after birth. A nine-month-old foal will have a full set of temporary baby, or milk, teeth.

Did You Know?

Regardless of their actual date of birth, all Thoroughbreds have an "official" birthday. In the northern hemisphere this is January 1, and in the southern hemisphere it is July 1. A Thoroughbred celebrates its first birthday in the year following its birth.

Adult teeth begin to appear when the horse is approximately two-and-a-half years old. The permanent teeth are called hypsodont, which means that they have very long crowns—up to three and a half inches (eight centimeters)—and short roots. By the age of five, all permanent teeth—12 molars and six incisors in each jaw—are in place. Canine teeth, two in each jaw, erupt in the male horse between four and five years of age—mares do not generally have canines.

At seven years, hooks appear on the corner incisor teeth; these disappear at eight and reappear at 11 years.

Glossary

A horse is said to be "rising six" when it is nearer six than five. It is said to be "six off" when it is nearer six than seven.

At ten years, a discolored longitudinal groove, called Galvayne's Groove, appears at the gum margin of the upper corner incisors. By 15 years, the groove extends halfway down the tooth. When it has reached the bottom, the horse will be approximately 20 years old. The groove will have disappeared by the time the horse reaches 30. The angle at which the upper and lower incisors meet, which becomes gradually more acute, and the appearance of the surface of the tooth also give an indication of a horse's age.

The newborn foal is toothless.

Did You Know?

A horse's tooth grows about one-eighth of an inch (2 mm) each year.

Colors and Markings

An accepted vocabulary to describe the markings and colors of horses is used for official identification papers, and all horse owners and riders need to be acquainted with these terms.

Main Colors

Bay Reddish to dark-brown coat with black points on the legs, muzzle, mane and tail, and the tips of the ears. Very dark bays may be mistaken for black.

Black Pure black coat. True black is uncommon.

Brown Dark-brown to black hair. No black points.

Buckskin Light to dark sandy-yellow or tan color with black points.

Chestnut Sometimes known as sorrel. Varies from pale gold through golden reddish-brown to a dark-liver chestnut. Flaxen chestnuts have a cream or silver-colored mane and tail.

Did You Know?

Lipizzaners, renowned for their snowy-white appearance, are actually born with dark coats. The color gradually lightens with each change of coat, becoming pure white by the time the animal is around seven years old. One in every 200 foals retains the dark coloration, and this is considered, surprisingly, a sign of good luck.

Dun Sandy-yellow or gold coat with black or brown points. They usually have a dark stripe down their back and may have zebra markings on the legs.

Gray Black skin with white or gray hair. A dapple-gray horse has distinct dark-gray circles on a lighter-gray base. A fleabitten gray has speckles of black or brown hair on an otherwise light-gray body. An iron- or steel-gray horse has a black base coat with mixed white or gray hairs. Rose-gray horses have gray hairs tinted with red. Gray horses often lighten with age.

Palomino Golden coat, with a white or light-cream-colored mane and tail.

Pinto Large patches of white on another base color, usually black, bay, or chestnut. The terms piebald (black and white) and skewbald (white and any other color, although usually brown or chestnut) are also used to describe the pinto coloring.

Roan A blue roan has a mixture of black-brown and white hairs; a strawberry roan has chestnut and white hairs; a bay roan has brown and white hairs.

Spotted A spotted coat has patterns of colored spots on another color, usually white or roan.

White The true white horse has pink skin and white hair.

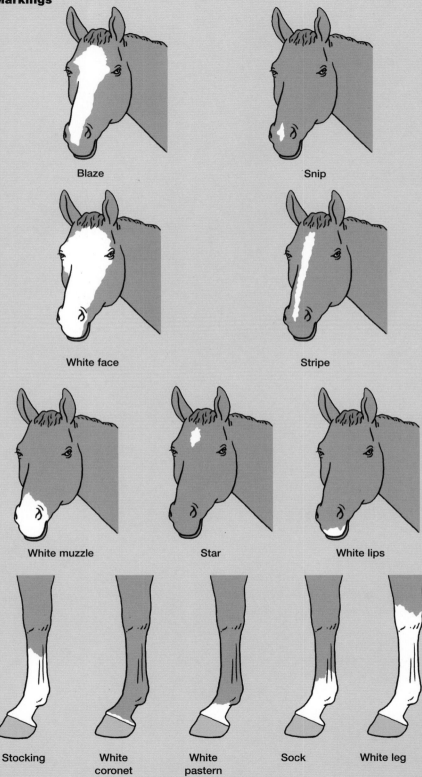

Blaze

Snip

White face

Stripe

White muzzle

Star

White lips

Stocking

White coronet

White pastern

Sock

White leg

The Natural Gaits

The natural gaits of the horse are the walk, trot, canter, and gallop.

The Walk

The walk is the slowest of the gaits. There are four beats to each walk stride, and each hoofbeat is distinct and can be heard easily. If the horse starts to walk from the right hind leg, the walk sequence will be: right hind leg, right front leg, left hind leg, left front leg.

The Trot

The trot is a two-beat gait in which diagonal pairs of legs move together, so, for example, the right hind and left front move together, and the left hind and right front move together.

The Canter

The canter is a smooth, three-beat gait. In the canter, one of the horse's hind legs propels the horse forward. If the canter begins on the left hind leg, the next beat in the sequence will consist of the left foreleg and the right hind leg. These should touch the ground simultaneously. On the third beat, the right foreleg touches the ground—this is termed the leading leg. When cantering on a circle, the horse should always lead with the inside leg. A horse that is leading with the outside leg is said to be on the "wrong lead."

The Gallop

The gallop is a fast, four-beat gait, and is very similar to the canter. As in a canter, the horse will strike off with its non-leading hind leg. However, the second stage of the canter becomes the second and third stages in a gallop sequence. This is because the hind foot hits the ground a split second before the front foot. If the horse strikes off with the left hind leg, the gallop sequence will be: left hind leg, right hind leg, left foreleg, right foreleg, followed by a moment of suspension when all four feet are off the ground.

The Gaited Horse

As well as the natural gaits, there are a number of specialized gaits that appear in particular breeds or specially trained horses. These include the pace—in which the legs move in lateral pairs—the slow gait, the rack, the tölt, the running walk, and the fox trot. Gaited horses include the American Standardbred, the American Saddlebred (see Plates 43, 44), the Peruvian Paso, the Icelandic Horse, the Tennessee Walker, and the Missouri Fox Trotter (see Plates 45, 47).

Did You Know?

The Tennessee Walker has a unique gait, the "running walk." This smooth, gliding gait retains the 4-beat cadence of a normal walk, but the hind foot overreaches the track left by the front foot by as much as 24 inches (60 centimeters).

Natural Gaits of the Horse

Walk

Trot

Canter

Gallop

"A canter is the cure for all evils."

BENJAMIN DISRAELI (1804–1881)

Behavior and Communication

In their natural state horses are social creatures, and much of their behavior can be understood from this perspective. Through a range of noises, body postures, facial expressions, and physical movements, horses communicate with one another and give out signals that we, as handlers and riders, can and should be aware of. By picking up the clues, we can tell at a glance whether a horse is feeling, for example, contented, anxious, or unwell, and we can treat the animal appropriately, making for a relationship that is both safer and more satisfying.

The Nature of the Horse

In order to cultivate a working relationship with the horse, it is necessary for the handler to appreciate the innate nature of the animal. We can best do this by studying the evolutionary pressures that shaped the horse, and also by looking at the present-day herds of wild and feral horses in their natural environments.

In the wild the horse lives in herds that have a strong social hierarchy. This particular type of social organization developed as a response to the basic evolutionary selective forces of survival and reproduction. The horse is a natural prey animal, and there is a greater degree of safety in numbers. As the horse's legs are designed for fast running, the horse's first instinct when faced with danger is flight, not fight, although a cornered horse will fight for survival. This is an important consideration for the rider.

When faced with something scary, the domesticated horse will want to turn and bolt. When a horse bolts, the adrenaline produced in its brain stops it listening to commands other than "Go." If a horse is to be a safe mount, it must be trained to listen to the rider at all times and to overcome the instinct to flee.

Leadership

The herd is protected and led by a dominant stallion, aided by an alpha mare, and the other members of the herd look to these two for leadership. In the domestic situation the horseman takes over the leadership role, simply by acting as the dominant member of the partnership. It is the naturally submissive nature of the horse that allows the rider to achieve dominance over the much stronger and larger animal.

In the wild the dominant stallion will sometimes face challenges from arrogant young males keen to take over leadership of the herd. The rider,

Horses are social animals, and in the wild they will band together in herds.

too, will be challenged from time to time by a young or poorly mannered horse. The handler should never lose the challenge or the horse will assume a position of dominance and its behavior may become dangerous to the handler. Biting, kicking, or striking out are normal ways for a horse to assert its dominance, but they are totally inappropriate ways to behave around humans. The key for the horseman is to avoid such confrontations, and not to ask more of a horse than it is willing to give at any one time.

The herd is hierarchical in nature, and every horse in the group has his or her place in the "pecking order." Horses kept at grass will also establish a hierarchy. The submissive horse will often be forced to wait its turn at the water trough or will be moved off its hay by the more aggressive horse.

Understanding the way a horse is likely to behave in response to natural stimuli is the key to training and the basis of natural horsemanship (*see pp. 138–139*).

Herdbound Horses

A herdbound horse is one that becomes stressed when its stable companions leave the field or barn. It will run up and down the fence line, frantically whinnying to the other horses. In the barn it may paw or weave in its stall.

Did You Know?

Over 30 herds of white horses run free on the salt marshes of southern France. The Camargue horse (see Plate 11), often referred to as the "Horse of the Sea," has roamed on this land since prehistoric times.

Horses will fight to establish dominance over one another, biting (top) and rearing.

A horse may rear in play or excitement, or it may be a defensive response to a stressful situation.

"Reading" a Horse

The body language of a horse reveals much about its moods and intentions, and many of the problems that humans encounter with horses can be avoided if we take the time to make the effort to understand what the horse is "saying." When trying to read a horse's body language, overall body posture is the first consideration. A tense, excited horse will have a raised head and tail, giving it a rounded outline. In contrast, the submissive or relaxed horse will have a lowered posture.

In the wild horses need to protect themselves against predators and defend their position in the herd hierarchy, so much of the horse's body language signals aggressive intent. Actual fighting among horses can exact a high price, even for the victor, so displays of aggression are designed to cause a horse to submit to the more dominant one without the need for physical conflict.

Face

The facial expressions of a horse are extremely revealing. An annoyed horse will screw up its nose in disgust. An anxious horse is "tightmouthed," and a worried horse will have wrinkles around the eyes. The aggressive horse will have wide open eyes, which are generally staring fixedly at the object of his aggression. If the horse is threatening to bite, it will extend its head, open its mouth, and bare its teeth. If a horse wants to show submission, it will try to back away, at the same time avoiding eye contact with the other horse. Young horses show a submissive behavior known as "mouthing." A horse that engages in mouthing extends its head, and has an open mouth with the lips drawn back.

It will then open and close the jaws, but without bringing the lips or teeth together. This is similar to the behavior shown by the horse who wants to engage in mutual grooming.

Ears

The ears are the most expressive part of a horse, and their position is a good indication of what the horse is feeling. The angry or aggressive horse will stretch its head forward slightly and pin the ears back flat against the neck. A horse with forward, pricked ears is interested, but inattentive to the rider. Floppy ears indicate relaxation. Flickering ears indicate that the horse is both attentive and listening.

If the horse's ears are facing backward, the horse is listening behind. A horse with flickering ears that are facing both forward and backward is aware of sounds from all directions.

Tail

The tail is also used as a tool of communication. An excited or aggressive horse will hold its tail up high, while a frightened one will put its tail flat between his legs, similar to a dog. Swishing the tail up and down or from side to side is a sign of annoyance or pain, and may be an indication that the horse is about to kick.

Body

The way a horse orients its body is also a telling signal. A horse that turns its quarters toward another horse or person or pushes with its shoulder is being a bully and is likely to lash out aggressively. A submissive horse will lower its quarters and try to turn away.

A foal will recognize its mother by the sound of her nicker as well as her smell.

Vocal communication

Horses also communicate with each other vocally. Recognizing what the horse is saying may give a forewarning of subsequent behavior:

Bellow The bellow is used to assert authority, particularly by dominant stallions.

Blow Gentle exhalation of air through the nose. Used by the curious horse, for example, when meeting another horse or smelling droppings.

Neigh/Whinny The neigh is the loudest and longest of the horse's sounds. It is made to attract attention, especially when separated from companions.

Nicker A friendly greeting, often in anticipation of food. Nickering may also be made by a mare to her foal. The sound is caused by a vibration of the vocal cords, and is made with the mouth closed.

Snort The snort is a loud sound made by the horse when it is particularly excited or frightened. It is made by exhaling through the nose with the mouth shut, and it causes a vibration in the nostrils. The sound normally lasts about one second.

Squeal The squeal is often used as a warning for a horse to back off or it can be used by a mare to scold her foal. Also, the sound is typically made by mares in heat. The squeal can be heard at a distance and may attract a stallion.

Plate 1: This model of a Persian chariot is part of the Oxus treasure, a collection of gold and silver items found by the Oxus River (now the Amu Darya River). It dates to c. 5–4th century BCE.

Plate 2: This classical Greek bronze was discovered at the site of a shipwreck off the cape Artemision in north Euboea. It is dated to c.140 BCE and is referred to as the Jockey of Artemision.

Plate 3: As this beautifully proportioned drawing of a rider on a rearing horse shows, Leonardo da Vinci (1452–1519) was a supremely talented observer of natural forms.

Plate 4 (right): A richly detailed example of Mongol art depicting Genghis Khan and his hordes. Using both horses and elephants as instruments of war gave the great leader the advantage.

Plate 5 The Horse in Art

Plate 5: Mare and Fillies, *by the English painter George Stubbs (1724–1806). Stubbs received many equine commissions, and his* paintings provide a clear indication of the importance of the horse to the aristocracy in 18th-century Britain.

Plates 6–7 The Horse in Art

Plate 6: The ill-fated Charge of the Light Brigade, as depicted by Richard Woodville (1825–1855), was led by Lord Cardigan at the Battle of Balaclava on October 25, 1854.

Plate 7 (right): The Plains Indians benefited from the reintroduction of the horse to North America. They became expert horsemen, as the US Cavalry would find to their cost.

Plate 8 (below): The Arabian horse is noted for its intelligence, beauty, spirit, and stamina. Breed characteristics include a "dished" face, large eyes, and an arched tail.

Plate 9 (bottom): The Akhal-Teke is a horse of the desert. The Turkoman peoples have long used the Akhal-Teke for racing, and the breed is also famed as an endurance horse.

Plate 10 (below): At 10–12 hands high, the Caspian is a pony, but its proportions and characteristics make it more horselike. It may be a descendant of the royal horses of ancient Persia.

Plate 11 (bottom): Feral Camargue horses live on the salt marshes of the Rhône delta in southern France. They are used to round up the black fighting bulls of the Camargue.

Plate 12 (below): The Quarter Horse is the quintessential horse of the American West. They are the most popular breed of cow pony on working ranches, but also make good pleasure horses.

Plate 13 (bottom): Hackneys have a high-stepping action, and carry their heads in a stylish, elegant manner, making them supreme harness horses in the showring.

Plate 14 Major Breeds

Plate 14: The Frieisian is a Coldblood from Friesland, in the Netherlands. Its ancestors were used as war horses in medieval Europe. The Frieisian is always black, and stands around 15 hands high.

Plate 15 (below): The feral Mustang is a tough, agile horse. Herds of mustangs still run free in the United States. The word "Mustang" comes from the Spanish word montesino, meaning wild.

Plate 16 (bottom): The small but strong, muscular Morgan can be traced back to one founding stallion, Justin Morgan, foaled in 1789. The breed is ideal for all kinds of riding.

Plate 17 (below): The Cleveland Bay originates from Yorkshire in England, and is the oldest indigenous breed in Britain. It has been used in farm work and as a hunt, coach, or pack horse.

Plate 18 (bottom): The popular Appaloosa is an American breed of spotted horse, whose ancestors were introduced to the Nez Percé Indians by the Spanish conquistadores.

Plate 19 Major Breeds

Plate 19: The Suffolk Punch may be the oldest and now rarest breed of heavy horse. They are always chestnut and average between 15.2 and 16.2 hh. They are used for draft and harness work.

Plate 20 (below): At 18 hh or more, the Shire is the tallest of the draft breeds, thought to be a descendant of the English medieval Great Horse. Shires have distinctive "feathers" on the lower legs.

Plate 21 (bottom): The Percheron is from Normandy, France. Thousands were imported into the United States in the late 1800s to be used as draft horses on the farm and in the city.

Plate 22 (below): The Irish Draught is strong boned with a willing temperament. Bred initially for farm work, the breed also makes a fine sport horse, and shows a natural jumping ability.

Plate 23 (bottom): The all-round Australian Stock Horse developed from breeding imported Thoroughbreds and Arabs with local horse strains. It is used for sports and general stock work.

The horse has a well-developed olfactory organ and will sniff at any unfamiliar object.

The Horse's Senses

Key to developing an understanding of the horse and its responses is a good knowledge of what the horse is experiencing through its senses.

Smell

The horse has a very good sense of smell, and uses it to investigate anything new or strange and to locate and select water and food. Smell has an important role in the equine social world, particularly in relation to sexual behavior. The pheromone produced by a mare in heat tells a stallion that she is ready to mate. It is detected by a stallion when he sniffs at the mare's vulva and urine.

A feral stallion will defecate and urinate over manure piles made by himself, other members of other herds, or rival stallions. Particular attention is paid to the manure piles of his own mares, and a stallion will first sniff at the pile, then step over it, and urinate or defecate directly on top. In the wild groups of bachelor male horses appear to take turns to defecate at a manure pile in hierarchical order, with the last to defecate assuming dominant status.

Taste

The senses of taste and smell are closely linked, and a horse will use both simultaneously, particularly in relation to the selection of food and water. The horse cannot vomit, so survival depends on the horse's ability to avoid harmful or poisonous food and water. Like humans, horses can differentiate between sweet and salty foods, and seem to have the same level of tolerance to salty, sour, and bitter tastes as humans, and are also attracted to sweet foods, such as sugar cubes, apples, and molasses.

Flehmen (curling back the lip) is often a sign of a response to sexual excitement.

Vision

Much of the horse's evolution has taken place in open grasslands, where vision often gives the first warning of danger, so it is not surprising that the horse has excellent sight. The horse's eye is one of the largest of all land mammals, and it possesses a tapetum—a layer at the back of the eye that reflects unabsorbed light back through the light-sensitive retina, thus improving night vision.

The eyes are positioned on the sides of the head facing slightly forward, giving the horse almost 340 degrees of vision horizontally. This means that horses can look all round for danger while grazing, with just a narrow blind area directly behind the head.

When a horse is ridden on the bit, as in dressage, it has no vision of what is ahead and must accept and trust its rider in order to move forward willingly.

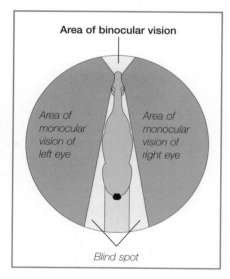

Area of binocular vision

Area of monocular vision of left eye

Area of monocular vision of right eye

Blind spot

The horse has good all-round vision, but only a small part of its field of vision is seen with both eyes. This means that the horse cannot perceive distance and depth on either side without turning to face the object. It may, therefore, overreact to anything that may seem to be a source of danger, possibly by bolting.

Head vertical, the horse sees best immediately in front of its feet and each eye sees clearly to the sides but forward vision is blurred.

To see a jump and judge the distance the horse must be able to raise its head and direct its focus as it approaches the obstacle.

The fields of vision of the two eyes overlap by about 60 degrees in front of the horse, giving it an area of stereoscopic vision that is smaller than that of humans but is nonetheless significant. In this area of overlap the horse is capable of fine distance judgment, but the nose obscures the area directly below and in front. This is worth bearing in mind when a horse approaches a jump—it will need to lower its head if it is unsure of what is ahead.

Hearing

A horse's sense of hearing is also acute, primarily as a defense against predators but also as an important part of its communication with others of its species. A horse can hear a wider range of vibrations than humans, and has extremely mobile ears that allow it to pinpoint the direction of a sound and "funnel" it to the inner ear. Windy conditions can make a horse nervous because it is no longer able to identify the direction of a sound. The horse is alert to sounds all the time, except during brief periods of deep sleep.

Touch

The horse's sense of touch is extremely sensitive, especially around the ears, eyes, and lips, and the animal does a lot of its investigation of the world with its mouth. Touch is an important part of a horse's social life, too, through courtship and through mutual grooming between adults, and mothers and foals communicate by touching each other constantly.

The upper lip and muzzle are particularly sensitive, and the horse

> **Did You Know?**
>
> *Horses have a "skin twitch" response that enables them to contract the surface of the skin and dislodge a fly or other source of irritation.*

uses the whiskers around its mouth, rather as a cat does, to judge close distances and protect its face, especially in poor light. For this reason it is unwise to shave a horse's whiskers for purely cosmetic purposes.

The skin of the whole body has abundant sensory nerve endings that transmit sensations of touch, pressure, vibration, cold, heat, and pain. The sensitivity depends on the thickness of the skin, which varies considerably, and to some degree on the breed of horse. Thoroughbreds, for example, are notoriously "touchy," and for this reason can be difficult to clip.

A horse with pricked ears is listening to the sounds around it.

The American West

The horse is so intimately connected with the history of the American West that the two are inseparable to this day. To see the North American breeds of horse is to recall their role in the changing lifestyle of the Plains Indians. To watch the drama of the rodeo is to be reminded of cattle ranches and cowboys, and to ride the trail on an Appaloosa, seated deep in a hand-tooled saddle, is to remember that the spirit of the West is still alive and kicking.

The Horse on the Plains

It is perhaps surprising to discover that, because the horse became extinct in North America in prehistoric times, the animal was unknown to the Native American peoples before the arrival of the Spanish conquistadores. The reintroduction of the horse in the sixteenth century totally transformed the Native American way of life, particularly on the Great Plains.

Spanish law at first prohibited any Native American from riding a horse. However, in 1541, Antonio de Souza, the Viceroy of New Spain, recognized the need to give horses to his allies among the Aztec chieftains so that they could better help him put down a revolt in central Mexico, and this is the first documented evidence of the relationship between Native Americans and the horse.

As the Spanish migrated northward, they took the horse with them, establishing horse-breeding settlements in the area now known as New Mexico. By the early seventeenth century, the horse had again become firmly established in North America. The Pueblo Indians were the first peoples of North America to acquire the horse in any great numbers. In 1680, the Pueblo Revolt drove the Spanish out of New Mexico, forcing them to leave many of their animals, including horses, behind. Although the Pueblo Indians learned to ride, they were not a great horse people, and valued the animal more as a trade or food item. By the mid 1700s, use of the horse had spread to other tribes, including those of the Plains Indians.

My horse be swift in flight.
Even like a bird;
My horse be swift in flight.
Bear me now in safety
Far from enemy arrows,
And you shall be rewarded
With streamers and ribbons red.

SIOUX WARRIOR'S SONG

Did You Know?

The Plains Indians referred to the horse as the Sacred Dog, Spirit Dog, or Medicine Dog.

The Plains Indians

The Native Americans of the Great Plains became the first true horse peoples of the Americas (*see Plate 7*). The animal transformed their way of life, giving them greater mobility and making hunting easier. Thanks to the horse, the Plains Indians were no longer forced

to live sedentary lives, subsistence farming on the banks of the rivers, and many of the tribes—including the Sioux, Cheyenne, Comanche, and Crow—adopted nomadic lifestyles. Buffalo hunting became central to the Plains Indian way of life. The buffalo was killed both for its meat and for its hide, which was used to make clothing, blankets, and shelter. The acquisition of horses allowed the Plains Indians to travel vast distances in search of the great buffalo herds.

Before the horse, the dog had been their only pack animal, and the amount a dog could carry was obviously very limited. The dog's harness and sled, the travois, was adapted to fit the horse, permitting much more weight to be carried. The sick and elderly were also sometimes transported in this manner.

Many Plains Indians rode bareback, with only a rudimentary rawhide thong wrapped around the horse's jaw for

Once they had acquired the horse, the Plains Indians became great buffalo hunters.

a bridle. Others used a blanket or small hide saddle stuffed with grass or buffalo hair. Sometimes the horse was adorned with feathers or fancy beadwork ornaments.

The horse came to be seen as a symbol of wealth for the Plains Indians, with some tribal chiefs owning up to a thousand animals, and they were often the cause of raiding parties between rival tribes.

The riding skills of the Plains Indians are legendary, particularly in battle. A warrior could shield himself from enemy fire by suspending himself from the flanks of his horse, at the same time shooting arrows at his foe. The Indian pony, although small, easily outpaced the larger mounts of the US cavalry during the Plains Wars of the 1800s, and had far greater stamina.

"There's nothin' in life that's worth doin', if it cain't be done from a horse ..."

RED STEAGALL, "BORN TO THIS LAND"

Cowboys and Cattle

The cowboy has come to epitomize the American West. The life of the nineteenth-century cowboy was hard and rugged, but the romantic image of the whip-cracking, sharpshooting, Indian-slaying white hero owes more to twentieth-century Hollywood. Moreover, the first cowboys were Mexican rather than North American, and were hired by the Spanish to work on their cattle ranches.

Large numbers of men were needed on cattle ranches: thus the cowboy legend was born.

Did You Know?

In the early days, the cattle driver had to carry all his food and bedding with him. Fortunately, in 1866, legendary ranchman Charles Goodnight came up with the idea of the chuckwagon, a mule-drawn wagon for carrying food, cooking utensils, and water, as well as tools and bed rolls.

Cattle in the early days were used more for their hides than for food, but all that changed in the mid 1800s. The demand for beef grew in response to the rapidly expanding population in North America, and the cattle business in the West began to flourish.

The Cattle Drive

Of all the tasks assigned to the cowboy, nothing was tougher than the cattle drive. Drives could last up to five months, and the drivers met many hazards. Native Americans continually posed a threat, and there was always the risk of cattle stampedes or dangerously swollen rivers.

The number of cattle in a drive varied, but between 1,000 and 2,000 head was not uncommon. A herd this size could be managed by a 12-man crew, each requiring eight to ten horses each. One driver, or wrangler, was put in charge of the spare horses while the others took up their post along the line of cattle. A large herd could stretch up to two miles along the trail, and men worked in pairs, one either side of the line. The most skilled drivers were placed at the head of the line, and it was their task to prevent the herd from stampeding. Others worked at the rear, keeping stragglers from getting left behind. The drive would cover 10–15 miles in a day.

The peak time for the cattle drives occurred after the US Civil War ended in 1865, and finished with the coming of the railroads to Texas and the advent of refrigeration in the 1880s, which meant that the cattle no longer needed to be brought to the cities for slaughter.

> **Did You Know?**
>
> *The cowboy was also known as a vaquero, cowpuncher, cowhand, or buckaroo, depending on the area in which he worked.*

Cowboy Poetry

Cowboy poetry originated around the campfire. At night, after a hard day's riding, there wasn't much else to do in the way of entertainment. Although most cowboy poetry is now written down, it was originally presented in oral form only. The themes of the poems focus on the lifestyle of the West, both past and present, and include the horse, the landscape, cattle, tall tales, humor, and cowboy values. Cowboy poetry is still written and recited today, and Baxter Black (born 1945) is probably the best known of today's poets.

Stetson

Concho

The Well-dressed Cowboy

Cowboy attire, past and present, is practical and designed to withstand the rugged life of a working ranchman. Indispensable items include a Stetson, a pair of Levis—often worn with chaps (leather leg coverings)—leather boots, and spurs.

The Stetson

The cowboy hat is usually referred to as a Stetson after one of the principal manufacturers, John Batterson Stetson of St. Joseph, Missouri. It is also known as a ten-gallon hat. The cowboy hat is traditionally made of felt, and has a tall crown and wide brim. The high crown allows for an insulating pocket of air for the head and the wide brim protects against sun, wind, rain, and snow. The lining is waterproof, and cowboy lore says the Stetson also makes an ideal water carrier.

Jeans

Jewish merchant Levi Strauss introduced the world to denim in the 1870s. Style and comfort took a turn for the better in the 1940s, when

Since the introduction of Levis, every self-respecting cowboy has worn denim jeans.

Polish tailor Bernard Lichtenstein, known as Rodeo Ben, designed a new style of jeans for the rodeo cowboy, the 13MWZ, for the Wrangler brand, and persuaded the great rodeo stars of the time, including Jim Shoulders, Bill Linderman, and Freckles Brown, to endorse the new design. In 1974, Wrangler Jeans became the "Official Jeans of the Pro Rodeo Cowboys Association." A pair of chaps gave added protection.

Cowboy Boots and Spurs
Cowboy boots have a high, angled heel, and often a pointed toe. They are usually made of leather and can be decorated with elaborate designs and accessorized with a pair of large, roweled spurs.

Buffalo Bill's Wild West Shows purported to show typical scenes from froniter life—but the actions of the white man were typically glorifed.

Boots   Chaps

Buffalo Bill
As the reality of the Wild West faded into history, it was replaced by a larger-than-life legend brought to the public through the pageant and performance of the Wild West Show. Presented as a true representation of America's history, the "historical" events the show re-enacted were embellishments of the truth, in which the white man was victorious against the hostile Indians. In 1883, William F. Cody, better known as Buffalo Bill, established his Wild West Show, eager to capitalize on America's nostalgia for the passing of the frontier era. His performers included Annie Oakley and a number of famous Native Americans, among them Sitting Bull, Geronimo, and Rains in the Face—the man said to have killed Lieutenant-Colonel George A. Custer at the Battle of Little Bighorn in 1876.

Cody's three-hour show depicted early settlers defending their homesteads, Native Americans attacking a wagon train, or historical events such as the Battle of Little Bighorn. Sharpshooting and daredevil stunts added to the spectacle. By the end of the nineteenth century, Buffalo Bill was one of the most famous and popular entertainers in the world.

Stars of the Silver Screen

The Western has long been a popular genre, paying homage to a uniquely American sentiment—a nostalgic yearning for the days of the frontier. Most Westerns are set in the latter part of the nineteenth century, after the Civil War. The rugged landscape portrays the border between civilization and wilderness. Settings often include the frontier town, the lonely homestead, saloons, and so on. Genre themes are typically black and white—good vs. bad, settlers vs. Indians, sheriff vs. gunslinger—and the hero often stands alone in his fight against evil. Behind every heroic cowboy you will find a trusty steed. Whether fighting Apaches, chasing trains, or pursuing villains, the horse is always there. Some of the horses that appeared with the Hollywood cowboys became stars in their own right, and have rightly earned their place in celluloid history.

Gene Autry and Champion

Gene Autry used several horses throughout his career as a film and television star, all billed as Champion. Champion also appeared in a children's television series, which had a catchy theme tune sung by Frankie Laine, "Champion the Wonder Horse":

Roy Rogers and Trigger

Trigger is perhaps the most famous horse in the history of moviemaking, starring in over 100 films with Roy Rogers and even having his own comic book. Rogers bought the horse for $2,500 in 1938 after spotting the actress Olivia de Havilland riding him on the set of *The Adventures of Robin Hood*. Trigger was a 15.3-hand stallion, with a stunning golden coat

Roy Rogers and his horse Trigger appeared in more than 100 movies.

Like a streak of lightnin' flashin' 'cross the sky,
Like the swiftest arrow whizzin' from a bow,
Like a mighty cannonball he seems to fly.
You'll hear about him ever'where you go.
The time'll come when everyone will know
The name of Champion the Wonder Horse!

The masked Lone Ranger was one of the most popular Western heroes in TV history.

and a white mane and tail, and he wore a $5,000 gold and silver saddle. He was known as the smartest horse in showbusiness, performing a great number of tricks, including counting, doing the hula, shooting a gun, and walking on his hind legs. Trigger died in 1965 at the age of 33.

The Lone Ranger and Silver

"A fiery horse with the speed of light, a cloud of dust and a hearty 'Hi-yo, Silver.' " These were the words that introduced the Lone Ranger and his horse Silver to a weekly television audience between 1949 and 1957. Clayton Moore played the masked Lone Ranger for most of the episodes, and Jay Silverheels played Tonto, his trusty Native American sidekick. In the story, the Lone Ranger and Tonto save the silver-white stallion from being gored by a buffalo, and nurse him back to health before setting him free. However, the horse follows them, and the Lone Ranger decides to keep him, naming him Silver.

Hopalong Cassidy and Topper

Topper was the white horse ridden by William "Bill" Boyd in his incarnation as Hopalong Cassidy during the 1950s. Boyd starred in over 60 films as the gentle, silver-haired hero who lived at the Bar 20 ranch. Topper was bought by Boyd in 1937 and named by his wife Grace after her favorite book series, "Topper," written by Thorne Smith. Topper died in 1961 at the age of 26, and is buried at the Los Angeles Pet Memorial Park in Calabasas, California.

Hopalong Cassidy rode a famous white steed called Topper.

The Western Bridle

The main difference between a Western and an English bridle (*see pp. 272–273*) is that the Western bridle has no a noseband. There are two styles of Western bridle, the browband headstall and the one-ear headstall. The one-ear headstall has a split on one side, through which the ear of the horse passes. It is a delicate bridle and complements a horse with a small, pretty head. Like the saddle, Western bridles can be quite fancy and many are decorated with silverwork and rhinestones.

Western Reins

Western reins are between six and eight feet (1.8–2.4 meters) in length, and are usually split, meaning that the reins are not joined together at the ends. Closed reins, called California reins, are joined together by a long romal, which is a piece of leather that hangs down the horse's neck that can also be used as a whip.

The Hackamore

A hackamore is a bridle that is used without a bit, pressure instead being applied to the nose, poll, and chin. Although there is nothing in the horse's mouth, the hackamore can be quite severe and should only be used by an experienced rider with good, soft hands.

Western Bits

Although the Western bridle may be used with any bit, including the snaffle, the one most commonly used in Western riding is the curb bit, which has long shanks—cheekpieces—that

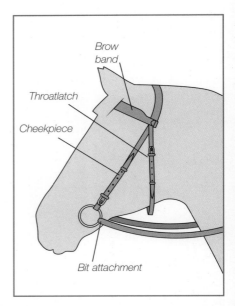

Brow band

Throatlatch

Cheekpiece

Bit attachment

The standard Western bridle does not have a noseband.

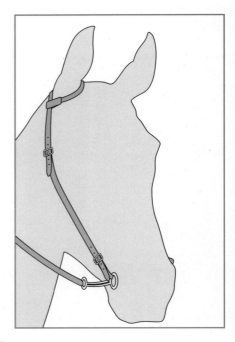

The one-eared version.

may be straight or curved. The bit applies pressure to the bars, tongue, lips, chin groove, and poll. All curb bits should be used with a curb strap or curb chain. With a Western bit, the higher the port—the part that goes in the mouth—and the longer the shank, the more severe the bit will be.

Western Stirrups

The Western horseman rides with longer stirrup length than his English counterpart. A straighter leg is more comfortable when riding over a lengthy period, and this riding style developed as a response to the many hours spent in the saddle by the cowboy.

There are many different types of Western stirrup, including the roper, the bell bottom, the ox bow, and the visalia, and choice is usually a question of personal taste. A leather "hood," called a tapadero, may be attached to the stirrup to protect the rider's foot from the brush when out on the trail and to prevent the foot from being pushed through the stirrup.

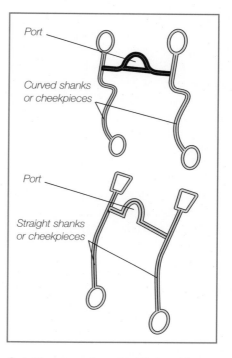

Port

Curved shanks or cheekpieces

Port

Straight shanks or cheekpieces

Curb bits are usually used in Western riding. They work using leverage: as the rider pulls on the reins the port lifts against the roof of the horse's mouth. Use only enough pull to make the horse respond.

Tapadero

Western stirrups can be made from leather, wood, or aluminum. They are often tooled or decorated with rhinestones.

Visalia

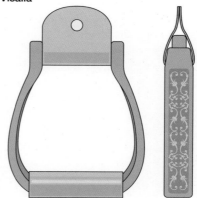

The Western Saddle

The Western saddle is to the English saddle what the Harley-Davidson Electraglide was to the Triumph Bonneville—the sacrifice of control and speed in favor of comfort over distance. The cowboy's saddle came to North America by way of the working cowboys of Mexico, and evolved from the saddles brought to Latin America by the Spanish conquistadores. Strong and durable, it has a flat-topped horn to which a roped calf can be tied, a high cantle and a deep seat, and may have a second girth strap, or flank cinch, to hold the back of the saddle down when a calf is tied to the horn or if the horse bucks.

Cutting Saddle

The cutting saddle is designed to position the rider correctly as the cutting horse makes quick, cat-like moves to follow the maneuvers of a steer, allowing the rider to stay in balance and on top of the action at all times. The seat is flat and the pommel is high and straight to keep the rider in contact with the horse while maintaining a relaxed position and preventing him from slipping forward. The rider keeps one hand braced against the tall, thin horn, not only to stop him being pitched forward but also to prevent him from interfering with the movements of the horse, which is trained to work independently when tracking a calf.

Barrel-racing Saddle

Small and light, the barrel-racing saddle is constructed with a relatively flat, deep seat and fairly wide swells to give a secure ride and help the rider to balance the horse in turns. The tall

horn offers the rider a firm hold. The barrel saddle is built strongly built to withstand the rigors and speed of barrel racing while still being safe and secure. Most barrel-racing saddles have only the front cinch and no back cinch.

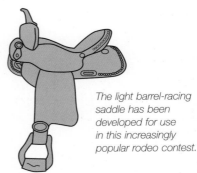

The light barrel-racing saddle has been developed for use in this increasingly popular rodeo contest.

Roping Saddle

The rider needs to be upright and well balanced to rope a steer, so the roping saddle has a deep seat and fenders positioned so the rider's legs are directly below him. Once the steer is roped, the horn and tree must be extra strong to take the pull, and the swells of the saddle are kept low to reduce the leverage of the rope on the horn. To help the rider remain secure during quick turns, the seat of the saddle is usually made of suede to give more grip.

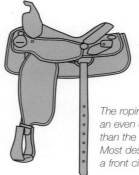

The roping saddle has an even deeper seat than the Western saddle. Most designs have only a front cinch.

The Western Saddle

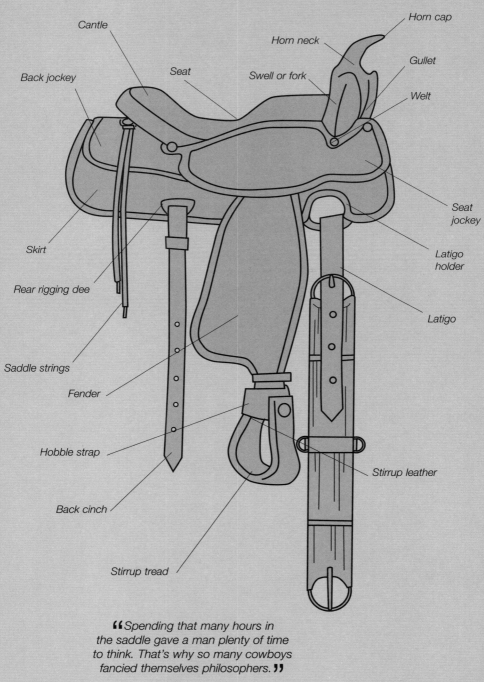

Cantle

Horn cap

Horn neck

Back jockey

Seat

Gullet

Swell or fork

Welt

Skirt

Seat jockey

Rear rigging dee

Latigo holder

Latigo

Saddle strings

Fender

Hobble strap

Stirrup leather

Back cinch

Stirrup tread

> **"**Spending that many hours in
> the saddle gave a man plenty of time
> to think. That's why so many cowboys
> fancied themselves philosophers. **"**
>
> C.M. RUSSELL

The Western Horse

Although almost any type of horse can be ridden in a Western saddle, there are a number of breeds that have particularly close association with the Western way of life, including the American Quarter Horse, the Appaloosa, the Mustang, and the Paint. Horses used in ranch work need to be strong and capable of traveling long distances without tiring. They also need to be agile, capable of quick turns and rapid acceleration, and be of sound temperament and not at all spooky.

The American Quarter Horse

The American Quarter Horse (*see Plate 12*) is the oldest breed in North America, dating back to the early seventeenth century. The first American Quarter Horses were bred by settlers in Virginia, who crossed horses of Spanish origin with those imported from England. The result was a stocky, muscular horse of medium height (between 15 and 15.3 hands). Its

Did You Know?

The American Quarter Horse gets its name from the fact that it was originally bred by Virginian settlers to race over a quarter-mile distance.

temperament, speed, and agility make it the ideal ranch horse, as well as a pleasurable trail horse.

The Mustang

The Mustang (*see Plate 15*) is a feral horse, found in the western USA. It is descended from escaped or freed horses brought to North America by the Spanish conquistadores. These horses successfully bred in the wild, and by the beginning of the twentieth century, the Mustang population was estimated as being between one and two million. Slaughter to supply the meat and pet-food trade drastically reduced the population almost to the

The working Western horse needs to be strong and hardy for ranch work.

point of extinction, but in 1971, the Wild Free-Roaming Horse and Burro Act was passed to protect these animals. The current population is estimated at between 30,000 and 40,000. Today the United States Bureau of Land Management runs an adoption program and, once broken (meaning schooled or educated for ranch work or pleasure riding), the Mustang is a sound, sure-footed, easy-to-keep mount.

The Appaloosa

The Appaloosa (*see Plate 18*) is a breed of spotted horse that originated from stock brought to the New World by the Spanish. The Nez Perce Indians acquired the spotted horse in the early 1700s, and through careful breeding practices developed an animal of exceptional intelligence, courage, speed, and stamina. The Appaloosa gets its name from the Palouse River, home to many of the Nez Perce Indians and a major horse-breeding area.

There are a number of different coat patterns, including the blanket Appaloosa, which consists of a dark body with a spotted white blanket over the rump, and the leopard Appaloosa, which has spots all over the body. As well as its distinctive coat, the Appaloosa has a number of unique characteristics, including mottled skin around the eyes, muzzle, and genitals, vertical strips on the hooves, and a white sclera, the part of the eye surrounding the iris.

The Paint and the Pinto

Like the Appaloosa, the Paint traces its ancestry back to the horses of Cortez and his conquistadores. The Paint is distinguished by large patches of color, rather than spots, on a white background over white skin. These distinctive horses were popular with the Plains Indians, particularly with the Comanche.

The most common coat patterns are tobiano—large rounded blocks of dark color and a colored face; white legs and white across the back and rump; the tail is often two colors—and overo—which has sharp, regular markings; the face is usually white, sometimes with blue eyes; at least one, and often all four, legs are dark; the tail is commonly one color. A horse exhibiting mixed characteristics is called tovero.

The Paint is a registered breed, with the conformation of the American Quarter Horse; horses with similar coloring but not from specific bloodlines are called Pintos (*see Plate 51*), derived from the Spanish word *pintado*, meaning "painted."

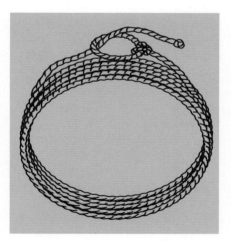

In the hands of a skilled operator, the lasso or lariat is an essential tool for ranch work.

Competitors may only use one hand in bronc-riding competitions.

The Rodeo

The modern rodeo is founded on the rich history of open ranching in the American West of the 1800s, when ranchers from the southwest would organize long cattle drives, bringing cattle to the stockyards in towns such as Kansas City, where trains would carry the cattle east. This was the golden age of the cowhand, whose duties included, as they do today, roping, horse breaking, riding, herding, and branding, and at the end of the long trails, these new "cowboys" would compete to see which outfit had the best riders, ropers, and all-round drivers. It was from these competitions that the rodeo was born.

With the expansion of the railroads and the division of the open-range lands, demand for the cowboys dwindled. While some took jobs with

the new American phenomenon, the Wild West Show, others supplemented their incomes by entering the cowboy competitions, or rodeos, that many towns had now begun to organize and promote. The Wild West Shows, which were expensive to stage, gradually died out, but the rodeo went from strength to strength, incorporating some of the theatricality of the Wild West Shows as it grew to become the unique blend of horse-riding skills and pageantry that we see today.

The professional rodeo consists of two types of competition—roughstock events and timed events.

The Roughstock Events

In the roughstock events—bareback riding, saddle bronc riding, and bull riding—a competitor's score is made up of marks awarded for both the rider's and the animal's performances. Points are awarded for the bucking pattern and power of the animal, as well as the spurring action, strength, and style of the rider. Two judges each award scores of up to 25 points for rider and animal. These two scores are then combined to

Did You Know?

Many cowboys believe that you should never set your hat on a bed, because it could presage a major injury or even death. This belief comes from the close association of sleep with death, and the dangerous lifestyle of a rodeo cowboy.

give the competitor a score out of 100. The rider only earns a score, however, if he manages to ride with one hand only and stay on the bucking bull or horse for at least eight seconds.

Saddle Bronc Riding and Bareback Riding

The essential difference between these two events lies in the equipment used by the competitor. In bareback riding, the competitor attempts to ride the bucking horse without the benefit of any type of reins, saddle, or stirrups—his only handhold is a leather-and-rawhide rigging that fits around the horse's chest. In saddle bronc riding, the competitor uses an approved rodeo saddle with stirrups and has a braided rein, which he may hold with one hand only.

In both events the competitor must come out of the chute with their spurs in a position above the horse's shoulders. They must hold them here until the horse's front feet have hit the ground. If the spurs are not in the correct position, then the rider will be disqualified.

Bull Riding

Bull riding is the most dangerous event in the rodeo, and it demands great physical prowess and courage from the competitor.

Once the bull has ditched the rider, rodeo clowns—known as bullfighters—distract the bull from mauling the dismounted rider, and cowboys on horseback then steer the bull out of the ring. The horses used in the ring show no fear when faced with an angry 2,000-pound (900-kilogram) bull.

Did You Know?

Bull rider Wade Leslie scored a perfect 100 for his ride on the bull, Wolfman, in Central Point, Oregon, in 1991.

The Calgary Stampede

The annual Calgary Exhibition and Stampede is the largest and most spectacular rodeo in North America. It lasts ten days, offers prize money totalling $1.6 million, and attracts over a million visitors every year.

In addition to the full panoply of rodeo events, the stampede features the famous opening parade, wild-cow milking, a wild-horse race, bullfighting, and the dangerous chuckwagon derby.

Las Vegas and the NFR

The largest rodeo event in the USA is the Wrangler National Finals Rodeo (NFR), the "Super Bowl of Rodeo" (*see Plate 42*), held since 1985 in the Thomas and Mack Center of Las Vegas. Cowboys from the USA and Canada work all year in the hope of qualifying for the championship, which is held each December, and for the big prize money. Established by the Professional Rodeo Cowboys Association in 1958, the NFR decides the world champion in each of the seven main rodeo events—bull riding, bareback riding, saddle bronc riding, steer wrestling, calf roping, team roping, and barrel racing.

Rodeo Timed Events

In the timed rodeo events—calf roping, steer wrestling, steer roping, team roping, and barrel racing—the winner is the competitor with the fastest time. In the roping and steer wrestling events, the quarry animal is given a head start, and the competitor waits in a boxed enclosure with a roped barrier. If the competitor "breaks the barrier," a ten-second penalty is added to his time.

Steer Wrestling

Steer wrestling matches a man against a wild longhorn steer. The wrestler is aided by another rider, known as a "hazer," who rides parallel to the steer to keep it straight. Once the competitor has caught up with the steer, he leaps across from his horse, grabs the bull by its horns, and wrestles it to the ground. Time is stopped once the steer is on its side, with all four feet pointing in the same direction. Champion steer wrestlers achieve this feat in less than four seconds from the release of the steer.

Tie-down Roping

Once the barrier has been dropped, the competitor gives chase and attempts to catch the calf with his lariat. Once the calf has been caught, the horse comes to an immediate halt, and the competitor leaps off and throws the calf to the ground. The roper then ties three of the calf's legs together with a rope, and throws up his hands to signal the end of the run. He must then remount the horse and wait six seconds to ensure that the calf does not get to its feet.

Team Roping

Team roping is the only team event in professional rodeo, and involves two ropers—a "header" and a "heeler." First, the header must rope the steer's horns. The heeler then attempts to rope both hind legs. If only one leg is roped, the team is awarded a five-second penalty. The clock stops when there is no slack in the ropes and the horses are facing one another.

Steer wrestling requires the competitor to launch himself off his horse onto a running steer.

Barrel racing gives the cowgirls the opportunity to show off their riding skills.

Barrel Racing

Barrel racing is a sport for youngsters and cowgirls, and fast, agile horses. Riding against the clock, each rider enters the arena at full speed, rides around three barrels in a cloverleaf pattern as close as possible to the barrels to shave precious seconds off the time, and then exits the arena at a full gallop. Touching a barrel is permitted, but knocking one over incurs a five-second penalty. The winning time in a barrel race can be as little as 13 seconds and timers register to the one-hundredth of a second. A horse with speed, acceleration, and the ability to turn quickly is essential, and a top-quality barrel horse can cost up to $50,000.

Did You Know?

Traditionally a Stetson was part of the dress code for barrel racing and a rider who lost her hat was fined. However, the fine is now less likely to be imposed, and some events request no hat.

The tie-down roping competition has its roots in the working cattle ranches.

In team penning, three riders work together in a race against the clock to separate and pen three numbered steers from a larger herd.

Western Competitive Events

In addition to the professional rodeo events, Western riders also participate in a range of classes designed to display the skills of the rider and the horse.

Cutting

On the ranch, the purpose of cutting is to separate an individual steer from the herd in order to brand, castrate, vaccinate, or ship the animal to market, and the task calls for special skills in both the horse and rider. In the arena, each contestant is allowed two and a half minutes to cut one steer from the

remainder of the herd. Once his choice of steer has been made, the contestant is not able to change animal without incurring a penalty. He is assisted by four riders of his choice—two herd holders to keep the cattle from drifting into the working area and two turnback riders to turn the animal back to the contestant if it tries to break away.

Once the rider has clearly separated one steer from the herd, he must slacken the reins and allow the specially trained horse to take over, heading the steer off with rapid footwork if it tries to return to the herd, matching the moves of the steer, but without being aggressive. Horses receive extra credit for their skill and style and the exertion used to keep the steer under control.

Team Penning

In the team penning event, three riders have up to 90 seconds to separate three identically numbered steers from a herd of cattle. Once they have been separated, the steers must be driven into a pen at the opposite end of the arena. During the competition, no more than four cattle from the remaining herd are permitted to cross a foul line or the team will be disqualified.

Reining

Like so many other Western riding events, the origins of the reining competition can be traced back to the ranch. Horses on working cattle ranches had to be quick and agile, responding to the lightest touch of the rein. The cowboys took pride in their animals, and would perform spins and turns to show off their horse to his best advantage. The modern reining contest is the natural development of these displays of machismo.

Often referred to as "cowboy dressage," the reining competition consists of a number of maneuvers performed in a set pattern. Movements include circles—large and fast, or slow and small—lead changes, spins, rollbacks, backups, and the sliding stop. The sliding stop is perhaps the most flashy of the reining movements, and is performed from a lope, or canter. When the horse comes to a stop, the hindquarters are tucked deep underneath it, and the hind feet begin

to slide. When performed correctly, the horse may slide up to 30 feet (nine meters).

Western Division Classes

Western classes include the Western Riding Horse, the Western Pleasure Horse, and Trail. In the Western Riding Horse class, the rider has to perform to a set pattern. In the Western Pleasure class the horse performs at a walk, trot, and lope around the ring, and the horse should appear relaxed, comfortable, and a pleasure to ride. Both classes are judged on a combination of performance, conformation, and turnout. The Trail horse has to negotiate a series of obstacles, such as it might meet when out on the trail, and they include gates, bridges, and ditches. Performance is judged on skills and obedience in negotiating these obstacles.

Western Games

These are fun events for all ages, and include baton relay, pole bending, musical chairs, roping the sack, and flag races.

The sliding stop is one of the most spectacular movements in the reining contest.

Stick or Carrot?

The horse is a large and, certainly in its natural state, highly nervous animal, wary of physical contact and ready to respond to any perceived threat by fleeing, or even biting and kicking—not a promising start for an animal that we want to ride.

The two very different ways of overcoming this initial problem are, on the one hand, to break the will of the horse and make it submit to being ridden and handled through the use of force, or, on the other hand, to become the horse's ally and, through building up trust, teach it to see the human not as a predator but as the head of the herd and a provider of food and security.

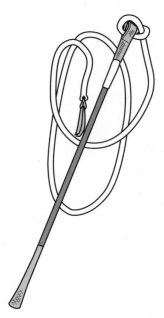

The carrot stick is 4 ft (1.2 m) in length, and is used as an extension of the horseman's arm.

66 If all I did was teach you to think like a horse and truly understand their psychology, you'd have the keys to be able to do whatever you want with horses, and to win their hearts. 99

PAT PARELLI

Xenophon (*see p. 35*) is the first person known to have recommended training the horse through sympathetic understanding of its natural instincts and building up such a relationship. Down the centuries, both schools of thought, and many in between, have had their proponents, but the gentler approach is now by far the most commonly used. Often referred to as "horse whispering" or "natural horsemanship," it is a training method that can produce dramatic results, making the horse even tempered, obedient, and responsive. Over the last hundred years, the technique has also been widely used to rehabilitate horses that have been abused or otherwise traumatized.

The term horse whisperer was first applied to the nineteenth-century Irish trainer Daniel Sullivan, whose face-to-face approach led onlookers to think he was talking to the horse, and has since been used to refer to the methods of such trainers as Buck Brannaman—whose techniques are portrayed being used by Robert Redford in the film *The Horse Whisperer*—John Solomon Rarey, Ray Hunt, Monty Roberts, Pat Parelli, and Bill and Tom Dorrance.

"Natural Horse-Man-Ship"

The teachings and training methods of Pat Parelli represent a codified form of horse whispering. A good horseman from an early age, and a successful rodeo rider in his late teens, Parelli started developing and refining a method of understanding horse psychology and communication in order to train horses and get the best results from them. Disappointed by the fact that the progress he made with individual horses was often lost when they returned to their owners, he developed the Savvy System, a learning program to lead students through successive levels of "Natural Horse-Man-Ship," as Parelli puts it.

The premises behind Pat Parelli's method are common to many horse trainers, but are spelled out in his teaching program, which uses six keys:

Attitude In order to progress with the horse, it is necessary to have an open-minded attitude and a willingness to work with, rather than on, the horse.

Knowledge The trainer needs to take on board the horse's point of view, which means understanding his evolutionary background, his instinctive responses, and his communication, especially through body language, which the trainer can use.

Tools Pat Parelli has developed such aids as the "carrot stick," halter, and short lunge line, specifically designed to work with his methods.

Techniques These are a program of exercises, based on "making the right thing to do the easy thing to do," designed to make the horse responsive and yielding to the lightest of cues.

Time The program places considerable emphasis on the amount of time actually spent working with the horse.

Imagination Being open to creating new and unlimited challenges for both the horse and oneself.

The Parelli rope halter has a loop that hangs below the jaw. This loop is for attaching lines and acts as a hinge.

Dressage

Dressage, which simply means "training" in French, is at once both art and sport, as well as a systematic means of training both the horse and the rider. The French master-horseman François Baucher once described dressage as "equitation in bedroom slippers," and it can certainly be considered the pinnacle of horse-riding finesse. The exercises, which focus on the horse's pace and bearing, and include specialized maneuvers, are designed to develop the horse's balance and suppleness and to make it highly responsive to the most subtle signals from the rider.

" A horse is a thing of such beauty… none will tire of looking at him as long as he displays himself in his splendor. "

XENOPHON, GREEK HISTORIAN (C. 430–355 BCE)

Classical Equitation

The art of classical equitation has its origins in the work of the Greek historian and horse trainer Xenophon (c. 430–355 BCE), who wrote *The Art of Horsemanship*, a treatise on the art of riding. The ancient Greeks realized the value of the well-schooled, obedient horse in warfare, and used dressage techniques in their training of the warhorse.

The knights of the Middle Ages built upon the equestrian traditions of ancient Greece, and it is thought that many of the advanced movements practiced by the great riding academies of today have their origins on the battlefields of medieval Europe. For example, a knight might have used the piaffe (*see p. 157*) to make a sudden forward movement on an enemy or the capriole (*see p. 147*) to leap over the heads of the infantry.

The roots of dressage can be traced to the horsemanship of the Ancient Greeks.

The Renaissance

The period 1400–1600 CE, known as the Renaissance—meaning "rebirth"— in Europe, saw a resurgence of interest in all things classical, including the work of Xenophon. The Italian city of Naples led the revival in classical equestrianism and in 1532 a Neapolitan nobleman named Federico Grisone opened the first of the great riding academies.

Federico Grisone

Grisone, considered by many as the first of the classical Masters, worked mostly with heavily built warhorses. His training methods differed, however, from the kind, gentle methods used by Xenophon, and he advocated the use of harsh bits and cruel punishments. In his book, *Gli Ordini di Cavalcare* (*The Rules of Riding*; 1550), Grisone suggests such barbaric training methods for a reluctant horse as attaching a cat to a long pole and placing it under the horse's belly and hind leg, or tying a live hedgehog under the horse's tail.

Antoine de Pluvinel

Fortunately for the horse, a more enlightened method of teaching was practiced by the later French Masters. Antoine de Pluvinel (1555–1620) studied at the Neapolitan School under Giovanni Baptista Pignatelli, a disciple of Grisone. Pluvinel was riding instructor to Louis XIII, and author of the posthumously published *L'Instruction du Roy en l'Exercice de Monter à Cheval* (*Instruction of the King in the*

Art of Mounting the Horse; 1629).
Pluvinel's training methods were gentle,
and he considered the use of the spur
or the whip as a failure on the part of
the rider. One of his training methods
involved attaching the horse's bridle
between two pillars and teaching it to
obey hand movements or the touch of
the whip. The Spanish Riding School
and the Cadre Noir still use the pillars
as a training aid.

*Antoine de Pluvinel's training methods are still
used to train horses to perform classical airs
above the ground.*

William Cavendish

Britain's contribution to classical
riding comes from the work of William
Cavendish, Duke of Newcastle (1592–
1676). Cavendish served as a Royalist
cavalry officer during the English Civil
War but after Cromwell's victory he
went into exile in Belgium, where he
acted as riding instructor to the future
King Charles II of England. During
this time, Cavendish wrote *Méthode
et Invention Nouvelle de Dresser Les
Chevaux* (*New Methods and Inventions
for Training Horses*; 1658), in which
he advocated that patience and
understanding, not coercion, should be
the basis of horse training.

François Robichon
de la Guérinière

Riding master to Louis XIV of France,
François Robichon de la Guérinière
must be considered the father of
modern *haute école*. He wrote *Ecole
de Cavalerie* (*School of Horsemanship*;
1733) and developed the techniques
for the half-halt, the shoulder-in, the
counter canter, and the flying change.

Robichon de la Guérinière (1688–1751).

The Spanish Riding School of Vienna

The Winter Riding School of the Hapsburg Palace is a stunning baroque-style building.

The *haute école* discipline of Guérinière is nowhere better exemplified than in the Spanish Riding School of Vienna. Founded in 1572 to train the nobility in the equestrian arts, the Spanish School is world-famous for its teaching and the spectacular performances of its riders and white Lipizzaner stallions. The name is taken from the Spanish horses with which the school was founded—the Lipizzaners are their descendants, bred for their temperament and amazing feats of athleticism.

Public performances in Vienna take place in the Winter Riding School of the Hapsburg Palace, which was founded by the Holy Roman Emperor Charles VI in 1735. This elegant building was designed by Fischer von Erlach, and with its white columns and ornate decoration it looks more like a ballroom than a riding arena. A painting of Charles VI hangs on the wall, and as the riders enter the arena they lift their caps in tribute to the school's founding patron. Watched from the gallery and illuminated by crystal chandeliers, the immaculate horses sport black, gold-

Did You Know?

During World War II, the School's Lipizzaners were evacuated to Czechoslovakia. At the end of the war, they were rescued from the advancing Red Army by US troops under the command of General George S. Patton. Without this heroic exploit, the tradition of the Spanish School would have come to an end. This moving story is retold in the 1963 Disney movie, Miracle of the White Stallions.

decorated bridles and white buckskin saddles, while their riders—elegantly dressed in traditional military-style uniforms of dark-brown tailcoat, white breeches, and tall black boots—take them through choreographed sequences, such as the quadrille, to music by the classical composers. For many people, this is the pinnacle of the art of riding.

The White Horse of Vienna

The famous white Lipizzaners are Europe's oldest domesticated breed of horse. They take their name from Lipizza (now Lipica in modern Slovenia), the town in which the Austro-Hungarian Archduke Charles established a stud farm in 1580, and more than 400 years of selective breeding from the finest Spanish and Karst bloodlines has produced a beautiful and noble horse, prized for its rare combination of courage, strength, temperament, and intelligence.

Although it has enormous presence, the Lipizzaner is not a large horse—usually between 15 and 16 hands—but it is compact, strong-limbed, and

The Founding Stallions

Of all the sires used during the eighteenth and nineteenth centuries, only six of these horses are accepted as the founding stallions of today's Lipizzaner:

Conversano (*b. 1767*) A black Neapolitan.

Favory (*b. 1779*) A dun of Bohemian origin, born at the Kladrub stud.

Maestoso (*b. 1819*) A white—not gray—crossbreed of a Neapolitan sire and a Spanish dam.

Neapolitano (*b. 1790*) A bay Neapolitan.

Pluto (*b. 1765*) A gray from the Royal Danish Court stud.

Siglavy (*b. 1810*) A gray Arabian.

powerful in the quarters and neck. With its high gait, innate ability to perform airs—leaps above the ground—and quick learning, this is a natural dressage horse, although it is also excellent in harness and some Lipizzaners are still used for general farm work.

The Black Squad of Saumur

The Cadre Noir school, based at Saumur in France, acts as the guardian of the art of French horsemanship as established by Guérinière. There has been an equestrian academy in Saumur for over 400 years, but the Cadre Noir did not come into existence until 1828. It was established as a cavalry school, but its riders are now chosen from both military and civilian life, and women are now admitted. However, tradition is still very much in evidence: the leading horseman is still known by the honorific title of "Grand Dieu" ("Great Lord"), the riders still wear the distinctive black uniform that gave the academy its name, and the horses still sport the ceremonial red saddles. The Cadre Noir uses mainly Selle Français, Thoroughbreds, and Anglo-Arabians for its displays, but also keeps Lusitano horses to demonstrate the sixteenth- and seventeenth-century baroque riding style.

The freezemark of the Selle Français breed.

Did You Know?

In 2002, the French team that won the Team Gold Medal in Show Jumping at the World Equestrian Games in Jerez, Spain, were all riding Selle Français stallions.

The Selle Français

The Selle Français, or French Saddle Horse (*see Plate 44*), is an all-round naturally athletic competition horse. It has an outstanding temperament and a willing attitude, making it suitable for all disciplines. Strong but elegant, the ideal Selle Français conformation is large-boned, with a strong back, a long neck, powerful quarters, and sturdy legs with good bones and joints. Selle Français horses are typically bay or chestnut, and they usually stand over 16 hands. The majority of Selle Français horses are sired by Thoroughbreds, Anglo-Arabians, and registered Selle Français stallions.

Airs Above the Ground

Many of the maneuvers seen at the Spanish Riding School and the Cadre Noir are performed at the higher levels of dressage competition, but these do not include the classical-school leaps. These "airs above the ground" are based on the natural jumps and kicks that a horse makes when running free. Only exceptionally talented horses can perform these leaps, and they are considered the ultimate manifestations of the *haute école*.

Dressage Classical-school Leaps

Traditionally, seven leaps were recognized, but today only three—the levade, courbette, and capriole—are performed. They require an enormous amount of strength and muscle control, and are first taught in-hand—that is, riderless—often using the pillar system devised by Antoine de Pluvinel. Once this has been perfected, the horse will be taught the movement with a rider.

The levade is regarded as the transitional movement between ground work and the airs above ground, and is therefore taught first. It requires the horse to balance on its haunches at a 45-degree angle, while holding the forelegs in a bent position. The levade should be held for a few seconds.

The levade, courbette, and capriole. Capriole means "leap of the goat," and derives from the Italian word for goat, capra.

The courbette follows on from the levade, and involves the horse springing forward on its hind legs while maintaining the levade position with its forelegs.

Most impressive of all is the capriole, in which the horse leaps clear of the ground and kicks out with its hind legs while appearing to float momentarily in mid-air.

The riders at the Spanish Riding School wear a distinctive uniform of black and gold and give a special salute during their performance.

The Dressage Test

Dressage tests consist of a series of prescribed movements that are designed to show off a horse's abilities and evaluate its level of training. There are many levels of test, and each level increases in difficulty, gradually preparing both horse and rider for the next stage in training.

The lower levels are set by the national board of the country in which the event is taking place. In the USA, for example, they are set by the US Equestrian Federation.

Pas de Deux and Quadrilles

There are two additional types of dressage competition, the pas de deux and the quadrilles. The pas de deux involves two horses, and the quadrilles, four horses. Competitors perform a personally choreographed test, usually set to music, and are judged on synchronization as well as technical and artistic merit.

Scoring

The judge(s) awards a score for every movement on the test. Scores are out of 10, and range from zero, "not performed," to 10, "excellent." The final score is calculated by adding the individual scores together and dividing this figure by the total number of points possible. The overall score is expressed in terms of a percentage.

The lower-level tests are:

Training level: Tests 1, 2, 3, and 4
First level: Tests 1, 2, 3, and 4
Second level: Tests 1, 2, 3, and 4
Third level: Tests 1, 2, and 3
Fourth level: Tests 1, 2, and 3

The more advanced tests are set by the Fédération Equestre Internationale (FEI), and are used in international competitions all over the world.

The advanced tests are:
Prix St. Georges
Intermédiaire I
Intermédiaire II
Grand Prix
Grand Prix Spécial

The dressage horse is as impeccably turned out as its rider. The requirement is small, neat braids to match its mane color.

Training Level: Test 1

Purpose:
- To confirm that the horse's muscles are supple and loose and that it moves freely forward in a clear and steady rhythm, accepting contact with the bit.
- All trot work may be ridden sitting or rising. Halts may be through the walk.

Arena (std or small):
Average time:
Maximum possible points: 220

		Test	Points	Remarks *(gaits, impulsion, submission, rider)*
1	A X	Enter working trot Halt, Salute Proceed working trot		
2	C E	Track left Circle left 20m		
3	Between K & A	Working canter left lead		
4	B	Circle left 20m		
5	Between centerline & B	Working trot		
6	C C-H	Medium walk Medium walk		
7	HXF F–A	Free walk Medium walk		
8	A	Working trot		
9	E	Circle right 20m		
10	Between H & C	Working canter right lead		
11	B	Circle right 20m		
12	Between centerline & B	Working trot		
13	A X	Down centerline Halt, Salute		

Dressage at the Olympics

The first modern Olympiad took place in 1896, but equestrian sports had to wait until the sixth games to be accepted. The 1912 Olympics were held in Stockholm, Sweden, and included dressage as an individual event only. The gold medal went to Swedish cavalry officer Carl Bonde on Emperor. This first Olympic dressage competition bore little resemblance to the modern test, and included jumping five small obstacles, one of which was a barrel rolled toward the horse. The dressage test in Stockholm did not include any advanced movements such as piaffe or passage and, indeed, these movements were not included until the 1932 Los Angeles games.

The early equestrian competitions were dominated by military personnel, but after World War II, more civilians began to take part. Women were allowed to compete in the dressage event at the 1952 Helsinki games, and equestrian sports remain the only Olympic discipline in which men and women compete against each other on an equal level.

The Kur

The road to Olympic gold at today's games consists of three phases: the Grand Prix, the Grand Prix Spécial,

The Olympic dressage rider and horse present a very elegant picture. Saddle pads are optional in a dressage test but, if used, they should be white.

and the Grand Prix Freestyle, also known as the Kur.

The Grand Prix and Grand Prix Spécial tests include the following movements from horse and rider: collected and extended walk, trot, and canter; trot and canter half-pass; passage; piaffe; one and two tempi changes; and pirouettes. The average test takes approximately six minutes.

The first round is the Grand Prix test, which also doubles as the team competition. The gold, silver, and bronze team medals are decided in this round. Each country has four riders, and the top three scores from each competing team count toward the team medal.

This team event serves as the first qualifier round for individual medals, and the top 25 competitors from the Grand Prix test then compete against each other in the Grand Prix Spécial test. The Grand Prix Spécial round consists of the same movements as the previous round but in a different pattern. The scores from both the Grand Prix and the Grand Prix Spécial rounds are added together, and the top 15 riders go forward to the third and final event, the Grand Prix Freestyle.

The Grand Prix Freestyle

The Grand Prix Freestyle was first introduced at the 1996 Atlanta Olympics, although the first World Freestyle competition had been held a decade earlier. For the Freestyle, horses and riders perform a choreographed test set to a chosen musical score that lasts up to six minutes. A rider will choose movements to enhance their particular horse's strengths, although there are a number of compulsory movements. The test is judged on artistic as well as technical merit.

Dressage Greats

Anky van Grunsven of the Netherlands currently holds the world record for the highest Grand Prix dressage score. On June 22, 2006 she achieved a record-shattering score of 81.333% on her horse Keltec Salinero (*see Plate 39*).

Danish rider Lis Hartel won the silver medal in the 1952 equestrian dressage event in Helsinki despite the fact that she was suffering from poliomyelitis at the time and had to be lifted on and off her horse.

The Dressage Arena

There are two sizes of dressage arena, small and standard. Dressage arenas have boards around the edges to act as a barrier. The dressage arena is marked with alphabetical markers to denote where the rider should begin and end certain movements in the test. There are markers on both the long and short sides, as well as the central line. The markers are set back from the arena, but pegs are located on the boards to mark the precise spot in the arena.

The small arena measures 40 meters by 20 meters (44 by 22 yards), and is used for the lower levels of dressage competition. The markers in the small arena, beginning from the point of entry (A) and moving clockwise, are: A–K–E–H–C–M–B–F. The center line markers are D–X–G, with X marking the center. Since the merging of the Canadian Equestrian Federation (CEF) and the United States Dressage Federation (USDF) tests in 2003, the small-size arena is no longer used for rated shows in North America.

The standard arena measures 60 meters by 20 meters (65 by 22 yards), and is used for higher-level dressage tests and also in the dressage phase of three-day eventing competitions. The standard dressage arena letters are A–K–V–E–S–H–C–M–R–B–P–F. The center line markers are D-L–X–I–G, with X again in the center. On the long side, the corner markers are six meters (19 feet nine inches) in from the corners. The other markers are set 12 meters (39 feet six inches) apart from each other.

The dressage horse always enters the arena at A. The judge is seated at C, although for international-level competitions there may be up to five judges sitting at different points around the arena.

" The beauties of the horse reside in the nobleness, the grace, the boldness of his movements, their splendid achievement, their energy. The beautiful horsemanship, in its delicacy and its good taste, seeks the development of these gifts belonging to the horse, and not in perverting them. It is nature which we take as a guide, and not the extraordinary, the eccentric which we seek. "

GENERAL ALEXIS L'HOTTE (1825–1904), RIDING MASTER AT THE CADRE NOIR

Standard Dressage Arena

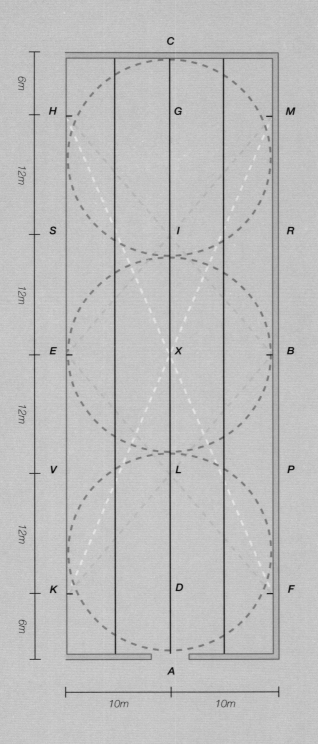

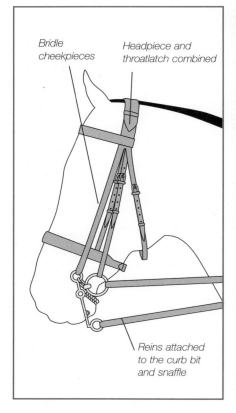

Bridle cheekpieces

Headpiece and throatlatch combined

Reins attached to the curb bit and snaffle

A double bridle is always used for advanced dressage work. It has two reins, attached to two bits: a snaffle bit against the corners of the mouth, and a curb bit below the snaffle.

The Double Bridle

A simple snaffle bridle is used in lower-level dressage tests, but for more advanced work, a double bridle is necessary, as it allows the rider to use more precise and refined aids. The double bridle has two bits—a snaffle and a curb—attached to two different sets of reins. The snaffle bit, which is sometimes referred to as a bridoon when used in a double bridle, acts on the corners of the mouth. The curb

bit acts on the lips, tongue, and chin groove. When the two bits are placed in the mouth, the snaffle sits above the curb, which rests on the bars of the mouth. The snaffle reins should be wider than the curb reins.

An ornate eighteenth-century interpretation of the curb bit showing the two bits.

The Dressage Saddle

The dressage saddle is cut differently from the forward-seat or jumping saddles. It has a deep seat, and straight, long flaps. The girth straps are lower down to allow for closer leg contact.

Rider's Equipment

The riding attire of top-level dressage riders is traditional and very elegant. For all tests above fourth level, the dressage rider should wear a dark tailcoat with top hat, a yellow waistcoat, white breeches, stock or tie, white gloves, and long black leather boots. Spurs are compulsory for all tests. Dressage whips are not permitted to be carried in competition.

Movements in Dressage

The dressage test consists of a series of linked movements, which are carried out at different paces.

Variation of Paces

The length of a horse's stride can be varied in all the paces, and this variation is an essential part of any dressage test. The novice rider or horse will start training in working trot, working canter, and medium walk. As training progresses, the movements will be performed in the collected or medium paces. Once these have been perfected, extension is introduced. At the very highest level, collection plus—the slowest pace—is necessary as preparation for such movements as piaffe and passage.

The Lateral Movements

In lateral movements, the horse is slightly bent laterally, and the forelegs and hind legs move forward on two separate tracks. The lateral movements encourage the horse to listen attentively to the leg and rein aids, while strengthening the quarters

The extended (lengthened) trot. Extended paces are the longest strides a horse can take.

and making them more supple. The lateral movements include shoulder-in, travers, renvers, and the half-pass.

Shoulder-in

When performing shoulder-in, the horse's forehand is approximately half a step inside the track of the hind legs, the horse is bent round the inside leg of the rider, and it is looking in toward the center of the ring rather than in the direction in which it is moving. The angle of the bend should not be greater than 30 degrees. The direction of flexion and bend is away from the direction of movement.

Travers

In both travers and renvers (see below), the horse moves along the track with a sideways movement of the body while looking in the direction of movement. In travers, the horse's shoulders remain on the outside track, while the quarters move along an inside track with the body at an angle of approximately 30 degrees, the outside hind leg moving in the track of the inside foreleg. The horse moves into the direction of flexion and bend, and the head is facing forward along the outside track.

Dressage Movements

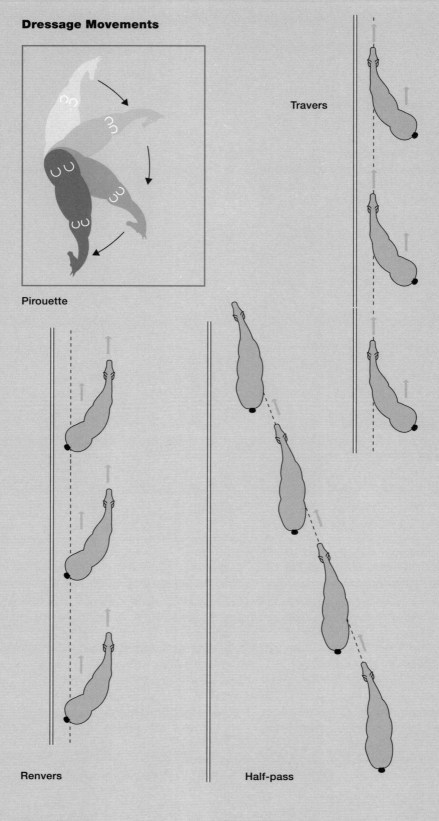

Pirouette

Travers

Renvers

Half-pass

Renvers

Renvers is essentially the same movement as travers, but with the opposite bend. The horse's quarters travel on the outside track, while the shoulders move along an inside track, the inside hind leg moving in the track of the outside foreleg. The bend in this case is around the outside leg.

Half-pass

The half-pass is similar to travers and renvers in that the horse travels sideways as well as forward, and moves in the direction of bend, but the movement is performed without the benefit of the track, and the bend around the leg is only slight. The horse moves diagonally in the direction of the bend, and the outside legs pass and cross in front of the inside legs.

Flying Changes

Put simply, the flying change is a change of lead in canter from one side to the other while in the air. For example, when a horse is cantering on the right lead, the order in which its hooves strike the ground is as follows: left hind, left fore and right hind together, right fore, and then a brief moment of suspension. For the flying change to occur, the horse must now take the weight on its right hind, followed by the right fore and left hind, and then left fore. The lead is now on the left. An essential part of dressage, the flying change is also used by show hunters and jumpers to change direction between jumps.

Tempi Changes

In tempi changes, the horse changes its lead with every canter stride.

Pirouette

As its name suggests, a pirouette involves the horse moving in a circle, but with the forehand moving around the quarters while one hind leg stays in place as a pivot. In this way, the forelegs complete a wide circle, while the hind legs complete a much smaller one. This can be performed at the walk, canter, or piaffe (see below).

Schaukel

Schaukel means "see-saw" in German, and it refers to a smooth and uninterrupted sequence of backward and forward movements. Starting from a square halt, the horse is reined back in regular two-time steps, and then moves forward in four-time, starting with the same hind leg that made the last backward step. In the next backward movement, the most advanced fore and hind legs step backward simultaneously.

Piaffe

This impressive movement is, in essence, trotting in place, and it requires a subtle balance of advanced collection and impulsion. Most of the weight of horse and rider is taken on the hind legs, and the quarters are slightly lowered. The rhythm is lively and the trot is elevated, with sufficient impulsion to maintain the moment of suspension, but without the horse showing any wish to move forward.

Passage

When the horse performs piaffe, but with a slow and steady progress forward, this is passage, a maneuver that imparts a stately, almost majestic, grace to the horse.

Show Jumping

A key element in the English-style equestrian events, show jumping attracts an enormous following among the viewing public, especially at the higher levels. It is a sport that brings out the graceful agility of the horse, as well as its strength, and the complexity of the communication between horse and rider that international competition demands has led to some famous partnerships. The best of the show-jumping arenas have become legends in their own right, combining history, atmosphere, and the most testing of jumps.

Early Jumping Competitions

Jumping competitions for horses made an appearance in the latter half of the nineteenth century. The 1869 Dublin Horse Show included a horse-leaping competition, involving both high and wide jumps. Jumps included a 12-foot (3.6-meter) water jump and a six-foot (1.8-meter) loose-stone wall, and competition rules merely stated that "the obstacles had to be cleared to the satisfaction of the judges." France was one of the first countries to include jumping as an equestrian sport.

Lepping

Early competitions, known as "Lepping," took place mostly outside of the arena. At the start, the competitors would parade before spectators, but once the jumping started the horses would disappear out of sight. Later competitions included a number of jumps in the arena to provide audience entertainment, By the start of the twentieth century, many of the important sporting events and large horse shows included Lepping classes, although it still attracted few competitors.

Rules governing the new jumping competitions were virtually nonexistent, and judges awarded marks based on random preferences, including style or severity of the jumps. Early competitions did not penalize for refusals, and sometimes competitors could miss a fence. Eventually, the need to formalize rules was recognized, and in 1917 the

> **Did You Know?**
>
> *The National Horse Show first took place at the original Madison Square Garden in 1883. In 1909, Alfred G. Vanderbilt, the president of the National Horse Show, invited British cavalry officers to compete for the first time, making the show truly international. The Show moved in 2004 to Wellington, Florida and is now held in an outdoor venue.*

American Horse Shows Association—now the United States Equestrian Federation—was formed to write a set of rules. International shows are now held under Fédération Equestre Internationale (FEI) rules.

Strange as it seems to us today, early riders were taught to sit back in the seat and pull on the reins when jumping.

Show Jumping Federico Caprilli

Early Riders

The jumping position of early riders was very different from that seen in the show-jumping arena today. Not only did the rider use long stirrups, but he was taught to adopt a backward seat and pull on the reins as he jumped. The idea was to encourage the horse to land on its hind, not forelegs. It was thought at that time that the shock of landing from a jump was more easily absorbed by the hind legs, which were flexible, as opposed to the straight forelimbs.

However, Italian cavalry instructor Captain Federico Caprilli (1868–1907) realized that this style of riding actually hampered the natural balance and rhythm of the horse, and made it harder for the animal to jump. Caprilli studied horses jumping freely, and deduced that they always naturally land on the forelegs, without injury.

Caprilli believed that the horse should be allowed more freedom when tackling a jump, and that the rider should interfere as little as possible. To make this possible, he came up with the idea of the more forward seat for jumping. Caprilli, who taught equitation at the Tor di Quinto and Pinerolo schools of cavalry, encouraged his riders to use shorter stirrups and to lean forward as the horse took off over a fence. Caprilli's innovative teachings revolutionized jumping techniques, and enabled the horse to tackle more demanding obstacles. The great Caprilli died in a riding accident at the age of 39, but his style of riding lives on in the world of show jumping.

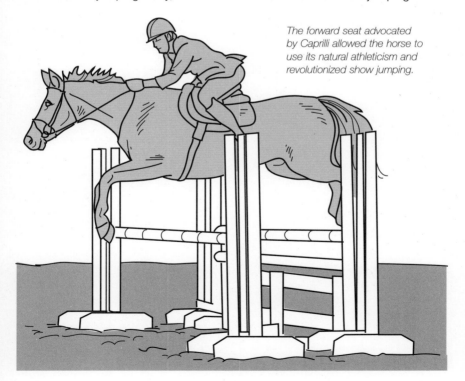

The forward seat advocated by Caprilli allowed the horse to use its natural athleticism and revolutionized show jumping.

Show Jumping at the Olympics

Show jumping first appeared at the 1900 Olympic Games in Paris, as an individual event only, and the gold medal was won by Aimé Haegeman of Belgium on Benton II. These Olympics also included a long-jump and a high-jump equestrian competition. The high-jump gold was won jointly by Dominique Maximien Gardères (France) on Canela and Giovanni Giorgio Trissino (Italy) on Oreste, with a jump of six feet ¾ inch (1.85 meters). Constant van Langhendonck (Belgium) on Extra Day won gold in the long jump with a distance of 20 feet ¼ inch (6.1 meters). However, these two competitions never again appeared in the Olympics.

There were no jumping events at the next two Olympics, but both individual and team show-jumping events were held 12 years later in Stockholm. Jean Cariou of France won the individual

Did You Know?

For the first time in Olympic history the four-member US show-jumping team at the 2000 Sydney Olympics were all women—Nona Garson, Margie Goldstein Engle, Lauren Hough, and Laura Kraut.

gold on Mignon, and Sweden won the team jumping competition. Since 1912, show jumping has been a part of every Olympic Games.

Olympic Greats

Olympic show jumping has been dominated by Germany: the nation has won 13 gold medals, more than any other country, and has a total of 22 medals in all.

Did You Know?

Brothers Raimondo and Piero d'Inzeo from Italy are the only Olympic competitors to have represented their country an impressive eight times. They first competed at the 1948 London Games, and took part in every Olympic Games thereafter up to, and including, Montreal in 1976. The brothers won six show-jumping medals each—Raimondo won one gold, two silver, and three bronze, and Piero took two silver and four bronze.

Hans-Günter Winkler

Hans-Günter Winkler of Germany has won more Olympic show-jumping medals than any other rider—seven, including five golds. His first Olympic medals came in the 1956 Stockholm Games, where he won gold in both the team and individual events on his Hanoverian mare, Halla. Four years later, in Rome, Winkler again won team gold on Halla. Although Halla retired, Winkler went on to compete in four more Olympics on a number of different horses, winning a team medal at each Games—gold in Tokyo (1964), bronze in Mexico (1968), gold in Munich (1972), and silver in Montreal (1976).

Marion Coakes and Stroller

Stroller (*see Plate 40*) was a bay gelding, sired by a Thoroughbred out of a Connemara pony. Ridden by 21-year-old Marion Coakes, Stroller was a member of the Great Britain show-jumping team at the 1968 Mexico Olympics. The pair won the silver medal in the individual show-jumping event, clearing a puissance fence of six feet 10 inches (2 meters)—despite the fact that Stroller was only 14.2 hands! The jumping course proved a stiff test for all the horses, and Marion and Stroller achieved one of only two clear rounds in the entire Olympics—gold-medalist Bill Steinkraus (USA) on Snowbound being the other. To this day, Stroller is the only pony to have competed at Olympic level.

Stroller and Marion Coakes won 61 international events in their career, including the famous Hickstead Derby in 1967. In 1986, Stroller died of a heart attack at the age of 36, after 15 years of retirement.

Show-jumping Individual Gold Medallists at the Olympics

1900 Aimé Haegeman, *Belgium*

1904–1908 NOT HELD

1912 Jean Cariou, *France*

1920 Tomasso Lequio di Assaba, *Italy*

1924 Alphonse Gemuseus, *Switzerland*

1928 Frantisek Ventura, *Czechoslovakia*

1932 Takeichi Nishi, *Japan*

1936 Kurt Haase, *Germany*

1948 Humberto Mariles Cortés, *Mexico*

1952 Pierre Jonqueres d'Oriola, *France*

1956 Hans-Günter Winkler, *West Germany*

1960 Raimondo D'Inzeo, *Italy*

1964 Pierre Jonquères d'Oriola, *France*

1968 William Steinkraus, *United States*

1972 Graziano Mancinelli, *Italy*

1976 Alwin Schockemöhle, *West Germany*

1980 Jan Kowalczyk, *Poland*

1984 Joe Fargis, *United States*

1988 Pierre Durand, *France*

1992 Ludger Beerbaum, *Germany*

1996 Ulrich Kirchhoff, *Germany*

2000 Jeroen Dubbeldam, *Netherlands*

2004 Rodrigo Pessoa, *Brazil*

The FEI World Equestrian Games

The World Equestrian Games are held every four years, two years either side of the Olympic Games. They are organized by the Fédération Equestre Internationale (FEI), which is based in Lausanne, Switzerland. There has been a show-jumping world championship since 1953, but in 1990 it became part of a much larger equestrian event. The Games now include eight equestrian sports: show jumping, dressage, eventing, driving, reining, vaulting, endurance, and para equestrian.

The show-jumping world championship consists of a team competition and an individual competition, but the individual championship ignites the most interest.

Did You Know?

A separate World Championship for women was held on three occasions. Marion Coakes (Great Britain) won it on Little Fellow in 1965, and Janou Lefebvre (France) won it twice, in 1970 and 1974, on Troubadour and Rocket respectively.

Did You Know?

To date, the World Equestrian Games have never yet been held outside Europe. However, the 2010 Games will in held in North America, and the Kentucky Horse Park in Lexington, Kentucky, will act as host.

Individual Show-jumping World Champions

1953 Paris, France Francisco Goyoaga (*Spain*) on **Quorum**

1954 Madrid, Spain Hans-Günther Winkler (*Germany*) on **Halla**

1955 Aachen, Germany Hans-Günther Winkler (*Germany*) on **Halla**

1956 Aachen, Germany Raimondo d'Inzeo (*Italy*) on **Merano**

1960 Venice, Italy Raimondo d'Inzeo (*Italy*) on **Gowran Girl**

1966 Buenos Aires, Argentina Pierre Jonquères d'Oriola (*France*) on **Pomone**

1970 La Baule, France David Broome (*Great Britain*) on **Beethoven**

1974 Hickstead, Great Britain Hartwig Steenken (*Germany*) on **Simona**

1978 Aachen, Germany Gerd Wiltfang (*Germany*) on **Roman**

1982 Dublin, Eire Norbert Koof (*Germany*) on **Fire**

1986 Aachen, Germany Gail Greenough (*Canada*) on **Mr T**

1990 Stockholm, Sweden Eric Navet (*France*) on **Malesan Quito de Baussy**

1994 The Hague, Netherlands Franke Sloothaak (*Germany*) on **S.P. Weihawaej**

1998 Rome Rodrigo Pessoa (*Brazil*) on **Gandini Lianos**

2002 Jerez de la Frontera, Spain Dermott Lennon (*Ireland*) on **Liscalgot**

2006 Aachen, Germany Jos Lansink (*Belgium*) on **Cavalor Cumano**

Competitors begin to accrue points from the first day of competition, which is the speed event. They then compete in the team event, the Nations' Cup. Following this, the top 25 riders go forward to the next round, from which the four top riders emerge. These four then go on to compete in the final—on each other's horses! The riders have to ride their own horse as well as those of their three rivals, and the champion is the rider who picks up the lowest number of penalty points from all four rounds.

The Nations' Cup

The Nations' Cup is a team event, and was first staged at Olympia, London in 1909. Women were allowed to compete for the first time in 1956. The modern Nations' Cup competition is held at various international venues throughout the year. Teams, consisting of four riders each, compete over two rounds. The highest score from each of a team's two rounds is disregarded and the country with the lowest number of penalties wins the competition. The President's Cup is awarded annually to the country with the greatest number of Nations' Cup wins in that year.

Show-jumping Scoring

First disobedience
4 penalties

Obstacle knocked down while jumping
4 penalties

One or more feet in the water jump or any imprint on the lath defining its limits on the landing side
4 penalties

First fall of horse or competitor or both in all competitions
Elimination

Second disobedience
Elimination

Exceeding the time limit
Elimination

Exceeding the time allowed in the first and second rounds and jump-offs not against the clock
1 penalty point for every four seconds commenced

Exceeding the time allowed in a jump-off against the clock
1 penalty for each second or commenced fraction of a second

The Jump-Off

If, after the first round of jumping, there is a tie for first place, there will be a jump-off. The jump-off takes place over a shortened course and the jumps are raised. The winner is the competitor with the least number of faults. However, in the event of a tie at this stage, the competitor with the fastest round wins.

What Makes a Show Jumper

To become a top-level show jumper, a horse needs to be extremely athletic and have nerves of steel. Jumping is very demanding on the horse's body, and a horse needs to have near-perfect conformation to withstand the pressures of high-class competition if he is to remain sound over the years. Good technique is important, too, especially over the big courses, and the horse should fold its legs well at the joints. The horse should also have a willingness and a desire to compete—watch the top show jumpers and see how much they seem to enjoy themselves at a competition.

The Warmbloods

Many different horse breeds are seen in the show-jumping ring, including the Thoroughbred, but Warmbloods (*see Plates 49–50*) of one breed or another are becoming more and more popular.

Warmbloods are the product of selective breeding that involves crossing a "hotblood" horse, namely a Thoroughbred or Arab (*see Plate 8*), with a "coldblood" horse, that is a draft- or heavy-horse breed. The result is a breed that combines the best qualities of both: an athletic ability with an easygoing temperament.

Although the term "warmblood" could be applied to any horse that is a cross between a Thoroughbred or Arab and a heavy-type horse, it has come to mean a certain type of performance horse that is bred in Europe. The Warmbloods include the Hanoverian, Holsteiner, Selle Français, Trakehner, Oldenburger, and Westphalian, and the Danish, Dutch, and Swedish Warmbloods. The

Some of the breed marks of show jumpers (left to right, top to bottom): Hanoverian, American Warmblood, Danish Warmblood, Oldenburg, American Trakehner, Holstein.

Warmbloods are suitable for all kinds of equestrian disciplines, but particularly dressage and show jumping.

Show-jumping Greats

The sport has its share of equine stars whose names will be remembered as much as their riders ...

Touch of Class

Touch of Class was a 16-hand bay Thoroughbred mare who began her career on the race track. Partnered by Joe Fargis, Touch of Class was a member of the 1984 US gold medal-winning show-jumping team in Los Angeles, where she posted the first double clear rounds in Olympic history. Touch of Class was also the first nonhuman recipient of the United States Olympic Committee Female Equestrian Athlete of the Year Award.

Snowman

Snowman was bought in 1956 for $80 by Harry deLeyer from a truck bound for the slaughterhouse. DeLeyer recognized his potential and turned the gray ex-plow horse into one of the leading show jumpers of the day. It was Snowman's laid-back personality, however, that made him so popular. Totally unfazed by anything, Snowman once went straight from appearing on the *Johnny Carson Show*—where Carson climbed onto his back—to The National Horse Show, where he won the Stake. In 1958 and 1959, he was named both the American Horse Shows Association Horse of the Year and the Professional Horseman's Association Champion.

Big Ben

Big Ben was a 17.3-hand liver-chestnut Belgian Warmblood gelding ridden by Canada's Ian Millar. Together they won over 40 Grand Prix titles, including six Spruce Meadows Derbys. Millar also became the first rider to win back-to-back World Cup Final titles in 1988 and 1989. In 1989, the pair ranked Number One in the world. Big Ben became a national icon, and in 1999 Canada Post issued a stamp in his honor.

Baloubet du Rouet

Born in 1989, Baloubet du Rouet (*see Plate 38*) is the mount of Brazilian rider Rodrigo Pessoa. The Selle Français stallion was sired by Galoubet A, also a champion show jumper. Pessoa and his horse have won many of the top international show-jumping events, including one individual gold and two team bronze medals at the Olympics.

Snowman's personality and his inauspicious start in life made him one of the most popular show jumpers of all time.

The Great Arenas

There are a great number of important international show-jumping competitions held throughout the year, and the top competitors travel to several different countries to compete. Although there are many magnificent venues, three stand out as the very best: Hickstead, Spruce Meadows, and Aachen.

Hickstead

Former show jumper Douglas Bunne built the All-England Jumping Course at Hickstead in the south of England in 1960, as Britain at that time had no outdoor arena to match those found in continental Europe or North America. Annual shows at the ground include the British Jumping Derby Meeting and the Royal International Horse Show. The British Jumping Derby is a particular favorite with the crowds. The 1,306-yard (1,195-meter) course is a test of supreme skill, and includes the Devil's Dyke—a three-fence combination with a water-filled ditch in the middle—and the famous Derby Bank, which has a ten-foot-six-inch (3.2-meter) slope down the front, followed by a tricky jump almost as soon as the horse reaches the bottom. Hickstead has also played host to a number of European and World Show Jumping Championships.

Spruce Meadows

The Spruce Meadows 300-acre (121.5-hectare) complex is located in Calgary, Alberta, in the foothills of the Canadian Rocky Mountains. It opened in 1975, and now draws in over 400,000 spectators annually to its events. Record attendance was 58,440 on Sunday September 7, 2003 during the Masters Tournament. With over CDN$6 million prize money on offer, the Spruce Meadows meetings attract top-class competitors from all over the world. Major show-jumping tournaments held there include the

Did You Know?

The Al Maktoum Memorial Challenge at the Dubai International Horse Show offers the largest purse in show jumping. The inaugural meeting in January 2006 had a prize fund of $1,250,000.

The Derby Bank at Hickstead is a test of skill and nerve on the part of horse and rider.

National, the Canada One, the North American, and the Masters. Spruce Meadows has twice been ranked the Number One venue in the world, in 2002–2003 and 2004–2005.

Aachen

The Aachen Soers competition facility is located in the heart of Germany's Eiffel mountains, close to the Dutch and Belgian borders. The city of Aachen has long been associated with the horse, and its annual CHIO (Concours Hippique International Officiel) was first held in 1924; it now attracts over 300,000 spectators to the ground. Aachen has been host to more World Championships and European Championships than any other venue, and in 2006 had the honor of holding the FEI World Equestrian Games.

Types of Competition

There are many types of show-jumping competition, including the following:

Grandprix The Grandprix is usually the most challenging event and has the highest prize money. The winner is the rider with the lowest number of penalties and the fastest time.

Speed Derby The winner in a speed derby is the rider with the fastest time. However, accuracy is still important, as a five-second penalty will be added to the total time for any fences that are knocked down.

Puissance The puissance is a short course of jumps, ending with a wall. In the final round, the wall may reach over seven feet (2.1 meters).

Six-Bar Riders have to take six vertical fences that are placed in a straight line. The first fence is the lowest, and each subsequent fence is higher than the previous one. The fences are raised after each round. As the event progresses, some of the fences are removed, and there may only be two fences in the final rounds. However, these fences may be well over six feet (1.8 meters).

Gambler's Choice In this event competitors choose their own course, and are awarded points, according to difficulty, for every jump cleared. The winner is the rider with the greatest number of accumulated points.

Design of the Show-jumping Course

In international competition, the show-jumping course usually consists of between15 and 20 fences, and these range in height from four feet three inches to around six feet (1.3 to 1.8 meters). The course designer sets a time limit for the course, and the rider will be penalized should he or she exceed this time. Courses are designed by professionals, and should be inviting but challenging for both horse and rider.

Types of Jumps

A typical international show-jumping course will include a variety of the following fences:

The Vertical This fence is made up of a number of poles set vertically. As a horse jumps naturally over a sloping fence, the vertical is one of the most difficult jumps for a horse.

The Wall This is a solid-looking jump, with a top line made up of sections that can be dislodged by the horse.

The Oxer This is a type of jump with two rails that may be parallel or ascending. The oxer takes its name from the wide fencing used to contain cattle, which will not jump over width.

The Triple Bar This is a spread fence composed of poles that graduate in height. Although it may be high, the triple is relatively easy for a horse to jump as it mirrors the natural jumping shape of a horse.

The Gate This is a vertical jump of solid appearance, usually made up of planks.

The Combination This is a series of two or three fences, with one or two strides between each fence. If the horse has a refusal at any part of the combination, the whole combination must be jumped again.

The Water Jump This is usually marked by a low hedge and can be up to 16 feet (4.9 meters) wide. The horse incurs a penalty if it puts a foot in the water.

The Winter Equestrian Festival

The Wellington showground in West Palm Beach, Florida is the most important hunter/jumping venue in the United States. Every winter, it plays host to a seven-week equestrian extravaganza – the Winter Equestrian Festival. During this festival more than $3 million in prize money is up for grabs. The ground has eight rings, which are often in simultaneous use throughout the festival. Wellington also holds the National Horse Show and the American Grandprix Association.

Typical Show-jumping Fences

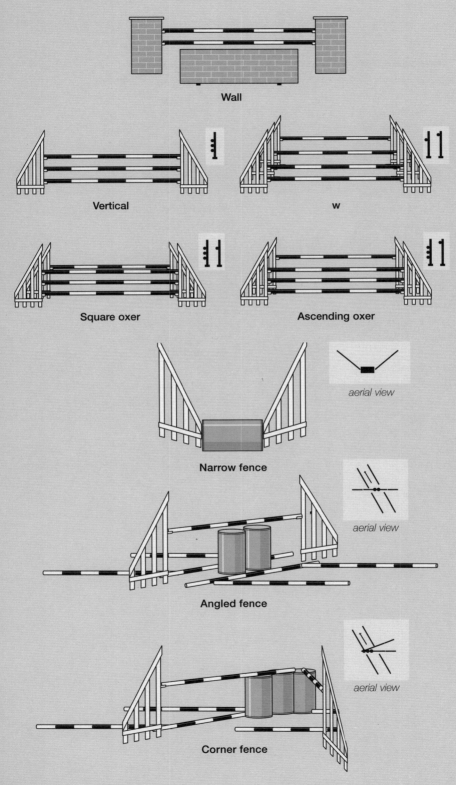

Wall

Vertical

w

Square oxer

Ascending oxer

Narrow fence

aerial view

Angled fence

aerial view

Corner fence

aerial view

The Hunter-jumping Style

Hunter jumping differs from show jumping in that it is judged primarily on jumping style, not speed. Judging begins the moment the horse enters the ring, and continues until it leaves. A good hunter moves in a smooth, relaxed manner, and should look a pleasure to ride. When the horse jumps, it should tuck up its knees high and evenly, and stretch its head and neck long and low over the jump. Each jump should be cleared easily, and the pace between jumps should be consistent. There is an optimum number of strides between combination jumps, and the horse will be penalized should it add or subtract a stride from this number. Unsafe or bad form over fences is penalized, whether or not the jump is knocked down or touched.

The ideal hunter has a small, neat head and correct conformation. In the ring, turnout of both horse and rider is very important, and both should wear regulation hunter-style dress.

Did You Know?

In 1937, the American Horse Shows Association (now USA Equestrian) founded the Equitation Medal program to honor young riders in the Hunter, Stock, and Saddle Seat disciplines. For the first decade, all three disciplines competed together in the Equitation Final but since 1948 there have been separate competitions for the three different seats.

Hunter Division

There are several hunter divisions at a show, based on various criteria including height of jump and the amateur or professional status of the rider. Each division has three or four jumping classes and one under-saddle class. Points are awarded for each class, the two riders with the highest divisional points winning Champion or Reserve ribbon for their division.

The Hunter Course

The hunter course is designed to simulate fences found in the hunting field, and these may include post-and-rail, brush, gate, oxer, and stone-wall fences. There are usually at least eight jumps, and these may include a one-stride in-and-out combination jump. The course always has at least two changes of direction (*see opposite*), designed to showcase the hunter's flying changes.

The Hunter-Seat Championships

Hunter-seat equitation classes originated in the US during the 1930s. Winners of the classes were presented with a medal, and these equitation classes have ever since been known as "Medal Classes."

Although there are now competitions for adult amateur riders, the medal classes are particularly popular with junior riders, classed as aged 17 and under. Throughout the year, young riders compete in medal classes at affiliated shows in an attempt to qualify for the year-end national championships,—notably the USEF Medal and the ASPCA Maclay Championships.

Typical Hunter-jumping Course

Table: A, article 238.2.2
Height: 14.5 m
Speed: 350 m/min

First round: 1-13
Time allowed: 82 secs
Time limit: 164 secs

Jump-off: ⑮, 3, 5ab, ⑯, ⑰
Time allowed: 52 secs
Time limit: 104 secs

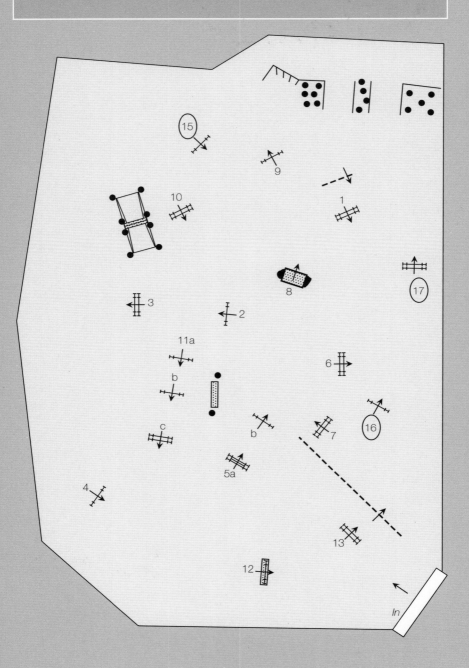

Eventing

The muscular elegance of a horse in action is nowhere better displayed than in the three very different equine sports that combine in three-day eventing. For the spectator, the full range of the horse's prowess is in evidence, from the fine and balanced movements of dressage, through the grueling challenge of the cross-country course, to the technical demands of the show-jumping arena. No wonder this sport attracts such an ardent following of both committed competitors and appreciative onlookers.

Eventing Origins

The Disciplines of Eventing

Aptly called *Le Cours Complet*, meaning "the Complete Test," by the French, the sport of eventing is indeed the ultimate test of horsemanship. The eventer must excel in three separate disciplines—dressage, cross-country, and show jumping—and the horse needs to be of exceptional ability, fitness, and courage.

Origins of Eventing

Eventing has its roots in the training exercises undertaken by European cavalry officers in the late nineteenth century. Cavalry horses had to be all-round performers, demonstrating obedience, stamina, speed, and courage. They had to be able to perform quietly and obediently on the parade ground as well as gallop over difficult and rough terrain, and it was also important that they remain sound at the end of the day.

Early cavalry exercises included arduous endurance rides. One such test, in 1892, involved Austrian and German officers riding from Berlin to Vienna, covering a distance of 360 miles (580 kilometers) in under 72 hours. Unfortunately, the winning horse died, as did 25 others out of the 199 competitors.

Did You Know?

The USA has won more medals in Olympic three-day eventing than any other country—23, including six golds.

The eventing horse must be able to perform advanced dressage movements.

The French developed these early military exercises into a sport, the *Championnat du Cheval d'Armes*. First staged in 1902, the *Championnat* resembled the modern three-day event, and included a dressage test, a steeplechase, a road-and-tracks phase, and arena jumping.

This new sport made its Olympic debut at the 1912 games in Stockholm, Sweden, under the name of "The Military." Only cavalry officers on active duty were allowed to compete, and they had to ride military chargers. The Military competition was divided into five separate phases: a 33-mile (53-kilometer) distance ride, a cross-country race, a two-mile (3.2 kilometer) steeplechase, show jumping, and dressage. Dressage came last, as it was believed at that time that the ultimate test of a horse's conditioning and obedience was best determined after two strenuous days of maximum competition. The Swede Axel Nordlander won individual gold in the event, and the Swedes also won the team event.

In 1924, civilian riders were allowed to compete in three-day events for the first time, but they remained barred from the Olympics until 1956. In 1964, Lana DuPont of the USA became the first female competitor to take part in Olympic eventing.

CCI and CIC Events

International eventing is regulated by the Fédération Equestre Internationale (FEI), based in Lausanne, Switzerland. The FEI is responsible for assigning categories and levels of competition to the various events that take place all over the world, and they are known by their French acronyms. An official three-day event is known as a CCI (Concours Complet International), and a one-day event as a CIC (Concours International Combiné). The events are "starred," from one to four, to indicate level of difficulty. A one-starred event is for horses that are just starting international competition, a CCI** is designed for horses that have some international experience of international competition, and a three-star event is for advanced competitors. Four stars denote the highest and most difficult level of competition, and is confined to the quadrennial World Championships, the Olympic Games, and five annual competitions—the Badminton Horse Trials and Burghley Horse Trials in Britain, the Rolex Kentucky Three-Day Event in the USA, the Adelaide International Horse Trials in Australia, and the Luhmühlen Horse Trials in Germany.

Olympic Eventing Gold Medallists

1912 Stockholm Axel Nordlander *(SWE)*

1920 Antwerp Helmer Morner *(SWE)*

1924 Paris Adolph van der Voort van Zijp *(NED)*

1928 Amsterdam Charles Pahud de Mortanges *(NED)*

1932 Los Angeles Charles Pahud de Mortanges *(NED)*

1936 Berlin Ludwig Stubbendorff *(GER)*

1948 London Bernard Chevallier *(FRA)*

1952 Helsinki Hans von Blixen-Finecke, Jr. *(SWE)*

1956 Melbourne/Stockholm Petrus Kastenman *(SWE)*

1960 Rome Lawrence Morgan *(AUS)*

1964 Tokyo Mauro Checcoli *(ITA)*

1968 Mexico City Jean-Jacques Guyon *(FRA)*

1972 Munich Richard Meade *(GBR)*

1976 Montreal Edmund Coffin *(USA)*

1980 Moscow Euro Federico Roman *(ITA)*

1984 Los Angeles Mark Todd *(NZL)*

1988 Seoul Mark Todd *(NZL)*

1992 Barcelona Matthew Ryan *(AUS)*

1996 Atlanta Blyth Tait *(NZL)*

2000 Sydney David O'Connor *(USA)*

2004 Athens Leslie Law *(GBR)*

The Three Phases

The three-day event consists of three phases—dressage, cross-country, and arena jumping—each of which takes place on a different day, and always in this same order.

Day One: The Dressage Phase

Dressage is the first discipline of the three-day event, and it showcases a horse's rhythm, suppleness, obedience, and gaits. In top-level competition, the horse will be asked to show collected, medium, and extended paces, and perform movements that include half-pass, shoulder-in, travers, flying changes, and countercanter. Grand Prix movements, such as piaffe and passage, are not part of the three-day event test.

The eventing competitor wears gloves to prevent the reins from slipping through his or her fingers.

Dressage Scoring

The dressage test is performed in a 65-by-22-yard (60-by-20-meter) arena (*see p. 153*), and is marked by one or more judges. Each movement is awarded a mark on a scale of zero to ten, by each of the judges, and these are known as "Good Marks." Marks are deducted for any errors or omissions in the test. These marks are then added together, and expressed in terms of a percentage, rounded to two decimal points. To convert the percentage mark into penalty points, the average percentage mark is subtracted from 100, and multiplied by 1.5.

Dressage Test Marks

The judge(s) will give a mark for each movement in the dressage test, from zero to ten, according to the following scale:

Excellent	10
Very good	9
Good	8
Fairly good	7
Satisfactory	6
Sufficient	5
Insufficient	4
Fairly bad	3
Bad	2
Very bad	1
Not performed	0

Errors and omissions receive the following penalties:

1st Error	**2 marks**
2nd Error	**4 marks**
3rd Error	**6 marks**
4th Error	**Elimination**

Day Two: The Speed-and-Endurance Phase

The second day of competition is the speed-and-endurance phase, and requires a display of stamina and courage from both horse and rider. At the higher levels of competition, day two consists of four phases: two sets of roads and tracks (A and C), the steeplechase (B), and the cross-country (D). In some competitions, the steeplechase phase is omitted.

Phase A—First Roads-and-Tracks

Section This is a timed hack, designed to be completed at a medium pace and acts as a warm-up for the next phase.

Phase B—The Steeplechase This

consists of a number of brush fences, which need to be taken at an extremely fast pace to stay within the time limit.

Phase C—Second Roads-and-

Tracks Section This is another timed

hack, but taken at a slower pace to allow the horse to be prepared for the demanding cross-country phase. After Phase C, the horse is inspected by a veterinarian to ensure that it is sound and fit enough to take part in Phase D.

Phase D—Cross-country The horse has

a ten-minute break before embarking on the tough cross-country course.

Safety

The cross-country phase has seen a number of fatal accidents among riders over the past few years. The most serious incidents occur when a horse hits a solid fence and somersaults, landing on top of the rider. To minimize the risk of serious injury, eventers must wear a body protector and helmet and harness during the cross-country phase.

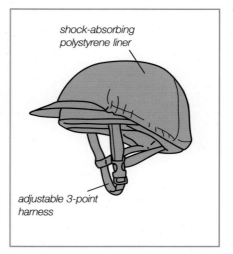

shock-absorbing polystyrene liner

adjustable 3-point harness

The eventing helmet is designed to withstand the heavy falls that sometimes befall the cross-country competitor.

The Three Phases contd
The Ten-Minute Box

After the compulsory veterinarian inspection at the end of Phase C on the second day, the horse is taken to the Ten-Minute Box, which is near the start of the cross-country phase. At this point, the horse is washed down and cooled off. The rider or helpers will check the horse's shoes, studs, bandages, and boots. The horse will be kept moving so that it does not get cold. The horse's legs should be greased. During this time, the rider will be briefed by his or her trainer as to the conditions of the course. With four minutes to go, the rider will remount and begin to get the horse moving again.

The solid obstacles encountered in the cross-country phase must be jumped with a good deal of impulsion.

Day Two:
The Cross-country Phase

In top-level competition, the cross-country course consists of between 30 and 40 obstacles, stretched over several miles. The Badminton course, for example, is 4½ miles (7 kilometers) long, and has 32 obstacles (*see* p. 186).

The Cross-country Course

Cross-country fences are solid and are usually constructed of natural materials, such as logs and stone walls. Unlike show jumps, cross-country jumps cannot be dislodged when knocked by a horse. There is also a variety of obstacles—including ditches, banks, and drops—that are designed to replicate obstacles found naturally in the countryside. In order to come in under the Optimum Time, the rider must complete the course at a fast gallop—approximately 20 miles per hour (32 kilometers per hour)—or time penalties will be incurred.

Banks

Banks occur all over the countryside, and are therefore an essential part of any cross-country course. A horse may be asked to jump up onto a bank or to jump down from a bank. Top-level competition may have a series of banks, or steps, to be ridden up or down, in the fashion of a staircase. The horse needs great impulsion when jumping banks, particularly when jumping onto them. When jumping off a bank, the rider needs to sit back and slip the reins, which allows the horse to move its head and neck freely. The horse should not be allowed to jump off a bank too fast, as it will be jarred upon landing.

A Normandy bank is a type that requires the horse to jump on and then off without taking a stride in between.

Spreads

"Spreads" are all the straightforward obstacles on the course. They come in all shapes and sizes and include a hay cart owned by a local farmer—which is a permanent fixture at Badminton—and a gnome's house at Burghley.

Combinations and bounces

Combinations come in various designs, but all require a balanced and controlled approach. On a cross-country course, there is often a choice of routes through combinations: for example, a rider may choose to take a shorter route by jumping out of a combination over a corner (see overleaf), as opposed to taking an "in-and-out" route.

A bounce is a combination that requires a horse to jump one obstacle and then take off again immediately for a second. It requires great athleticism.

Cross-country Scoring

The cross-country phase is scored in terms of penalties, and the horse with the fewest penalties at the end of the competition is the winner.

Faults at Cross-country Obstacles:

First refusal, run-out, circle at an obstacle	**20 penalties**
Second refusal, run-out, circle at the same obstacle	**40 penalties**
Third refusal, run-out, circle at the same obstacle	**Elimination**
First fall of rider	**65 penalties**
Second fall of rider	**Elimination**
Fall of horse *(The horse is considered to have fallen if his quarters touch the ground)*	**Elimination**
Fifth refusal, run-out, circle on the cross-country	**Elimination**
Error of course not rectified	**Elimination**
Omission of obstacle or compulsory passage	**Elimination**
Jumping an obstacle in the wrong order	**Elimination**
Jumping an obstacle in the wrong direction	**Elimination**
Retaking an obstacle already jumped	**Elimination**

Time Faults:

A competitor is also penalized a 0.4 penalty point for each second in excess of the Optimum Time, up to the Time Limit, which is twice the Optimum Time.

Types of jump contd
Ditches

Ditches may be jumped alone or in combinations, such as the coffin. Although they appear daunting, they cause few problems if ridden correctly, as a horse naturally covers twice the height of a jump from point of take-off to point of landing. CCI**** ditches may, however, be up to 11 feet ten inches (3.6 meters) wide. The golden rule in jumping ditches is to look ahead and ride forward. A ditch in front of a jump may appear quite frightening for a horse and will require strong, positive riding to help it overcome the fear.

Trakehner

A trakehner consists of a rail over a ditch, and is often perceived as a spooky jump by the horse.

Drop Fences

A drop fence is a bank-style jump. With a drop fence, the horse is required to jump a log obstacle and land on a level lower than that of the take-off. A drop is often part of a combination, so that after landing, the horse will take one or two strides and then jump another obstacle.

Did You Know?

The Badminton Horse Trials have been canceled three times—in 1966, 1975, and 1987—on each occasion because of bad weather. They were also canceled in 2001 owing to an outbreak of foot-and-mouth disease.

Brush Fences

The brush fence is found in both the steeplechasing and the cross-country phases. It is made up of brushwood on a wooden base and is designed to be jumped through, rather than over.

Bullfinch Fences

The bullfinch is similar to the brush fence, but the sprigs of brush are higher and the horse cannot see through to the other side of the fence. This jump, therefore, is a test of trust between horse and rider.

Coffin

The coffin is a combination jump that consists of a set of rails, a ditch—sometimes two—and then another set of rails. The ditch is normally downhill from the first set of rails. The closer the components and the steeper the incline to the ditch, the more difficult the combination. The coffin requires plenty of impulsion.

Arrowhead Fences

An arrowhead is a narrow, triangular-shaped fence. Arrowheads are usually only a few feet wide, and require a straight, correct approach to prevent a horse from running out.

Corner Fences

The corner fence is commonly offered as an alternative to an "in-and-out" route in a combination. The angle of the corner may be as severe as 90 degrees in top-level competitions, and is usually filled in to make the obstacle safer. The jump requires a very positive approach, as an uncommitted horse may tend to run out.

Typical Cross-country Jumps and Obstacles

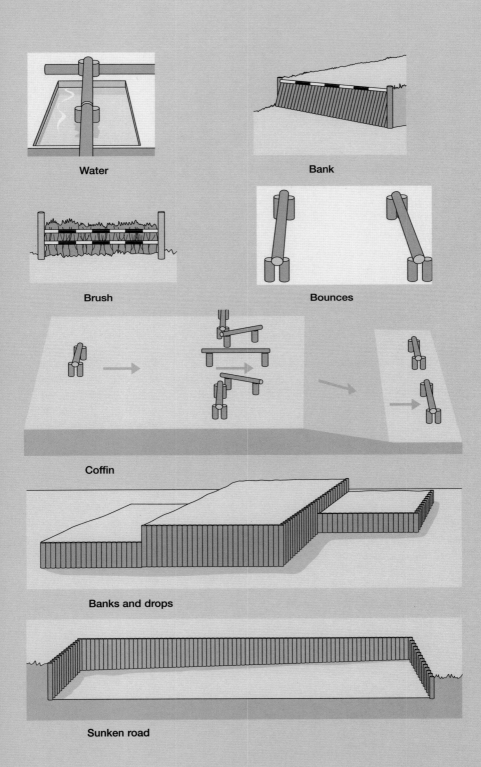

Water

Bank

Brush

Bounces

Coffin

Banks and drops

Sunken road

Types of jump contd
Sunken Road

A sunken road is a combination involving banks and rails. At the more advanced competitions, the sunken road may consist of a set of rails, one stride, a drop down, followed by a stride at the bottom of the "road," a jump onto a bank, followed by a stride, then a final set of rails.

Rolltop Fences

This is a solid fence with a rounded top. Although they can be quite wide, rolltops do not normally give the experienced eventer any problems.

Lidded Jumps

As the name suggests, these jumps have a raised roof to them, and the horse is required to jump under this lid. They do not usually cause the horse any problem.

Water Jumps

The water combination can be one of the most demanding parts of the entire

Many a famous rider has received an icy dunking in front of a large audience.

cross-country course, and many a rider has found himself in the water. In the more advanced competitions, the horse is expected to jump a drop fence into the water, take a stride or two, and then jump up onto a bank.

Veterinary Inspection

There is a mandatory veterinary inspection on the morning of the third day. This is a very formal affair, and both horse and rider should be impeccably turned out. The horse will be examined for any signs of injury or lameness incurred during the cross-country phase. If a horse fails the veterinary inspection, it will not be allowed to take part in the show-jumping phase.

Day Three:
The Show-jumping Phase

The show-jumping phase takes place in an arena, and the jumps are standard, colored show jumps, which will fall down when knocked by the horse. The horse has to jump the course cleanly, within a certain time, or it will incur penalties. The jumps are not large in comparison with pure international show jumps, but they none the less demand a high degree of technical skill.

The principal aim of the show-jumping phase is to test a horse's obedience and suppleness, and to ensure that it is sufficiently fit and conditioned to continue performing despite the previous day's cross-country. Horses jump in reverse order of merit, so the horse with the

Show-jumping Scoring

Knocking down an obstacle	4 penalties
First disobedience—refusal, run-out, circle	4 penalties
Second disobedience in the whole round	Elimination
First fall of rider	8 penalties
Second fall of rider	Elimination
Fall of horse	Elimination
Exceeding the time allowed	1 penalty per second
Jumping an obstacle in the wrong order	Elimination
Error of course not rectified	Elimination

> " The final show-jumping phase is a bit like going to the dentist. It's an absolute necessity, few relish the thought, most dread every minute, and it's a great relief when it's all over! "
>
> ROBERT LEMIEUX, BRITISH AND CANADIAN EVENT RIDER

lowest number of penalties goes last. Frequently, the riders in the top positions are separated by very few penalties, and a single pole knocked down in the show-jumping arena can cause a competitor to drop several places down the prize list. Therefore, the event can often be won or lost even at the very last jump of the competition; this creates a very tense atmosphere.

Brushwood fences are designed to be jumped through and not over.

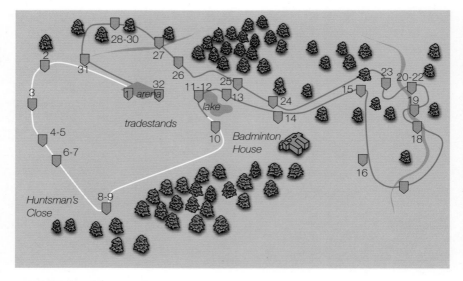

Badminton Horse Trials

The Badminton Horse Trials is one of the toughest and most exciting events in the equestrian calendar. Together with the Burghley Horse Trials and the Rolex Kentucky Three Day, Badminton forms the Rolex Grand Slam of Eventing. The Trials take place annually in May in the park of Badminton House, the home of the Duke of Beaufort, in Gloucestershire, England. It is a four-star CCI event—one of only five in the world.

The Badminton Horse Trials were inaugurated in 1949 by the 10th Duke of Beaufort, who wanted to provide a course that would allow riders to gain experience for Olympic competition. The first Trial was won by John Shedden riding Golden Willow. Only 22 competitors from just two countries—Britain and Ireland—contested the first event. In 1949 the winners received the equivalent of $270 in prize money—but by 2006 this sum had increased to $90,000!

The cross-country day at Badminton can attract a crowd of up to a quarter of a million, the largest for any paid-entry event in the UK.

Burghley Horse Trials

The Burghley Horse Trials take place in late August or early September, and are held at Burghley House in Lincolnshire, England. The first Burghley Horse Trials took place in 1961 at the invitation of Michael Cecil, the 8th Marquess of Exeter, an Olympic gold medallist in athletics, when he learned that the three-day event at Harewood House was

Did You Know?

In 1988, Ian Stark produced an extraordinary display of horsemanship to take first and second place at the Badminton Horse Trials, on Sir Wattie and Glenburnie respectively.

being discontinued. Burghley is now the longest continuously running international three-day event, and it is also one of the four-star CCI events.

Virginia Elliott (née Holgate) and Mark Todd are the two most successful riders at Burghley, each winning the title an amazing five times. Only one horse has won the competition twice, Priceless, Virginia Elliott's mount in 1983 and 1985. There have been six Burghley course designers in its history, including Captain Mark Phillips, who won the event in 1973 on Maid Marion. His former wife, HRH Princess Anne has also won the event, in 1971 on Doublet.

Badminton and Burghley Greats

The Horse Trials have their share of equine stars, of which two competitors stand out:

Lucinda Green Britain's Lucinda Green (née Prior-Palmer) is the undisputed queen of Badminton. The Hampshire-born British rider has won the event a record six times, and on six different horses: Be Fair (1973), Wideawake (1976), George (1977), Killaire (1979), Regal Realm (1983), and Beagle Bay (1984). In 1981, she also won the Burghley Horse Trials on Beagle Bay. She was European Champion in 1975 and 1977, and World Champion in 1982. In 1982, she was a member of the gold-medal-winning British team at the World Championships in Luhmühlen, Germany. Two years later, she represented Britain at the Los Angeles Olympics, where the team won silver.

Lucinda Green is also the seven-times winner of the Tony Collins Memorial Trophy, which is awarded to the British rider with the most points in an eventing season.

Mark Todd New Zealander Mark Todd was voted Event Rider of the Twentieth Century by the Fédération Equestre Internationale. When Todd entered the 1980 Badminton Horse Trials, he was unknown to the general public, but his surprise victory on Southern Comfort made him a household name. Todd won two more Badminton titles and a total of five Burghley titles. Riding the small Anglo-Arabian Charisma (*see Plate 41*), Todd also won back-to-back individual Olympic gold medals—in Los Angeles (1984) and Seoul (1988)—only the second rider in history to do so, and the first for 60 years. He also won a team silver in Barcelona (1992) and two team bronze medals in Seoul (1988) and Sydney (2000).

The Rolex Kentucky Three-Day Event

The Rolex Kentucky Three-Day Event is held in the last week of April, one week before the Kentucky Derby, at the Kentucky Horse Park in Lexington. Commonly referred to as "The Rolex," after its principal sponsor, it is the only four-star CCI event in North America.

The history of eventing at Kentucky Horse Park can be traced back to 1974, when Bruce Davidson and the US eventing team won individual and team gold at the World Championships. Their victory meant that the USA had the right to host the next World Championships four years later. At the time, the country

The back of the Kentucky quarter.

did not have a suitable venue for such a prestigious event, so plans were laid to develop a course at the Kentucky Horse Park. The first horse trials took place in 1976, and, two years later, the World Championships were held at the Park. The competition proved so popular that it was decided to hold an annual three-day event. The horse trials began as an advanced event, but were awarded a four-star rating in 1998.

World Champions

1966 Capt. Carlos Moratorio (ARG) **Chalan**

1970 Mary Gordon-Watson (GBR) **Cornishman**

1974 Bruce Davidson (USA) **Irish Cap**

1978 Bruce Davidson (USA) **Might Tango**

1982 Lucinda Green (GBR) **Regal Realm**

1986 Virginia Leng (GBR) **Priceless**

1990 Blyth Tait (NZL) **Messiah**

1994 Vaughan Jefferis (NZL) **Bounce**

1998 Blyth Tait (NZL) **Ready Teddy**

2002 Jean Teulère (FRA) **Espoir de la Mare**

2006 Zara Phillips (GBR) **Toytown**

The Rolex Grand Slam of Eventing

Three four-star CCI competitions—the Rolex Kentucky Three-Day Event, the Badminton Horse Trials, and the Burghley Horse Trials—make up the Rolex Grand Slam of Eventing. To be eligible for the award, which carries prize money of $250,000, a rider must win all three events in succession. In 2003, the fifth year of the Grand Slam, Pippa Funnell of Great Britain became the first, and so far the only, Grand Slam winner, with wins at Badminton on Supreme Rock, and Burghley and Kentucky on Primmore's Pride.

Eventing World Championships

There has been an Eventing World Championship since 1966, and it is now part of the FEI World Equestrian Games, which are held every four years. The current World Champion is Zara Phillips of Great Britain, who rode Toytown to victory at the 2006 Equestrian Games in Aachen. Zara Phillips is the daughter of former eventing champions Her Royal Highness Princess Anne and Captain Mark Phillips, and a granddaughter of Queen Elizabeth II.

Bruce Davidson

Bruce Davidson (b. 1949) is one of the most successful American riders in eventing history, and has twice led the FEI eventing rankings—in 1993 and in 1995. He is also the winner of a record five Rolex Kentucky Three-Day Event titles—he won the event in 1983 (J.J. Babu), 1984 (Dr. Peaches), 1988 (Dr. Peaches), 1989 (Dr. Peaches), and 1993 (Happy Talk). As a member of the United States eventing team, he has won four Olympic medals: two silvers—at Munich (1972) and Atlanta (1996), and two golds—at Montreal (1976) and Los Angeles (1984). Davidson is also the only back-to-back winner of the World Championships, winning the title in 1974 and 1978. In 1995, Bruce Davidson won the Badminton Horse Trials on Eagle Lion, and remains one of only two American riders to have done so.

Adelaide International Horse Trials

Held annually in early November, the Adelaide International Horse Trials in Australia is the only four-star CCI competition in the southern hemisphere. The event takes place at the Adelaide Parklands, which is located in the heart of the city.

The Adelaide International Horse Trials were created in 1997 as a replacement for the Gawler Horse Trials. The competition made its debut as a three-star event, but in 1999 it was upgraded to a four-star competition. Natalie Blundell won the inaugural four-star CCI riding Billy Bathgate.

The cross-country course at Adelaide was designed by Michael Etherington-Smith, an Olympic course designer, and includes some of the most challenging water jumps in international competition.

The biannual Trans Tasman Championship is also held on alternate occasions at Adelaide, the event being shared between Australia and New Zealand.

The Luhmühlen Horse Trials

The Luhmühlen Horse Trials are held annually in Luhmühlen, Germany, and are the only four-star CCI competition in continental Europe. The competition only became a four-star event in 2005, when it was won by Bettina Hoy of Germany on Ringwood Cockatoo.

Horse Racing

We can't know who was the first person to say, "I'll bet my horse can run faster than yours," but we can be sure it was a very long time ago. Now, horse racing, in all its many forms, is a multibillion-dollar international business that allows every one of us, if only for a few minutes at a time, to identify with "our" horse, share the thrill and the danger, and experience the elation or dejection that the race result brings.

Charles II had William Samwell build a pavilion at Newmarket from which to see the race.

❝'Tis delightful to see two, or sometimes more, of the most beautiful animals of the creation, struggling for superiority, stretching every muscle and sinew to obtain the prize and reach the goal! To observe the skill and address of the riders, who are all distinguished by different colors of white, blue, green, red, or yellow, sometimes spurring or whipping, sometimes checking or pulling, to give fresh breath and courage!❞

LORD BATH, ON RACING ON NEWMARKET HEATH (*THE WORLD*, VOL. 1, NO. 17, 1753)

Did You Know?

The Jockey Club established a registry of racing colors in 1762. In the first list published in the Racing Calendar, 18 owners shared 17 sets of colors.

The Sport of Kings

Although horse racing has been practiced in one form or another since man first learned to ride, the origins of modern-day horse racing can be traced to the seventeenth century. Riding and hunting were already aristocratic pastimes, and racing soon enjoyed the patronage of royalty and nobility—

English kings James I (1566–1625) and Charles I (1600–1649) both took an interest in horse racing. James I was responsible for introducing the sport to the little market town of Newmarket, Suffolk, but it was Charles II who really transformed Newmarket into the headquarters of English racing. He was so enamored with the sport that he moved his entire court from London to Newmarket for the race season. His influence is still felt today in the town, and one of the racecourses is known as the Rowley Mile, after Charles II's favorite black stallion Old Rowley.

The first flat races in England were over a course of four or five miles, and were often run in heats involving just two horses. In the latter half of the eighteenth century, however, races became shorter—a mile-and-a-half (2.4 kilometers) or so—and involved larger numbers of horses.

The Jockey Club

The Jockey Club was formed in England in 1750, initially as a friendly forum at which wealthy and influential racing enthusiasts could meet and do business. The group originally met in the Star and Garter Tavern at Pall Mall, London, but in 1752 the Club leased a plot of land in Newmarket to build a members' Coffee Room.

In 1757, the Jockey Club was called upon to settle a dispute at Curragh in Ireland. The following year it drew up an initial set of racing rules, and it gradually evolved into the sport's governing body. The Club published a complete set of rules in 1762, and sanctioned racecourses to hold meetings under their regulations. In 1791, the Jockey Club published the first stud book, *An Introduction to the Stud Book*.

The Jockey Club is still based in Newmarket, although it also has offices in London. It now owns over 4,000 acres (1,690 hectares) of land on Newmarket Heath, most of which is used for training, as well as the Rowley Mile Racecourse and the July Racecourse.

> **Did You Know?**
>
> *The Newmarket Town Plate, which was instituted by an Act of Parliament in 1665, is the oldest surviving flat race in the world. It is run over a distance of 3 miles and 6 furlongs (10.9 km), and is restricted to unlicensed amateur riders. The winning prize is indeed a relic of a bygone era—a pound of sausages and a voucher for the local tailors!*

Full-length boots need to be flexible and elastic to be comfortable in the jockey's racing position.

The Champion Breed

Think of the racehorse, and one breed comes to mind—the Thoroughbred. Averaging a little over 16 hands, with a long neck, deep well-muscled shoulders, high well-defined withers, long thigh bones, and strong, muscular hindquarters, the Thoroughbred is built for speed and for glory, but as a breed it is less than 300 years old.

Racing was popular in seventeenth-century England, where handsome prize money attracted the Scottish Galloway ponies, with their speed and stamina, to compete over distances of several miles. As the stakes increased, so did the bid to produce champion racers, as well as faster, lighter steeds for hunting, and aristocratic horse owners soon began to refine the techniques of selective breeding that were making an impact on agricultural livestock production at the time.

Andalusians were brought in from Spain to add their fine qualities, but the determining factor proved to be the purebreds imported from Arabia, Turkey, and North Africa, whose strength and stamina was so well suited to the long races of the time. A great many Arabian stallions were brought into the English stables, but all the world's Thoroughbreds today are descended from just three of these.

Founding Fathers

The "foundation" stallions of the breed were the Byerly Turk, the Darley Arabian, and the Godolphin Arabian, all three of which were bred to native sprinting mares—probably Galloways—and part-Arabian mares to sire the first Thoroughbreds.

Selective breeding produced the Thoroughbred, the equine equivalent of the sports car.

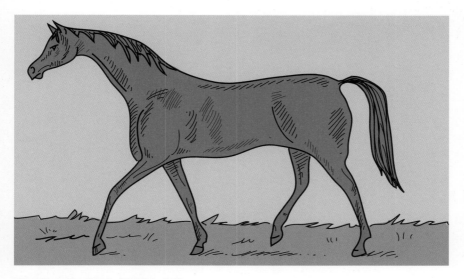

The Byerly Turk (1680–96)

Captured from the Turkish forces at the siege of Buda, Hungary, in 1686 by Captain Robert Byerley of the 6th Dragoon Guards, under King William of Orange, The Byerly Turk was the first of the three foundation stallions to come to Britain. (Captain Byerley's name accidentally lost its second "e" when the name was registered.) It is said that Captain Byerley rode this horse at the Battle of the Boyne, Ireland, in 1690, when William III defeated King James II. Although The Byerly Turk was bred to only a few mares, his line includes some distinguished Thoroughbreds, including Basto, Jigg, and Herod, the latter of which was foaled in 1758 and was another successful sire.

The Darley Arabian (1700–33)

The second, and most influential, of the founding stallions, this horse was bought in Aleppo, Syria, as a four-year-old by Thomas Darley, and was brought to Yorkshire, England. This bay horse, standing about 15 hands,

The first Thoroughbred horse to come to America was sired by the Darley Arabian.

was bred to many mares, but his most notable offspring were Childers and Bartlet's Childers, both out of Betty Leedes. Childers was held to be one of the fastest horses ever, and some 90 percent of all Thoroughbreds are descended from Bartlet's Childers' great-grandson, Eclipse.

The Godolphin Arabian (1724–53)

The third of the foundation stallions made a circuitous journey from Syria to England. Going first of all to Tunisia, he was given by the Bey of Tunis as a gift to the King of France before being bought by Edward Coke and taken to England. He was then acquired by the second Earl of Godolphin, who bred him to several distinguished mares, including Roxana, who foaled Lath—one of the greatest English racehorses—and Cade, who sired Matchem, through whom the Godolphin Arabian line continued.

Breeding and Breeders

The process of selective breeding that began around the end of the seventeenth century, and which has led to the fine, athletic Thoroughbred we know today, has left little to chance. Although in the early days the breeding records were poorly kept, it was soon clear that such records were vital in the quest to produce champion horses.

James Weatherby took on the task of compiling *The General Stud Book*, based on his own research and such records as he could obtain. Published in 1791, it listed the pedigrees of over 350 mares, all of which were descended from Herod, Eclipse, or Matchem (*see p. 195*). It was to become the

A Thoroughbred's bloodlines can be traced in The General Stud Book.

authority on Thoroughbred bloodlines and the basis on which breeders continue to bring together the best genes to create the finest performers. Weatherby's descendants continue to publish volumes on behalf of the UK Jockey Club. Up until 1948, unless all of a horse's ancestors could be traced to those listed in *The General Stud Book* it was not allowed to race in Britain.

The English National Stud

Much of the responsibility for maintaining standards and facilitating the continued improvement of the

Thoroughbred in Britain is shouldered by the National Stud. The Stud was originally founded in 1916 at Tully, County Kildare, Ireland, with bloodstock donated to the British Government by Colonel Hall Walker, later Lord Wavertree.

In 1943, the horses were moved to the Sandley Stud in Dorset, England, and an additional facility at West Grinstead in Sussex was bought a few years later. When the stud's priorities changed to providing more stallions, the National Stud moved to a new purpose-built facility at its present 500-acre (200-hectare) location at Newmarket, Suffolk.

One role of the National Studs is to educate and inform the public about the Thoroughbred.

The Irish National Stud

In 1945, after it was handed over to the Irish Government, the property of the Irish National Stud now provides facilities and the services of commercial stallions for breeders, as well as promoting the famous Irish bloodstock nationally and internationally. Like the Newmarket National Stud, the Irish Stud is a popular tourist attraction.

The Thoroughbred in the US

The bay stallion Bulle Rock was the first Thoroughbred to reach North America (probably imported at age 21 by James Patton in about 1731). He was followed by over 180 more that formed the basis of the Thoroughbred breeding stock in the American colonies. Horseracing flourished after Independence, and the first *American Stud Book* was published in 1873, compiled by Colonel Sanders Bruce of Kentucky. After 1896, the task was taken over by the newly formed Jockey Club, whose database now holds the pedigrees of some three million horses. The Jockey Club continues to register all Thoroughbreds in the US, Canada, and Puerto Rico, as well as imported animals.

Lexington, Kentucky

Over the last 200 years, the city of Lexington has become synonymous with the world-famous American Thoroughbred bloodstock industry. Set amid the lush pasturelands of Kentucky's Bluegrass country, home to hundreds of vast horse farms, Lexington justifiably calls itself the Horse Capital of the World. The 1,200-acre (485-hectare) Kentucky Horse Park—home to the International Museum of the Horse, an establishment dedicated to the entire history of the horse—has been chosen by the FEI to host the 2010 World Equestrian Games.

The Classic Races and Courses

The UK Classics consist of five races: the 1,000 Guineas, the 2,000 Guineas, the Derby, the Oaks, and the St. Leger—run annually for three-year-olds. The classic races are held on just three courses: Epsom, Newmarket, and Doncaster.

The 1,000 Guineas and the 2,000 Guineas

The 1,000 and 2,000 Guineas are one-mile (1.6-kilometer) races that take place on the famous Rowley Mile racecourse at Newmarket. The 2,000 Guineas is open to three-year-old colts and fillies and is run on a Saturday in April. The 1,000 Guineas, which is for three-year-old fillies only, is held the following day. The inaugural 2,000 Guineas took place in 1809, and was won by Bill Clift on Wizard. The same jockey won the first 1,000 Guineas in 1814 on the filly Charlotte.

Musjid and Summerside, winners of the Derby and the Oaks at Epsom Downs in 1859.

The Oaks and the Derby

The Oaks and the Derby take place in June at the Epsom Downs racecourse in Surrey. The Oaks was initiated in 1779 by Edward Smith Stanley, the 12th Earl of Derby, who challenged a group of friends to race their three-year-old fillies against him over a mile-and-a-half (2.4-kilometer) course. Derby won the race on his filly, Bridget, and named the race The Oaks after his estate. The race is still open only to fillies.

The following year, the Earl of Derby and his friend, Sir Charles Bunbury, decided to introduce another race, this time for colts and fillies. A coin was

> **Did You Know?**
>
> *The Triple Crown is considered flat racing's great achievement, and the accolade is given to a horse that wins the 2,000 Guineas, the Derby, and the St. Leger.*

Jockeys on the final leg of the St. Leger at Town Moor, Yorkshire in 1886.

tossed between the two friends as to which of them should have the honor of naming the race. The Earl of Derby won the toss, giving his name to the most prestigious flat race in England. Bunbury had the consolation, however, of winning the very first Derby on May 4, 1780, when his horse Diomed was first out of a field of nine. The first four races were run over a mile, with the starting point beyond the current five-furlong (one-kilometer) marker. The famous Tattenham Corner was introduced in 1784, and the race was lengthened to its current distance of a mile and a half.

The St. Leger

Originally known as the Doncaster Cup, the St. Leger is the oldest of the Classic races. It was first held on September 24, 1776, at Cantley Common near Doncaster in the north of England, and was won by Allabaculia. In 1778, the race was renamed the St. Leger, after Lieutenant-Colonel Anthony St. Leger, an Irish soldier and later the Governor of St. Lucia. Shortly afterward, the race

moved to its current venue at Town Moor in Yorkshire. Since that first race, the St. Leger has been canceled only once, in 1939, at the outbreak of World War II. The St. Leger is the longest of the English Classics, and is run over a distance of one mile, six furlongs, and 132 yards (2.97 kilometers), making it a test of stamina more than speed. Held in September, the St. Leger is the last Classic race of the British flat-racing season.

Did You Know?

Although fillies are allowed to enter the 2,000 Guineas as well as the 1,000 Guineas, only four have ever won both. Sceptre was the last horse to complete the double, in 1902. This filly also won the Oaks and the St. Leger.

English Racing Icons

English flat racing has many heroes, but two jockeys and one horse stand out above them all.

Lester Piggott

Lester Piggott (b. 1935) is considered one of the greatest flat-racing jockeys ever (*see Plate 37*). He was certainly one of the most successful, winning more than 5,300 races in his career, both in the UK and elsewhere. Although a man of few words—Piggott is partially deaf and has a slight speech impediment—he became known as the "housewives' favorite," and did much to popularize a sport that had hitherto been seen as elitist.

Lester Piggott won 30 English Classics and was seen as the best jockey of his generation.

“In terms of raw ability, Nijinsky was probably the best. He got nervous before his races, and I was always anxious until he had jumped out of the stalls. Then he'd drop the bit and you could put him anywhere in a race.”

LESTER PIGGOTT

Piggott won his first race in 1948, at Haydock Park, at the tender age of 12, on a horse called Chase. His first Classic win was in 1954, when, age 18, he won the Derby on Never Say Die. Piggott went on to win eight more Derbys, 21 other Classic races, and three Prix de l'Arc de Triomphe. He was also Champion Jockey 11 times.

Piggott retired in 1985 and became a trainer, but two years' on he was jailed for tax evasion, and served 366 days in prison. On release, he resumed riding, winning the Breeders' Cup Mile on Royal Academy in 1990 and the 2,000 Guineas on Rodrigo de Triano in 1992. Piggott retired in 1995 at the age of 60.

Nijinsky

Nijinsky is considered by many to be one of the best racehorses of the last century. Piggott, his regular jockey, regarded him as the most naturally talented horse he had ever ridden.

By Northern Dancer, out of Flaming Page, Nijinsky was bred at E.P. Taylor's Ontario Farm. He was bought at auction for $84,000 by US industrialist Charles W. Engelhard, Jr. and was sent to Ireland to train under the legendary Vincent O'Brien (*see Plate 37*).

As a two-year-old, Nijinsky won his first five races, including three of Ireland's biggest: the Railway, Beresford, and Angeles Stakes.

Nijinsky started the 1970 season with an impressive win in the Gladness Stakes. This was followed by victories in the 2,000 Guineas, the Epsom Derby, and the Irish Derby. He also beat a field of much older and more experienced horses to win the King George VI and Queen Elizabeth Diamond Stakes at Ascot by an impressive two lengths.

By winning the St. Leger at Doncaster in September that same year, Nijinsky became the first horse for 35 years to win the elusive Triple Crown. It also gave him an 11th consecutive career win. Sadly his career ended with two surprise defeats later that year, at the Prix de l'Arc de Triomphe at Longchamp, in Paris, France, where he was beaten by Sassafras, and at the Champion Stakes, when he again finished second, this time to Lorenzaccio.

With well over 4,000 wins, Gordon Richards is the all-time leading UK jockey.

The racing saddle is very light. Jockeys do not sit in the saddle, but ride in a perched position.

Nijinsky was retired to stud in Kentucky, USA, for a then record syndication fee of $5,500,000.

Sir Gordon Richards

Sir Gordon Richards (1904–1988) is the leading British flat-racing jockey of all time, winning 4,870 races in the UK alone. He also holds the record for the most championships, 26, as well as the most wins in a flat-racing season, 269. The son of a miner, Richards taught himself to ride on pit ponies. He won four out of the five UK Classic races in 1942, but he had to wait until 1953 to win the Derby on the horse Pinza. Richards is the only jockey ever to have received a knighthood.

Kentucky Derby

Kentucky has a rich tradition of racing, and the first racetrack was opened in Lexington in 1789. Nearly a hundred years later, while traveling in England and France, American Colonel M. Lewis Clark conceived the idea of building a new track to hold races based on the UK Derby, Oaks, and St. Leger. On his return to the USA, Clark developed the idea, and on May 17, 1875, the Churchill Downs track was opened (*see Plate 24*), and the first Kentucky Derby took place. The winner of the inaugural Derby was Aristides, ridden by African-American Oliver Lewis.

Did You Know?

Eddie Arcaro (1916–1997) enjoyed prolific success in the Triple Crown races—he won the Kentucky Derby five times, the Preakness six times, and the Belmont Stakes six times.

The Kentucky Derby (*see Plate 25*) is held on the first Saturday in May, and is the first leg of the American Triple Crown races. The track is one and one-quarter miles (2.012 kilometers) long, and the race is for three-year-old fillies and colts. Known as "the most exciting two minutes in sport," the Kentucky Derby attracts a large crowd, and is one of the most prestigious events in the American social calendar. As well as $2 million in prize money, the winner is awarded a garland of red roses by the governor of Kentucky in a tradition that goes back over a century.

The Preakness Stakes

The Preakness Stakes is the second race in the Triple Crown, and it takes place on the third Saturday in May, just two weeks after the Kentucky Derby. The race is held at the Pimlico racecourse in Baltimore, Maryland, and is run over one and three-sixteenths miles (1.91 kilometers), making it the shortest of the three races.

The inaugural Preakness Stakes, named for the winner of the Dinner Party Stakes and an early favorite at Pimlico, took place in 1873, two years before the first Kentucky Derby. Seven horses contested the first Stakes, with Survivor winning by ten lengths, the largest margin of victory until 2004.

The Belmont Stakes

The Belmont Stakes is named for August Belmont (1816–1890), an eminent financier and the first President

Mint Julep

The mint julep is the official cocktail of the Kentucky Derby, and almost 120,000 are served at the meeting. In 2006, 50 custom-made mint juleps were sold for a staggering $1,000 each, with the proceeds going to retired racehorses. The cocktail, which was served in gold-plated cups and sipped through silver straws, was made with ice from the Arctic Circle, fresh mint from Morocco, sugar from Mauritius, and, of course, the finest American bourbon.

Triple Crown winners

1919 **Sir Barton** Johnny Loftus

1930 **Gallant Fox** Earl Sande

1935 **Omaha** Willie Saunders

1937 **War Admiral** Charley Kurtsinger

1941 **Whirlaway** Eddie Arcaro

1943 **Count Fleet** Johnny Longden

1946 **Assault** Warren Mehrtens

1948 **Citation** Eddie Arcaro

1973 **Secretariat** Ron Turcotte

1977 **Seattle Slew** Jean Cruguet

1978 **Affirmed** Steve Cauthen

Did You Know?

Once the Preakness winner has been officially declared, a painter climbs to the top of a replica of the Old Clubhouse cupola, and paints the colors of the winning owner's silks onto the jockey and horse weather vane.

of the American Jockey Club. The first Belmont Stakes was held at Jerome Park, in the Bronx, in 1866. It moved to its present home, Belmont Park, Elmont, New York, in 1905.

As the last in the three-race series, the Belmont Stakes holds the key to Triple Crown glory. Since its inception, there have been 26 possible Triple Crown winners coming into the Belmont Stakes, but only eleven have succeeded, the most recent being Affirmed in 1976. At one and a half miles (2.4 kilometers) the race is the longest of the three, and it tests the staying power of the three-year-olds that contest the event.

The Pimlico racecourse opened in 1870.

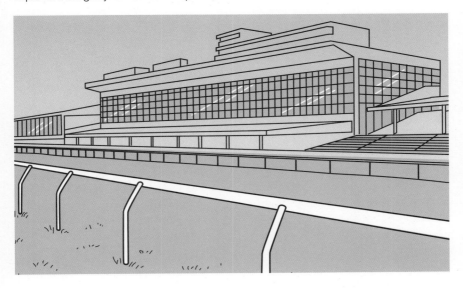

Legendary American Horses

Many horses have distinguished themselves on the dirt tracks of America, and every racegoer has their favorite. Great names of the twentieth century include Seabiscuit (*see Plate 30*), Citation, Northern Dancer, Affirmed (*see Plate 35*), and Cigar, but two great horses stand even above these names: Man O'War and Secretariat.

Man O'War

Although he raced for only 16 months, Man O'War (*see Plate 32*) became one of the most famous horses of the last hundred years. Nicknamed "Big Red," Man O'War won 20 out of his 21 races, including a seven-length victory over Triple Champion Sir Barton. At the time of his retirement in 1920, the great horse held the US record for five different distances—the mile, one and one-eighth miles, one and three-eighths miles, one and a half miles, and one and five-eighths miles (1.6, 1.8, 2.2, 2.4, and 2.6 kilometers)—and had earned $249,465 over his career, a record at the time. When he died in 1947, Man O'War was embalmed and lay in state for several days in a casket lined with his racing colors. He is buried at the Kentucky Horse Park.

Secretariat

Secretariat (*see Plate 29*) was a big chestnut, sired by Bold Ruler out of the dam Somethingroyal. In 1973, he won the Triple Crown in spectacular fashion, beating his nearest rival in the Belmont Stakes by 31 lengths. He set course records for each of the three races, although his time in the Preakness Stakes is not recognized officially, as the course timer malfunctioned. His records in the Kentucky Derby (1 minute 59.2 seconds) and the Belmont Stakes (2 minutes 24 seconds) remain unbeaten. As a two-year-old, Secretariat won the Eclipse Award for Horse of the Year, the first horse to be honored at that age. He also won the award the following year.

Secretariat's win at the 1973 Belmont Stakes remains a world record for a mile and a half on a dirt track—and a course record.

Important American Racecourses

The Santa Anita racetrack, which opened in 1934, is located in Arcadia, California. It is renowned for its fall and winter racing, and offers some of the highest purses in all of North America. Prestigious races include the Santa Anita Derby and the Santa Anita Handicap.

The Saratoga Racecourse in New York is the oldest in the USA—it opened in 1864. It is nicknamed "The Graveyard of Champions."

The great Man O'War suffered his only defeat there and Triple Crown winners Secretariat and Gallant Fox also suffered defeat there, Gallant Fox to a 100–1 outsider.

The Breeders' Cup World Championships

The Breeders' Cup is a one-day event that takes place in October or November, and is a year-end celebration featuring the very best Thoroughbred horses in the world. The event is sponsored by the National Thoroughbred Racing Association, and has been held annually since 1984. It is held at a different location every year, although all have been in the USA bar one—the 1996 event, which was held at the Woodbine Racetrack in Toronto, Canada. With $20 million in purses on offer, the Breeders' Cup World Championship is the single richest day in horse racing.

The Eight Championship Races

There are eight races on the Breeders' Day, each attracting top horses from all over the world. The order of the first six races listed below varies from year to year, but the Turf and the Classic are traditionally the last two races of the day. In 2006, the first six races carried a purse of $2 million each, the Turf $3 million, and the Classic $5 million.

Breeders' Cup Juvenile Fillies: 1$\frac{1}{16}$-mile race for 2-year-old fillies.

Breeders' Cup Juvenile: 1$\frac{1}{16}$-mile race for 2-year-old colts and geldings.

Breeders' Cup Filly and Mare Turf: 1$\frac{3}{8}$-mile or 1$\frac{1}{4}$-mile race for fillies and mares, 3-years-old and up.

Breeders' Cup Sprint: 6-furlong race.

Breeders' Cup Mile: 1-mile race.

Breeders' Cup Distaff: 1$\frac{1}{8}$-mile race for fillies and mares, 3-years-old and up.

Breeders' Cup Turf: 1$\frac{1}{2}$-mile race.

Breeders' Cup Classic: 1$\frac{1}{4}$-mile race.

The Steeplechase Course

Although steeplechasing—horse racing over jumps—does take place in the USA and continental Europe, it is most popular in Britain and Ireland, where it attracts a large following. Steeplechase courses are much longer than flat-racing courses, and require a horse to demonstrate stamina and athletic ability as well as speed. Many steeplechase horses begin their career on the flat and move onto steeplechasing.

The origins of the steeplechase lie in the field of hunting, where horses were required to jump any ditches, hedges, and walls that lay in the way of the hunt. The term "steeplechasing" evolved from the practice of racing between appointed landmarks, commonly the spires of the village churches. One of the earliest known references to steeplechasing concerns two Irishmen, Mr. Cornelius O'Callaghan and Mr. Edmund Blake, from County Cork. The men are said to have raced four and a half miles (7.2 kilometers) across country, from the steeple of St. Buttevant Church and on to that of St. Leger Church in Doneraile in 1752.

The first known prepared steeple-chasing track opened in Bedford,

The sport of steeplechasing has its origins on the hunting field.

England, in 1810, and consisted of eight four-to-six-foot (1.2-to-1.8-meter) fences over a three-mile (4.8-kilometer) course. Only certified hunters were eligible to compete. The St. Albans Steeplechase began in 1830, and proved so popular with the public that within a decade more than 60 other meets had sprung up all over the country. In 1839, the first Grand National at Aintree, Liverpool, took place.

Early steeplechase races were not subject to regulation, but, in 1882, the Grand National Hunt Committee—now called the National Hunt Committee—was formed to control the sport.

Steeplechasing in America

In the United States, the sport is regulated by the National Steeplechase Association (NSA), which was founded in 1895. The first recorded steeplechase in the United States occurred in 1834 when the Washington Jockey Club held a race at the National Race Course in Washington, DC. In the post-Civil War period, steeplechasing became a popular sport, and steeplechase and hurdle races were established on tracks from Louisiana to San Francisco.

In 1908, an anti-gambling bill was passed in New York and several important steeplechase racetracks were closed, including Saratoga, New York. Although the sport had been dealt a severe blow by the anti-betting laws, the steeplechase tradition was kept alive at local hunt meets and at "betless" meetings. In 1941, pari-mutuel betting became legal and racetracks across the country, including Saratoga, reintroduced hurdle racing.

Steeplechasing now takes place in 12 US states, at 32 National Steeplechase Association stops. There are more than 200 sanctioned steeplechase races every year, offering approximately $5 million in purse money. Saratoga is probably the most notable racetrack to hold steeplechasing meets. Most of the races are run over NSA sanctioned portable hurdles, which travel from event to event.

Many of the oldest and most prestigious races are still run, among them The Maryland Hunt Cup, the American Grand National, and the National Cup in Radnor. In the United States. The Maryland Hunt Cup (established 1894) and the Virginia Gold Cup (established 1923) are timber races that have been supported by generations of local hunt families, and are the closest type of race today to the Grand National (see p. 226), although they are held over open ground, not a turf course, and the fences are solid post-and-rail type.

Did You Know?

The Maryland Hunt Cup is considered the sternest test in American steeplechasing. The race is run over a 4-mile (6.4 kilometer) course, and consists of 22 obstacles. Two Maryland Hunt Cup winners have gone on to win the English Grand National—Jay Trump in 1965 and Ben Nevis II in 1980.

The Cheltenham Gold Cup is the most prestigious prize in English steeplechasing.

Cheltenham Gold Cup

The Cheltenham Festival in Gloucestershire, UK, is the top National Hunt meeting in England, and is held annually in March. The meeting includes the Champion Chase and the Champion Hurdle on its card, but the star attraction of the four-day event is the Cheltenham Gold Cup. First held in 1924, the Gold Cup is for horses five years old and above. It is run over a distance of three miles and two and a half furlongs (5.3 kilometers), with a demanding half-mile (0.8-kilometer) uphill finish.

The most successful horse in Gold Cup history was Golden Miller, who won five times from 1932. Three other horses have won the race three consecutive times: Cottage Rake in 1948–1950, Arkle in 1964–1966 (*see Plate 31*), and Best Mate in 2002–2004.

> **Did You Know?**
>
> *In 1983, the first five finishers in the Cheltenham Gold Cup—Bregawn, Captain John, Wayward Lad, Silver Buck and Ashley House—were all trained by Michael Dickinson.*

> **Did You Know?**
>
> *In 1934, Golden Miller became the first, and so far the only, horse to win both the Cheltenham Gold Cup and the Grand National in the same year.*

Cheltenham Gold Cup Winners for the last 20 years

1986 **Dawn Run** Jonjo O'Neill

1987 **The Thinker** Ridley Lamb

1988 **Charter Party** Richard Dunwoody

1989 **Desert Orchid** Simon Sherwood

1990 **Norton's Coin** Graham McCourt

1991 **Garrison Savannah** Mark Pitman

1992 **Cool Ground** Adrian Maguire

1993 **Jodami** Mark Dwyert

1994 **The Fellow Adam** Kondrat

1995 **Master Oats** Norman Williamson

1996 **Imperial Call** Conor O'Dwyer

1997 **Mr Mulligan** Tony McCoy

1998 **Cool Dawn** Andrew Thornton

1999 **See More Business** Mick Fitzgerald

2000 **Looks Like Trouble** Richard Johnson

2001 *race cancelled due to foot and mouth crisis*

2002 **Best Mate** Jim Culloty

2003 **Best Mate** Jim Culloty

2004 **Best Mate** Jim Culloty

2005 **Kicking King** Barry Geraghty

2006 **War of Attrition** Conor O'Dwyer

Plate 24 Famous Races

*Plate 24: Horses on the
back straight of the famous
track in Louisville—home
to America's most famous
horse race, the prestigious
Kentucky Derby.*

Plate 25 Famous Races

Plate 25: The wearing of silks dates back to the 18th century, when they were used to distinguish jockeys and their horses before the age of television and commentators came to the spectators' rescue.

These are the silks of the jockeys in the 2006 Kentucky Derby, together with the names of the horses. The 132nd "Run for the Roses" at Churchill Downs was won by Lael Stable's 3-year-old Barbaro with a 6$\frac{1}{2}$-length victory over Bluegrass Cat. The race was jockey Edgar Prado's first Kentucky Derby win after seven attempts. It was also the first victory Derby for Barbaro's breeders, Roy and Gretchen Jackson, and for his trainer Michael Matz.

Barbaro

A.P. Warrior

Cause to Believe

Deputy Glitters

Lawyer Ron

Point Determined

Showing Up

Sinister Minister

Bluegrass Cat

Bob and John

Brother Derek

Flashy Bull

Jazil

Keyed Entry

Private Vow

Seaside Retreat

Sharp Humor

Stephpenwolfer

Storm Treasure

Sweetnorthernsaint

Plate 26 (right): Trotters on the Red Mile harness race track, Kentucky, the second oldest racetrack in the United States. The track earned its name from the fast, red clay that forms the one-mile (1.6-km) course.

Plate 27 (below left): The Grand Pardubice is the most notorious and dangerous steeplechasing race in continental Europe, famous for its breathtaking post-fence drops. It takes place in the Czech Republic during the fall.

Plate 28 (below right): The English Grand National is held at the Aintree Racecourse in Liverpool, England. Only horses of exceptional courage and stamina manage to stay the four-and-half-mile (7.2-km) course.

Plate 29 (below): Secretariat is, for many, the greatest racehorse of all time. He was certainly a horse with a big heart—his autopsy revealed a heart three times bigger than the average Thoroughbred.

Plate 30 (bottom left): Celeste Susany painted Seabiscuit winning his most famous race against Triple Crown winner War Admiral (sired by Man O'War) at Pimlico on November 1, 1938.

Plate 31 (bottom right): The Cheltenham Cup (three times), King George VI Chase, the Irish Grand National, and Hennessey Gold Cup winner, Arkle is deemed the greatest steeplechaser of all time.

Plates 32–37 Famous Horses and Riders

Plate 32 (right): The memorial statue of Man O'War.
Plate 33 (below): Shergar won the Epsom Derby in 1981 by a record 10 lengths.
Plate 34 (center left): Texan-born jockey Willie Shoemaker.

Plate 35 (center right): Affirmed, the 11th and most recent winner of the Triple Crown. Plate 36 (btm left): Red Rum, Grand National champion. Plate 37 (btm right): Lester Piggott and Nijinsky.

Plate 38 (below): Olympic gold medallist Rodrigo Pessoa on Baloubet de Rouet. In 1992, age 19, Pessoa became the youngest person ever to appear in an Olympic equestrian event.

Plate 39 (bottom): Anky van Grunsven has twice won the Individual Olympic Gold Medal for dressage, her first gold in 2000 with Bonfire and her second in 2004 with Keltec Salinero (shown here).

Plate 40 (below): Marion Mould and Stoller stole the hearts of horse lovers at the 1968 Mexico City Olympics, when the 14.2 hh pony won the Individual Silver Show Jumping medal for Britain.

Plate 41 (bottom): Mark Todd's partnership with the small Anglo-Arab Charisma won him two individual Olympic Eventing gold medals—at Los Angeles in 1984 and Seoul in 1988.

Plate 42 Rodeo

Plate 42: The Wrangler National Rodeo Finals take place in December at the Thomas & Mack Center in Las Vegas. Cowboys the length and breadth of North America prepare all year for this event. Billed as a rodeo "super series," the finals determine the world champion of each rodeo event. Here, Fred Whitfield shows how the world champion ropes a calf.

Plate 43 (below): American Standardbreds are the fastest harness racing horses. They may be trotters or pacers. Standardbreds are good as endurance or trail horses, but do not excel at show jumping.

Plate 44 (bottom left): The Thoroughbred originated in 17th-century England, when Arabian stallions were bred to English stock mares. No breed can match the Thoroughbred for speed over distance.

Plate 45 (bottom right): The Tennessee Walker moves in three distinctive gaits—the flat walk, the running walk, and the canter. The "running" walk is an inherited trait, unique to this breed.

Plate 46: (below): The Selle Français is a naturally athletic horse, strong but elegant, normally between 16.0 and 17.0 hh. The Selle Français is a good show jumper, but excels as a dressage horse.

Plate 47 (bottom): The Missouri Fox Trotter is an American breed of gaited horse. Its gait is such that the rider feels little movement in the saddle, making it an extremely comfortable mount.

Plate 48 Further Breeds

Plate 48: Dutch horse breeders crossed German, French, and English horses with native stock, notably the Gelderlander and Groningen breeds, to produce the Dutch Warmblood. The result is a sport horse of exceptional quality. "Warmblood" distinguishes this type of horse from the "coldbloods" (draft horses) and the "hotbloods" (Thoroughbreds and Arabians).

Plates 49–50 Further Breeds

Plate 49 (below): The "Thoroughbred" of all the warmbloods, the Trakehner is renowned for its grace, power, intelligence, and ability to perform—the ideal show and riding horse.

Plate 50 (bottom): The Hanoverian was founded in 1735 by George II, King of England and Elector of Hanover. This German warmblood excels at dressage and show jumping.

Plate 51 Further Breeds

Plate 51: A Paint is a colored horse with two registered Paint parents or one registered Paint parent and one American Quarter Horse or Thoroughbred parent. The colors and markings can vary.

Racing Terminology

Common Racing Terms

Apprentice Jockey A jockey at the start of his or her career. A horse ridden by an apprentice jockey is allowed to carry less weight.

Card The day's racing program.

Blinkers (blinders) Eye patches attached to the bridle to prevent the horse from seeing sideways and thus being distracted.

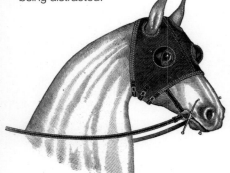

Claiming Race A race in which any of the horses may be purchased for an amount specified beforehand.

Conditioned Race A race where eligibility is based on age, sex, amount of money, or number of races won.

Handicap A race in which horses carry weights according to their form.

Home Stretch The straight length of track leading to the finish line.

Inquiry A stewards' inquiry is held to determine whether there has been an infringement of the rules during a race.

Maiden A horse that has never won.

Photo Finish When two horses cross the finish line together, officials look at a photograph taken at the finish line to determine the winner.

Scratch A horse that is withdrawn from a race before it starts.

Silks The colored shirts worn by the jockeys that carry the colors of the horse's owner.

Stake Race A race in which a horse's owners make a series of payments to keep a horse eligible for the race.

Tote Board An electronic board that posts the odds for each horse, amount of money bet, results of a race, and the wagering pay-offs.

Betting

In the USA, betting is through parimutuel pools, which can be described as "betting among ourselves." In parimutuel betting, the racetrack takes a commission from all bets wagered, and the remainder of the money taken on a particular horse is then distributed among the winning bets. This means that the odds change continuously, and depend on how the bets are placed. The racetrack makes the same amount of commission no matter what the outcome of the race.

Betting is organized differently in Europe and elsewhere, where bookmakers pay out according to the odds offered either at the time of accepting the bet or at the time of the start of the race. In this instance, the bookmaker does care whether or not a long-shot wins!

Grand National Winners of the last 30 years

2006	**Numbersixvalverde**	N. Madden
2005	**Hedgehunter**	R. Walsh
2004	**Amberleigh House**	G. Lee
2003	**Monty's Pass**	B.J. Geraghty
2002	**Bindaree**	J. Culloty
2001	**Red Marauder**	R. Guest
2000	**Papillon**	R. Walsh
1999	**Bobbyjo**	P. Carberry
1998	**Earth Summit**	C. Llewellyn
1997	**Lord Gyllene**	A. Dobbin
1996	**Rough Quest**	M.A. Fitzgerald
1995	**Royal Athlete**	J.F. Titley
1994	**Minnehoma**	R. Dunwoody
1993	*race void*	*n/a*
1992	**Party Politics**	C. Llewellyn
1991	**Seagram**	N. Hawke
1990	**Mr Frisk**	Mr. M. Armytage
1989	**Little Polveir**	J. Frost
1988	**Rhymen'Reason**	B. Powel
1987	**Maoriventure**	S. Knight
1986	**West Tip**	R. Dunwoody
1985	**Last Suspect**	H. Davies
1984	**Hallo Dandy**	N. Doughty
1983	**Corbiere**	B. de Haan
1982	**Grifftar**	Mr. C. Saunders
1981	**Aldaniti**	R. Champion
1980	**Ben Nevis**	Mr. C. Fenwick
1979	**Rubstic**	M. Barnes
1978	**Lucius**	B.R. Davies
1977	**Red Rum**	T. Stack
1976	**Rag Trade**	J. Burke

The Grand National

The Grand National (*see Plate 28*) is the world's biggest steeplechase, and it attracts over $186 million in bets every year. The race is held in early April at the Aintree Racecourse in Liverpool, England.

The first Grand National was held in 1839, and was won by Lottery. In the same race, Captain Martin Becher fell at the sixth fence in spectacular fashion, ending up in the brook that still bears his name.

The horses run twice around the Aintree course, covering four and half miles (7.2 kilometers). There are 16 jumps on the course, 14 of which are jumped twice, making a grand total of 30 fences. There are 40 horses at the start, but few manage to stay the course. Notorious jumps include Becher's Brook and the Chair, both of which claim many fallers.

Red Rum

Red Rum (*see Plate 36*) is the only horse in Grand National history to win

Did You Know?

The 1993 Grand National was declared a void race, after problems at the starting line. Many riders were unaware, however, that a false start had been called, and seven horses completed the race. The unlucky "winner" was Esha Ness, ridden by John White and trained by Jenny Pitman.

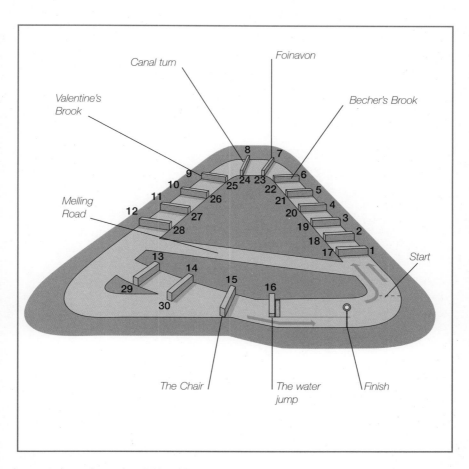

Foinavon

Canal turn

Valentine's
Brook

Becher's Brook

Melling
Road

Start

The Chair

The water
jump

Finish

the race three times, in 1973, 1974, and 1977. He also came second on two occasions.

Red Rum was bred by Martyn Molony at Rossenarra Stud in County Kilkenny, Eire. His sire was Quorum, and his dam was Mared.

Coincidentally, his first outing on the tracks was a flat race at Aintree on April 7, 1967, when he tied for first place. In his ten-year career, Red Rum ran in more than 100 steeplechasing races, winning 21 and coming second 37 times. Red Rum died in 1995, and is buried in a grave next to the winning post at Aintree racetrack.

The Grand National race is two full circuits of the Aintree Racecourse: 1–16 is the first circuit, 17–30 the second.

Did You Know?

Battleship, a son of the famous Man O'War (see Plate 32), won the American Grand National in 1934 and the English Grand National in 1938.

Quarter Horse Racing

Quarter Horse racing can be traced back to the seventeenth century, when early settlers to the Americas began to race their horses through forested tracks. Quarter Horse racing in the United States is well attended and prize money is extremely attractive.

Did You Know?

The world's richest Quarter Horse race is the $2 million All-American Futurity held at Ruidoso Downs, New Mexico on Labor Day. The first Futurity was held in 1959 and was won by a filly called Galobar.

Point-to-Pointing

Point-to-point racing is steeplechasing for amateur riders, run on courses dedicated to this sport. The first point-to-point meetings were organized by local hunts to cater for amateur riders once steeplechasing had become a professional sport, and to be eligible to compete in point-to-point a horse must have ridden with a recognized hunt for a least four days in the season preceding the race. In Ireland, trainers use point-to-point as an introduction to professional racing, while in Britain the sport is a proving ground for many trainers, owners, and up-and-coming young jockeys. The point-to-point season runs from January to June, and meetings are run under Jockey Club regulations.

Apart from maiden races for young horses, all point-to-point races are run over a minimum of three miles (4.8 kilometers) and there are usually a minimum of 18 fences to be jumped, with at least two ditches on the course. The fences are approximately four feet six inches (1.4 meters) high.

Point-to-point races are popular for competitors and spectators in Britain and Ireland.

Lady riders

From the early days of point-to-point, in the late 1870s, lady riders competed on an even footing with men, often riding side-saddle, but from 1929 they were restricted to "ladies only" races. In 1967, the rules were changed to allow them to ride against men in certain races, and, in 1976, they once again became eligible to compete in all races. However, some men-only and ladies-only events are still held.

The Grand Pardubice

The *Velká pardubická*—or the "Grand Pardubice," as it is more commonly known—is a challenging cross-country race that is held annually on the second Sunday in October (*see Plate 27*). It takes place in Pardubice in the Czech Republic, 62 miles (100 kilometers) east of Prague. The race was the idea of Count Oktavian Kinsky, who wanted to create a steeplechasing race in Bohemia to rival the English Grand National.

The first Grand Pardubice took place in 1874, and it soon gained a reputation as the longest, hardest, and most dangerous horse race in the world. Over the years, numerous fatalities have occurred, and in 1992 the decision was made to reduce the severity of the

Palio racers ride bareback. It is the horse, not the rider, that wins, provided its head ornaments remain intact.

course. The fourth jump, known as the Taxis, used to have a 16-foot (5-meter) drop onto uneven ground, but it has now been made much safer. Despite the changes, the Grand Pardubice remains the second longest race in the world, after the Grand National, and richly deserves its fearsome reputation.

The Palio di Siena

The Palio is an Italian horse race that takes place annually on July 2 and August 16 through the streets of Siena, Tuscany. It is a frenzied affair. The first Palio took place around 1650, and the race is dedicated to the Virgin Mary. Each horse and rider represents one of the 17 *Contrade*—city wards—of Siena, and both are dressed in the colors and arms of their *Contrade*. The race consists of three laps of the Piazza del Campo, and the winner is the first horse to cross the finishing line with its head ornaments intact, whether or not the rider is still on board!

> **Did You Know?**
>
> *The Grand Pardubice has only once been won by a woman. In 1937, the Countess Lata Brandisova led the field on the mare Norma.*

The Origins of Harness Racing

Racing horses in harness has its roots in the chariot races of ancient Rome, but modern-day harness racing evolved in the USA in the eighteenth century from friendly rivalries between owners as to who had the fastest horse. Competitions took place on the streets. (This is why so many US towns have a street called Race Street.) The first specially prepared tracks were built in the early nineteenth century.

The early 1900s saw a decline in the sport, as the horse gave way to the car, and the nation became more urbanized. The introduction of night time racing and parimutuel betting in 1940 at the Roosevelt Raceway, Long Island, New York began a boom in the sport, peaking in the 1970s. However, interest later declined and the Roosevelt Raceway closed in 1988. Most harness racing today takes place at country fairs. The United States Trotting Association, created in 1939, is the governing body for the sport. Harness racing is also widely followed in Europe and Australasia.

Harness racing evolved on the streets and country roads of 18th-century America.

The Sulky

The two-wheeled cart pulled in harness racing is known as a sulky. The nineteenth-century sulky had high wheels, with the result that the driver was positioned above the horse. This early version weighed about 100 pounds (45 kilograms). In 1892, the vehicle was altered dramatically with the introduction of pneumatic tires, giving rise to the "bike-sulky," the forerunner of today's model. Subsequent innovations in materials and design have brought the sulky to its current weight of about 40 pounds (18 kilograms).

The Standardbred

The Standardbred (*see Plate 43*) is a medium-built horse, with a larger, plainer head than the Thoroughbred. The body is long, muscular, and powerfully built, and the horse has a characteristically high croup that gives it massive thrusting power. They have placid temperaments and show a willingness to please. Most harness races are restricted to Standardbreds, although other breeds race in Europe.

The origins of the American Standardbred go back to a gray English Thoroughbred, Messenger, who was foaled in 1780 and exported to the USA eight years later. He stood at stud for many years, and gave rise to many lines. One line led to his great-grandson, Hambletonian 10 (1849–1876), a strong muscular horse, with powerful quarters that were two inches (5 centimeters) higher than his withers. This downhill conformation gave Hambletonian 10 a particular "trotting pitch," which he passed on to many of his offspring.

Hambletonian 10 sired more than 1,300 foals, and all registered Standardbreds can be traced from his line. Dexter, one of his sons, broke the world's trotting record in 1867, by clocking up a time of 2 minutes 17.25 seconds.

Dan Patch

Dan Patch (1897–1916) was one of the greatest harness racers in the history of the sport. In 1906, he ran a mile in one minute 55 seconds at the Minnesota State Fair racetrack, setting a new world record that stood for 32 years. His owner, Marion Savage, paid $60,000 for him. It proved a wise investment, as Dan Patch became a national celebrity, and earned around $3 million in stud fees, exhibitions, and advertising endorsements. He retired in 1909, the holder of nine world records.

The harness racing driver sits in a two-wheeled cart known as the sulky.

Trotters and Pacers

There are two types of gaits in harness racing, the trot and the pace. Trotters move in a diagonal gait, as does the naturally gaited horse. In this gait, the foreleg moves in unison with the diagonally opposite hind leg. Pacers move in a lateral gait, which means that they move both legs on the same side forward in unison. This is not a natural gait for the horse, although it is not unnatural for those Standardbreds that inherit a propensity to move at that gait. A trotter will only take part in trotting races, and a pacer will only take part in pacing races. Pacing is

The trotter moves its legs in diagonal pairs, unlike the pacer which moves its legs in lateral pairs.

the faster gait of the two. A horse that breaks its gait in a race will be penalized. Pacers are less likely to break stride than trotters because they wear plastic loops called hobbles, which connect the fore and hind legs on the same side of the horse, so helping to maintain the gait.

In continental Europe, trotters are more prevalent, whereas in North America and Australasia, most of the harness races are for pacers.

Did You Know?

Ontario-born John Campbell has won six Hambletonian titles, two more than his nearest rival. He is also the leading money-winning driver in the history of harness racing, with career earnings of more than $219 million.

Harness Racing in North America

The Northeast and Midwest are the main harness-racing centers in the US, although it is also popular in Florida and California, as well as in Canada. The premier locations include Meadowlands Racetrack and Freehold Raceway, both in New Jersey, and the Woodbine Racetrack and Mohawk Raceway, both in Ontario, Canada.

Pacers and trotters have their versions of the Triple Crown. The Pacing Triple Crown comprises the Cane Pace, the Messenger Stakes (both Yonkers Raceway, New York State), and the Little Brown Jug (Delaware, Ohio). Trotters compete in the Hambletonian (Meadowlands), the Yonkers Trot (Yonkers Raceway), and the Kentucky Futurity (Lexington's Red Mile, *see Plate 26*) for their Triple Crown. The main Canadian races include the North America Cup, the Canadian Pacing Derby, and the Maple Leaf Trot.

There is also a Breeders' Crown series of races, in which the top horses from various divisions race against each other. The 12 races are worth over $4 million in purses.

Harness Racing in Europe

Harness racing enjoys great popularity in Italy, France, and Scandinavia. The Hippodrome de Vincennes, near Paris, hosts the Prix d'Amérique, the most prestigious event of the European racing year. Other important races include the Elitloppet at Solvalla track near Stockholm, Sweden, and the Gran Premio Lotteria di Agnano in Naples, Italy.

Racing in Australasia

Australia and New Zealand both have a long tradition of harness racing, and the sport generates considerable interest in both countries. New Zealand produced Cardigan Bay, winner of 80 races and the first pacer to win $1.8 million in prize money.

Major events in Australia include the Miracle Mile, A.G. Hunter Cup, Victoria Cup, and the Australian Pacing Championship. In New Zealand the major races include the Auckland Cup, the New Zealand Cup, the Noel J. Taylor Memorial Mile, and the New Zealand Messenger Championship.

Racing Under Saddle (RUS)

At the beginning of the nineteenth century, nearly all trotting was done under saddle, meaning the horse was ridden, not driven in harness. Harness driving, however, became more popular as the roads improved, and under-saddle racing became a thing of the past.

The sport, however, has enjoyed a recent revival, beginning with the thrilling display by Brooke Nickells on Preferential in 1994, who set a world record for the mile with a time of one minute 58.4 seconds.

Since then, RUS has grown in popularity, and there is now a United States Trotting Association-sponsored Boots and Saddles Racing Under Saddle Series.

Did You Know?

In 2000, world champion mare, Moni Maker, ridden under saddle by Julie Krone, broke Preferential's record mile of 1:58.1. Julie, the only woman to win the Triple Crown, is also the first female jockey elected to the Thoroughbred Racing's Hall of Fame.

Other Sports

Bring together the horse's mental and physical potential and the human imagination and you have a recipe for an unlimited number of competitive sports. The roots of a number of sports are centuries old, while others have been around for just a few generations and still others are in their infancy. Whether they are based on hunting, ball sports, or cavalry exercises, and whether riders compete as individuals or as members of a team, these activities demand the utmost from the horse-and-rider partnership.

The hunt follower typically has to jump a variety of fences during the pursuit of the quarry.

Hunting for Sport

Prior to the growth of horse racing in England, the sport of kings was stag hunting on horseback with hounds, which was brought to Britain from France by William the Conqueror in 1066. Indeed, William's third son may have died as the result of a stag-hunting accident, and the "Rufus Stone" memorial in the New Forest in the south of England bears the inscription: "Here stood the oak tree, on which an arrow shot by Sir Walter Tyrell at a stag, glanced and struck King William the Second, surnamed Rufus, on the breast, of which he instantly died, on the second day of August, anno 1100." (Skeptics suggest that his brother Henry, soon to be King Henry I, may have been nearby.)

In the Pink

Stag hunting was always limited to relatively few areas of England, and in the late seventeenth century the hunting of foxes began to grow in popularity, and was welcomed by farmers as a means of reducing the numbers of an animal seen as a pest. Fox hunting soon largely replaced stag hunting, while adopting many of its traditions, and by the nineteenth century the hunt was seen as emblematic of the land-owning classes. The mounted men and women, dressed in hunting "pink," downing a "stirrup cup" on a frosty Boxing Day morning or leaping the hedgerows of the English countryside accompanied by a pack of baying hounds form a classic English image of yesteryear. In the last few years, however, issues of cruelty, animal rights, and a certain amount of class war have led to legislation in the UK, curbing the practice of hunting foxes to the death, and the sport in its traditional form is disappearing.

Fox Hunting in North America

The sport was brought to Maryland in the mid-1600s, and flourished in the Colonies. After Independence, hunting on horseback spread throughout much of North America and developed its own character and traditions; it remains especially popular in the mid-Atlantic and southern states, where the landscape is well suited to the chase. Instead of the red fox, the coyote is often the quarry, but the emphasis is on the chase and the animal is generally hunted until it goes to ground rather than being killed by the hounds.

The Kentucky Iroquois Hunt, named after the first US-bred winner of the Epsom Derby, is particularly well known and keeps some 80 hounds.

Pig Sticking

While the greatest danger for the fox hunter is falling from his horse, British cavalry officers in India came up with a somewhat more risky form of hunting, pig sticking. This sport, which was felt to be good training for both rider and horse, involved sending out beaters to flush wild boar from the undergrowth. Once the animal—no more than five feet (1.5 meters) in length, but extremely powerful and armed with sharp tusks—broke cover, the mounted hunters would attempt to overtake the beast and run it through with a nine-foot (2.7-meter) spear. Throwing the spear, which would have enabled the riders to

The tusks on a ferocious wild boar are capable of being used with fatal effect.

remain at a respectful distance, was considered unsporting. The greatest nerve and courage of both man and horse were required if the boar turned and attacked the hunter, who then had to hold his position and skewer the charging animal. Until the beginning of World War II, an annual championship hunt was held, and the winner was awarded the coveted Kadir Cup.

Pig sticking was a test of skill and bravery, and required horse and rider to get near to the boar, running the risk of the boar charging.

"In the cosmic game of polo
you are the ball
The mallet's left and right
becomes your call
He who causes your
movements, your rise
and fall
He is the one, the only one,
who knows it all."

THE RUBÀIYÀT OF OMAR KHAYYÀM (1048–1122)

Polo originated in the Orient, over two thousand years ago.

History of Polo

Claimed by some to be the oldest organized sport in the world, polo may have originated in Persia over 2,500 years ago. It was certainly being played in many parts of Asia by the middle of the first millennium CE, and there are references to the game in Persian literature and art from the ninth century.

The sport eventually spread to the royal courts of several far-flung countries, including Japan, China, India, and Tibet. During the sixteenth century, Shah Abbas the Great had a polo field built in front of the Ali Ghapu Palace in Isfahan, the capital of Persia at that time. The same size as a modern-day polo field, it can still be seen, complete with the original stone goal posts, as can the polo stables in Agra, built by the sixteenth-century ruler of India, Akbar the Great.

During the 1850s, when British tea planters were introduced to polo in the remote province of Manipur, on India's border with Burma, they were so enamored with the sport that they founded the world's first polo club at Silchar. The Calcutta Club, which is now the oldest polo club in the world, was founded in 1862.

Within 20 years, clubs were established in Malta, Britain, the USA, Argentina, and Australia, and today almost 80 countries play polo.

Did You Know?

Mounts in polo are always called ponies, despite the fact that they are almost invariably over the determining height for a pony: 14.2 hh.

The Principles of the Game

Once dubbed "hockey on horseback," polo is played by two teams of four mounted riders each, on an outdoor field measuring 300 yards by 160 yards (275 by 146 meters). The aim of the game is to score the most goals by hitting the ball through the opposing team's goal posts, which are set eight yards (7.3 meters) apart. A game comprises four, six, or eight periods, called chukkers, each lasting for seven minutes. There is a three-minute break between chukkers to allow players to change horses. An indoor version of the game is played on a smaller field, with only three players on each team, using a larger ball made of rubber.

Players wear protective helmets and faceguards, as well as protective kneeguards. Each player carries a mallet, traditionally made of bamboo and willow, but now often made of polyresins. The ball, which is three and a half inches (8.9 centimeters) in diameter and weighs about four and

a half ounces (127.5 grams), is struck with the side of the mallet head and not the end. The ponies are fitted with protective leg bandages, and their tails are braided or taped to keep them out of the way.

The four players in each team play prescribed positions: Number One plays a forward, goal-scoring offensive position; Number Two's role is to break up the defensive plays of the opposition; Number Three needs to hit long balls and make the play for the team; and Number Four plays defensively, guarding the goal.

> **Did You Know?**
>
> *Between 1900 and 1939, polo was an Olympic sport and, following recent recognition by the International Olympic Committee, it may soon be again.*

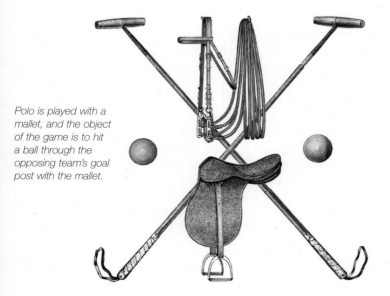

Polo is played with a mallet, and the object of the game is to hit a ball through the opposing team's goal post with the mallet.

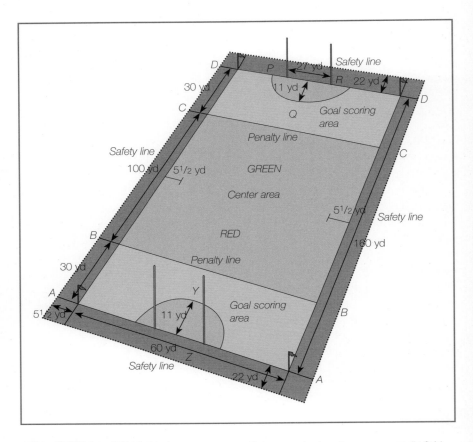

Safety line · 30 yd · 11 yd · 22 yd · Goal scoring area · Penalty line · Safety line · 100 yd · 5½ yd · GREEN · Center area · 5½ yd · Safety line · 160 yd · RED · Penalty line · 30 yd · 11 yd · Goal scoring area · 5½ yd · 60 yd · Safety line · 22 yd · D · P · R · Q · C · C · B · A · Y · Z · B · A

The Origins of Polocrosse

If polo is hockey on horseback, this is lacrosse on horseback. The concept began as a training aid at an English riding school, where riders used polo mallets with squash racquet heads to pick up balls and deposit them in hoops at the ends of an indoor arena. The idea was taken up in Australia in 1939, when a demonstration was given at a sports ground near Sydney, and the first polocrosse club was founded later that year, complete with a defining set of rules.

The sport quickly spread throughout Australia, and in 1946 the Polocrosse Association of Australia (PAA) was

Polocrosse is played on a grass or dirt field, measuring 160 yards long and 60 yards wide.

formed. The International Polocrosse Council (IPC), was formed in 1976, and polocrosse is now played in Canada, France, Germany, Ireland, New Zealand, Norway, South Africa, Spain, Great Britain, the USA, Vanuatu, and Zimbabwe. The American Polocrosse Association (APA) was founded in 1984.

Rules of the Game

Polocrosse is played on an outdoor field, about half the size of a polo pitch, with a goal at each end. Unlike polo, in which a player is allowed up to seven horses, each polocrosse rider is only allowed one horse, except in the event of an injury. The stick, with its loose net head, has changed little since the early days, and the ball is made of hard-cased rubber.

Each team consists of six riders, divided into two sections of three each—a Number One (attack), a Number Two (center), and a Number Three (defense). Only the Number One player can score, and this must be done from within the goal-scoring area. Sections play alternate chukkas of up to eight minutes each. A full match consists of six or eight chukkas.

Horseball: A Growing Sport

This fast young sport has a lot in common with buzkashi (see p. 242), with a dash of American football, and more than a hint of basketball. Horseball was invented in France in the late 1970s and, as with polocrosse, the intention was to create an enjoyable, inexpensive, and easily organized activity that would help to train riders and horses. The result was so successful that a National League soon developed, and the sport has now spread throughout Europe, Canada, the USA, and South America. The Fédération Internationale de Horseball, which is based in Paris, was founded in 1999.

Rules of the Game

The game is played in a standard-sized riding arena, and all breeds of horse are used. Much of the riding is done using the legs only, so horses need to be well trained. A team is comprised

of four players, and the game lasts for just 20 minutes, most of which is spent at a canter or gallop. Speed and maneuverability are key, as the aim of the game is take possession of the ball and to pass between at least three players without dropping the ball before shooting through a vertical ring at the end of the arena.

Contact between players is allowed, within limits, and players often barge each other when trying to grab the ball. When the ball falls to the ground it must be picked up "on the run," and a belly strap links the stirrups so that the player can swing down the side of the horse to reach the handles of the ball.

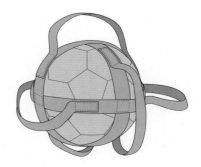

The horseball is a junior-sized soccer ball, which fits within a harness that has six leather handles.

Buzkashi

Best known as Afghanistan's national sport, buzkashi probably originated as a hunting or raiding tactic in the thirteenth century among the Mongol-Turkic horsemen of the Asian steppes, and may first have been played as a sport in the valley of the Oxus, or Amu Darya, river, which flows into the Aral Sea. It is now played under a variety of names and in various forms throughout south Central Asia. It requires teamwork and communication, and demands the highest skills of both horse and rider.

The name buzkashi comes from the Persian word for "goat killing," and the aim of the game, which can last for several days, is to seize and ride off with the beheaded carcass of a goat or calf. The body of a calf is preferred, as the carcass tends to stay intact for longer. Traditionally, the game was played over a huge open area with two teams of unlimited number, but it is now held on a marked-out field and a degree of regulation has been introduced. Teams usually number ten riders, weapons are limited to small whips, and the buzkashi players wear strong boots and thick clothing to protect themselves. The horses—all stallions—undergo five years of training before being allowed on the field, and can fetch prices of up to $2,500.

In one version of the game—tudabarai—the aim is simply to take possession of the carcass and to ride away clear of the opposition. In the more complex version—quarajai—the player must carry the carcass around a flag at one end of the field, ride back, and throw the animal into the scoring circle at the opposite end.

Tent Pegging

As a modern-day sport, tent pegging involves a galloping rider, armed with a lance or sword, spearing, and carrying

The aim of the Afghani sport of buzkashi is to ride off with the carcass of a goat, calf, or sheep, despite fierce and rough opposition from the rival team.

off symbolic tent pegs stuck into the ground. The origins of tent pegging date back even further than those of buzkashi, possibly as far back as the invasion of India by Alexander the Great in 326 BCE when, it is said, his horsemen gained an advantage against the elephants of the opposing army by riding past at a gallop and spearing their feet.

The sport derives its name from the practice of launching a dawn cavalry raid on the enemy encampment and causing their tents to collapse on the sleeping troops by uprooting the tent pegs, although there are very few accounts of this tactic actually being used. Nonetheless, as one of several cavalry sports designed to hone the skills of the horse and the armed rider, tent pegging was certainly practiced in medieval India, and from here it spread around the world to become the popular modern sport that it is today.

The tent peg is picked up at a gallop by a competitor armed with a lance or sword.

Competitive Tent Pegging

Tent pegging also encompasses such skill-at-arms cavalry sports as ring jousting, in which the rider must lance a suspended ring, and lemon sticking, using a sword to slice a lemon that is suspended on a string or sitting atop a pole. Competitions include individual, pairs, and team events.

Competitions are hosted in the USA, Canada, Great Britain, Australia, and South Africa, but India and Pakistan remain the true homes of the sport. It was accepted as an official event at the 1982 New Delhi Asian Games, and the International Tent Pegging Competition in Bangalore, India attracts contestants from around the world. In 2004, the Fédération Equestre Internationale granted tent pegging recognition as a Regional Discipline.

Competitive Horse Driving

Although the horse in harness is no longer used as an everyday means of transport, the skills required to drive a horse and carriage are still very much alive and well. Competitive driving has been popular in both America and Europe throughout the twentieth century, but, in 1968, the sport took a big leap forward.

The Modern Sport

His Royal Highness Prince Philip, himself a keen driver, was watching the four-in-hand cross-country and obstacle-driving trials at the International Horse Show at Aachen, Germany, and realized the potential for a sport combining several elements. The Fédération Equestre Internationale, the international governing body for all horse sports, worked with the Prince to draw up rules for these competitions, and combined Horse-Driving Trials became one of the FEI sports.

The first international event took place in 1970, the first European Championships came a year later, and the first ever World Four-in-Hand Driving Championships were held in 1972. They are now an established part of the World Equestrian Games. Competitive driving is not yet an Olympic equestrian event.

Designed to highlight the skill of the driver and the training of the horse, competitive driving has also encouraged the breeding of horses for competition as well as improving vehicle design. The sport consists of three very different stages that test every quality of the horse in harness—dressage, marathon, and cone—or obstacle—driving. Competing classes can include any of the following: single pony, pony pairs, pony tandems, pony teams, single horse, horse pairs, horse tandems, and horse teams.

The Horse-driving "Triathlon"

There is a three-day event in competitive driving which is modeled on ridden eventing (*see p. 178*):

Day 1, Dressage The dressage phase consists of a sequence of set movements that display the schooling and obedience of the animal. These include circles, half-circles, and serpentines at various speeds and paces, as well as halts and rein-backs. Judges award marks for the accuracy of the prescribed movements and penalize errors of course or dismounting of grooms—all turnouts must carry a groom (two grooms for teams of horses or ponies) who must remain seated throughout the test and may not speak or sign to the driver.

Para-equestrian Driving

The International Paralympic Equestrian Committee (IPEC) was set up in 1991 by the International Paralympic Committee to develop equestrian sport worldwide for athletes with a disability, in which it succeeded admirably, with some 38 nations now involved in competition. In April 2004, the National Federations of the FEI voted for IPEC to join the FEI, which it has now done, as Para Equestrian, the eighth FEI discipline. Para-equestrian driving is now one of the FEI World Championship Sports.

Many shows for competitive driving host competitions for a particular horse breed or type of carriage.

Day 2, Marathon The cross-country marathon course comprises five timed sections, the last of which is six and a quarter miles (ten kilometers) long with up to eight obstacles, lettered gates constructed around natural features such as ditches and banks. Time is everything, so high speeds and tight turns are needed in order to avoid time penalties.

Day 3, Cone Driving The equivalent of the show-jumping phase of a ridden event, this phase is a real test of the team as they fly, in sequence, between up to 20 narrowly spaced pairs of cones in a course that is between approximately 550 and 875 yards (500 and 800 meters) in distance. Penalties are awarded for exceeding the allowed time or for knocking any of the cones.

Endurance Riding

Endurance rides vary in length from 50 to 100 miles (80.5 to 161 kilometers) for one-day rides. National- and international-level riders compete over 100 miles, only stopping for veterinarian checks. Longer-distance rides usually take place over several days, when a distance of 50 or so miles is covered every day. A horse must be five years old before he is allowed to compete in races of 50 or more miles. Novice horses usually begin competing at a limited distance of between 25 and 30 miles (40.25 and 48.25 kilometers).

Although the winner of an endurance race is the horse with the fastest time, it must also be in a fit condition at the end of the race. There are compulsory veterinarian stops along the route, when the horse is assessed for soundness and general condition. During this stop, the horse's respiration, pulse, and temperature must return to normal or they will not be allowed to continue.

Endurance riding is recognized by the FEI and has been included in the World Equestrian Games, although it is not yet an Olympic sport.

Ride and Tie

Ride and tie is a sport in which two riders compete with one horse, each competitor alternately riding while the other runs. The distance of the course ranges from 10 to 40 miles (16 to 64 km).

The Endurance Horse

Although any breed of horse can be used for endurance riding, Arabians and Arabian crosses dominate the sport at the top level. The Arabian is a lightweight animal, yet it is also very fast and has incredible stamina, ideal

Endurance riding tests the limits of both the horse and the rider.

qualities for the endurance horse. Other characteristics that make the Arabian a favored mount include intelligence, courage, and a willingness to please his rider. Being a "horse of the desert," the Arabian also performs well in hot, dusty conditions.

The Tevis Cup

The Western States Trail Ride is a grueling 100-mile (160-kilometer) ride through the Sierra Nevada, starting in Robie Park, near Lake Tahoe, Nevada, and ending in Auburn, California. More popularly known as the Tevis Cup, this endurance race was first held in 1955. The ride was the idea of Auburn businessman Wendell Robie, who, along with a few of his friends, first proved that the trail could be completed in less than 24 hours using a single horse.

The trail is dusty and rugged, and temperatures can reach 100 degrees Fahrenheit (38 degrees Celsius). It is also very up and down—there is a climb of approximately 17,000 feet (5,200 meters) and a descent of about 22,000 feet (6,700 meters).

Although Tevis Cup winners typically complete the course in under 16 hours, all riders who take less than 24 hours are awarded the coveted Tevis Cup belt buckle. The overall winner is the rider who completes the course in the fastest possible time, and whose horse is considered "fit to continue." The first ten horses are also eligible for the Haggin Cup. This trophy is awarded to the horse judged by veterinarians to be in the best condition on the day following the ride.

The silver belt buckle is the prize for all Tevis Cup riders who complete the grueling course in under two days.

The Stand is one of the seven compulsory movements in vaulting competitions.

The Origins of Vaulting

Vaulting, which is most aptly described as gymnastics and dance on horseback, is of ancient origin. The Romans performed acrobatic movements on horseback 2,000 years ago, and the knights and noblemen of the Middle Ages practiced vaulting movements as part of their equestrian education.

The modern sport of vaulting was developed in Germany after World War II as a means of introducing children to equestrian sports. The FEI now recognizes vaulting as one

of the seven equestrian disciplines, and it is now part of the FEI World Equestrian Games. Enthusiasm for the sport is high in Germany, and interest is growing in the USA, Brazil, and Australia. American vaulters have been successful in competing on the world stage.

> **Did You Know?**
>
> *Vaulting featured in the 1920 Olympic Games, when it was known as "Artistic Riding."*

The Competition

Competitors are assisted by a longeur, who controls the movement of the carefully trained horse with a longe line and longe whip. The horse moves in a 16-yard (15-meter) circle. Competitors then vault onto the cantering horse, perform various movements, and then dismount from the horse.

The top-level vaulting competition consists of two elements, the compulsory test and the kur, or freestyle, both of which are performed to music.

The Compulsory Test

The vaulter must perform seven compulsory movements in a prescribed order, and each movement is given a score out of ten by the judges. In the individual competition, the movements are performed without dismounting from the horse. In team vaulting, however, the team members perform the first four movements in turn, then remount and complete the remaining three exercises. The seven movements are:

Mount The initial mount onto the back of the horse.

Basic Riding Seat The rider sits astride the horse, with arms out to the side. The movement should be held for four full strides.

Flag The rider kneels on the horse and extends the right leg out behind, so that it is parallel to the horse's spine. The left arm should be stretched out in front, in line with the right leg. This movement is also held for four full strides.

Mill Starting in the astride position, the vaulter swings the right leg over the horse's neck, then brings the left leg over the rump, followed by the right leg. Finally, the left leg swings back over the neck, and the rider is again in the starting position. Each leg movement should take one stride, and the movement is completed in four strides. The mill requires the vaulter to let go of the grip with each leg movement.

Scissors Again beginning in the astride position, the vaulter performs a handstand. Once in position, the vaulter's body should be turned inward, toward the longeur, and the inner leg should be crossed over the outer. The vaulter twists her body and lands facing the tail of the body. The movement is repeated, but this time the vaulter will land facing forward

once again. The vaulter should land gently on the horse's back.

Stand The rider stands on the horse's back for four full strides, arms held out to the sides as in the astride position.

Flank The flank is the dismount from the horse. From the astride position, the vaulter swings her legs forward and then back and up into the air until she is almost in a handstand. She then jackknifes her body, turning to the inside, and sits facing into the circle. Swinging her legs up and back over the horse's croup to the outside, she then pushes herself off the handgrips and lands on the offside of the horse, facing forward.

The Kur

The kur is the freestyle phase of the competition, and vaulters perform their own choreographed movements. In the team competition, all eight members of the team must perform, with a maximum number of three on the horse at any one time. The kur is marked on performance, technical difficulty, and artistic interpretation.

Did You Know?

Therapeutic, also known as Interactive, vaulting is also showing benefits for treating children or adults with balance, attention, gross motor skill, and social deficits.

From the Age of Elegance

After a period of relative obscurity, side-saddle riding, or riding aside, is now enjoying a comeback. For many riders, the appeal lies not so much in the comfort that the saddle offers but in the old-fashioned femininity of a riding style that harks back to a more elegant era.

Early History

There are examples of women depicted riding horses in a sideways position in paintings and bronzes from ancient Greece and Rome, but the forerunner of the modern side-saddle came into being in Europe in the Middle Ages. In a period when female attire made sitting astride a horse virtually impossible and the social mores of the time made it unacceptable, at least for someone from the nobility, a form of saddle developed on which the rider sat sideways with the feet resting on a wooden ledge called a planchette, French for "small plank." Although it would have been comfortable enough, this kind of saddle gave the rider little

Side-saddle riding permitted women of an earlier era to ride in a dignified and elegant manner.

stability—despite having a pommel that the rider could grip onto—and offered poor control over the horse, which was therefore generally led at a steady walk.

The Modern Saddle

The form of the saddle changed in the late sixteenth century with the addition of a second pommel, positioned off-center, around which the right leg could be hooked, giving additional security and enabling the rider to sit in a more forward-facing position. In the early 1800s, a third pommel, or leaping head, under which the left leg could be hooked to give a secure position for jumping, was added, and the original central pommel was gradually discarded. In the late 1870s, encouraged by Elizabeth, Empress of Austria, who often traveled to England and rode with aristocratic friends in the Pytchley Hunt, in Northamptonshire, an increasing number of women took up hunting side-saddle.

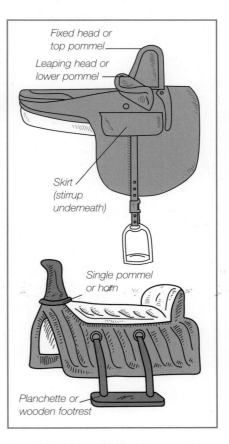

The modern side saddle (top) gives control in this riding position. The first side saddle (bottom) was little more than a seat and women were led, traveling at walking pace.

A Return to Favor

In the USA, too, women responded to the development of the side-saddle, and this form of riding was adopted throughout the nineteenth and early twentieth centuries for pleasure riding, hunting, and competition, but in America and Britain the side-saddle all but disappeared after World War II. However, thanks to dedicated female riders on both sides of the Atlantic and in Australia, and the foundation of such groups as the International Side-Saddle Organization in the USA and the Side-Saddle Association in Great Britain, the skill and art of riding aside has not only seen a resurgence but has been extended into an even wider range of competitive events. Riders in the USA can now compete in divisions that include Hunter, Saddle Horse, Dressage, Western, and Period Costume, and these are found at a growing number of major shows.

Dress

In side-saddle events, the rider's dress is all important, consisting of a traditional, dark-fabric outfit in the style of the early 1900s: skirt, cutaway jacket, vest, breeches, and a silk top hat, with an apron covering the rider's legs. Leather gloves are worn, and a pair of white string gloves must be properly positioned on the right side of the saddle. Riders carry a hunt whip in the right hand.

Caring for your Horse

PETRI PELS N.Y.

A horse is totally dependent upon others for all the essentials of life—its nutrition, health, shelter, safety, and comfort—and the well-being of the horse should be the prime concern of any owner or rider. As well as feeding and taking care of the basics, this means daily contact with the horse through grooming and handling. This not only ensures that your horse remains fit and healthy, it is also the best possible way to build up a relationship of mutual trust and understanding.

The Barn

A purpose-built horse barn should have the required number of stalls, a separate tack room, a feed storage area, and a work area.

Stalls must be sturdily built to withstand any kicking or pushing from the horse. The barn should be well ventilated and have good lighting.

Stalls

Stalls are typically built of wood or cement block, and the walls must be strong enough to withstand any kicking. Kick boards can be placed at the bottom of the walls for additional strengthening. The stall floor should be non-slip—hard-packed dirt or roughened concrete is adequate, although many horse owners now prefer to have rubber matting as it is comfortable for the horse and acts as a cushioning for its legs. Floors should slope slightly, preferably to the back of the stall, to allow adequate drainage.

Stalls should be at least ten feet (three meters) square for ponies, and 12 feet (3.6 meters) square for horses, and ten feet (three meters) high. If more space is available, make the stalls even larger. Foaling or nursing mares should have a double stall.

The stall door should be at least four feet (1.2 meters) wide, and should open outward. There should be bolts on both the top and bottom of the door, as many horses can manage to open the top latch.

The ceiling of the barn should be a minimum of 12 feet (3.5 meters) high—although 15 feet (4.5 meters) would be better—to prevent the horse from banging its head.

If the stall has metal bars, they should not be more than four inches (ten centimeters) apart, to ensure that a hoof cannot be passed between them or get stuck.

Ensure that there are no protruding nails or sharp edges that could harm the horse. Fixtures and fittings should be kept to the absolute minimum, as most horses have an uncanny way of hurting themselves on the most innocuous items. However, there should be a ring fixed approximately 5 feet (1.5 meters) off the ground for tying the horse up. There may also be a fitted feed manger and/or hayrack in the stall, and there must be a water bucket or automatic water system.

Ventilation and Lighting

The barn should be warm, dry, and waterproof, but not stuffy. Horses need a constant supply of fresh air, so make sure that your barn has good ventilation. Ideally, each stall should have a window. If your barn smells stuffy, you do not have adequate ventilation. On the other hand, make sure that your horse is not exposed to excessive drafts.

A well-lit barn is essential, and there should be light in every stall as well as an outside light. All switches and wires should be well out of the horse's reach.

Feed Room

Feed should ideally be kept in a separate room with a closed door (this also helps to keep rodents out). As well as keeping the barn tidy, it also prevents any loose horse from gorging on feed, which could have disastrous results.

Tack Room

A well-run and tidy tack room is a must (see p. 286).

The Work Area

The barn should have a place to groom and wash the horse, and it should be located near to a water supply. A hot-water supply is a welcome bonus.

Barn Tools

Essential items include a wheelbarrow, shavings fork, pitchfork, stable brush, and yard broom. Tools should always be stored away when not in use, as the carelessly dropped pitchfork can cause a great deal of harm!

When you have finished your barn duties for the day, put away all tools tidily.

Bedding

Bedding provides warmth and comfort for the stall-kept horse, and also absorbs much of the horse's urine. There are a number of different bedding options, and these include straw, wood shavings, shredded paper, and rubber matting. Factors to consider when choosing the type of bedding include cost, disposal of muck, and the health of your horse. Whatever type of bedding you use, the stall should be thoroughly cleaned every day. A dirty bed is not only uncomfortable for the horse but it is also unhygienic.

Straw bedding is very popular, as it provides a warm, comfortable bed for the horse and is easily disposed of for garden manure. Wheat straw is preferable to barley or oat straw, as it drains well and, more importantly, is not palatable, so it will not be eaten by the horse. Some horses, however, are allergic to the dust spores found in straw bedding.

Wood shavings make an economical and comfortable bed. Shavings will not be eaten by the horse, and they are good for horses with respiratory problems. However, it is important to know what type of wood is in the shavings, as some are toxic to the horse. Woods to avoid include black walnut, oak, and hickory. Droppings and wet patches need to be removed frequently, as shavings are quite porous and soon become saturated.

Straw is the traditional bedding for the horse. Some horses do, however, like to eat straw bedding, so it is not suitable for every animal.

Shredded paper is dust-free and is therefore a good option for the horse with allergies. It is difficult to muck out, however, as it becomes very heavy when wet.

Rubber matting is also dust-free and is easily cleaned with water. However, it does not provide a warm, comfortable bed for the horse to lie down on, and it is generally used with another form of bedding. Rubber matting is very expensive, but it does last a long time.

Mucking Out

Always tie up your horse before mucking out. Remove all soiled bedding with a four-pronged fork or shavings fork, depending on the type of bedding, and place in a wheelbarrow. Toss the dry bedding to the sides of the box. Sweep the floor clean, and allow it to air and dry. Once the floor is aired, replace old bedding and top up with new bedding. This should be banked up around the walls, as it will prevent a horse from becoming stuck, or cast, against the walls should it roll. Every few weeks, thoroughly wash the floor down with disinfectant.

The Manure Pile

The manure pile should be situated well away from the barn. Not only is this more hygienic, it is also safer, as manure piles can overheat and catch fire. There should be three muck heaps on the go, one that is rotted and ready for use on the garden, one that is in the process of rotting, and one that is currently in use.

Disposal of manure is a big problem in semi-rural and suburban areas. A typical arrangement is to contract with a local farmer, especially a mushroom grower, to haul away the manure.

Deep-litter Bed

A deep-litter bed is easy to manage and provides a deep, warm bed for a horse. It is usually made with a deep layer of shavings or straw. Droppings and wet patches are removed regularly and fresh bedding is sprinkled on top of the old bed, but the bed is mucked out completely only every three to six months. This method of bedding is not so popular nowadays, as it is thought that fungal spores thrive in the wet environment and may cause respiratory problems and hoof diseases such as thrush.

The stall floor should be swept clean on a daily basis and allowed to air.

Grooming

The stabled horse should be groomed daily to promote health and condition. Grooming removes dirt, sweat, dead skin cells, and loose hair, and gives a healthy sheen to the horse's coat. The daily grooming sessions act as a massage that helps tone the body. It also stimulates the blood and lymphatic systems, and aids the removal of waste products. At the same time, it gives the owner the opportunity to inspect the horse closely for any signs of illness or injury, for example, heat or swellings in the legs. Grooming removes ticks and bots and will also help to prevent skin diseases and infections. Finally, grooming helps to build up a relationship of trust between horse and handler.

Grooming Kit

Every horse owner and rider should possess their own grooming kit. The following items are essential:

Hoof pick For the removal of mud and stones from the feet. Always work from heel to toe to avoid harming the frog.

Dandy brush Used to remove sweat marks and caked mud from horse's body. Avoid using on thin-skinned horses and sensitive parts of the body, for example, the bony parts of the leg.

Rubber curry comb Use in a circular motion to remove mud, sweat, and loose hair.

Body brush Used to clean the whole of the body. Should be used in conjunction with the metal curry comb (*see below*).

Metal curry comb Cleans the body brush. After every four or five strokes, clean body brush by wiping it across the teeth of the metal curry comb. Bang curry comb on stable floor to remove dirt. Never use on the horse.

Water brush Used to dampen down mane or tail before braiding, or to clean mud off hooves.

Mane and tail combs There are two types of mane comb. The larger-toothed type is used to clean the mane and tail, and the thinner type for pulling the mane. The body brush may also be used to clean the mane and tail, and is a more gentle option.

Stable rubber Used after the grooming session to remove last traces of dirt.

Wisp Used for stropping (*see box*).

Sponges There should be two sponges, one to clean the eyes and one to clean the dock.

Sweat scraper Used to remove excess water after hosing down or bathing the horse

Braiding the Mane

A braided mane is often a requirement at a horse show or horse trials, and every competitive rider needs to know how to braid. For braiding, you will need a large yarn hook, wool as close in color as possible to your horse's mane, elastics, and scissors.

First, dampen the mane slightly to make it easier to handle. Divide the mane into equal sections and tie with elastic bands. Then, working from the head down, remove elastic from first section of hair and start to braid. Approximately halfway down the braid, add wool into it. Braid as far down as possible, then wrap the wool around the end of the braid and secure with a half-hitch knot. Thread the wool through the eye of the needle and pass the needle through the mane as near as possible to the roots. This will halve the length of the braid. Fold the braid

Horses need to be groomed daily, and every horse owner should put together a basic grooming kit. Essential items include the hoof pick, metal curry comb, mane and tail combs, body brush, and sponge.

in half again and put the needle back through the root. Stitch through the braid several times to secure, and cut the wool. Continue until all sections of the mane are braided. Finish by braiding the forelock.

Using a Wisp

Traditionally, wisps were simply made out of a handful of hay, but nowadays there are massage pads or gloves specifically designed for the job. A wisp is used at the end of the grooming session for a massage technique known as "stropping." In stropping, the wisp is used to bang the muscles on the neck, shoulders, and quarters. This causes the muscles to relax and contract alternately, helping to condition and tone the muscles and improving the horse's circulation.

Clipping

In the winter months, the horse grows a thick layer of hair as a natural defense against the cold. However, the horse at work will sweat heavily if it has a woolly coat, so many owners clip their horses. The clipped horse is easier to keep clean. The first clip of the season is in the fall, and the horse will probably need clipping monthly for four months. The clipped horse will need appropriate stable and/or turnout blankets to keep it warm. Clipping requires skill, and some horses object strongly to the process. If you are unsure of your ability, get it done professionally.

Tying Up a Horse

Never tie a horse directly to a fixed object, such as a fence or gate. The horse may pull back in panic and injure himself. Tie a piece of baling twine or string to the fixed object and attach the lead rope to the twine. If the horse does pull back, the twine will break easily. Always use a quick-release knot to tie the lead rope to the twine. This way, the lead rope can be released easily should the need arise.

Different Types of Clip

Full clip The whole coat is removed. Used for show horses.
Hunter clip The legs and saddle patch are left unclipped.
Blanket clip The neck and belly only are clipped. Used for horses in light work and for those kept out by day and in at night.
Trace clip The belly and area under the neck are clipped. Used for horses and ponies at grass.

Cross Ties

Cross tying in a stall or aisle is one of the safest and easiest ways to secure a horse when it is being groomed, clipped, or tacked-up. The ties should be attached at one end to a ring, which should be placed on facing walls at approximately the height of the withers. The other end of the tie is attached to the horse's halter. The ties should just be long enough to meet in the center.

How to Tie Quick-release Knots

Pass the rope through the ring or round the bar, and then create a loop in the free end of the rope and lay it over the standing part of the rope.

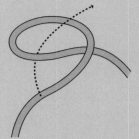

Now create a second loop in the free end, pass this under the standing part and through the first loop. A pull on the standing part will tighten the knot. A pull on the free end will undo it.

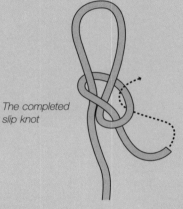

The completed slip knot

Slip knot
Quick release for tying horses

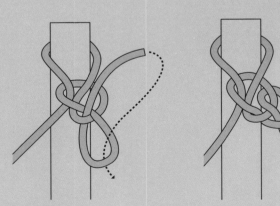

Slip knot with release loop
(Stable Tie)

Shoeing

Shoes help to protect the horse's feet from damage and concussion, and the importance of good and correct shoeing cannot be overstated. Ill-fitting shoes can damage a horse and make him permanently unsound. All too often, a farrier will try to make the horse's foot fit a ready-made shoe. Remedial shoeing by a skilled farrier, on the other hand, can correct conformational faults and relieve the pain caused by diseases of the foot, such as laminitis. Even horses that don't wear shoes need to have their feet trimmed regularly.

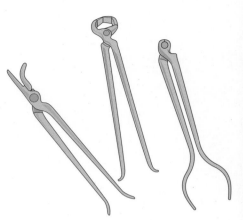

Horse owners should have a basic farrier kit in case a shoe needs to be removed urgently.

Studs

Studs can be screwed into a horse's shoe to provide more grip in slippery conditions. The size, shape, and number of studs varies according to ground conditions. Show jumpers and eventing horses usually wear studs.

Pulling Shoes

There are times when a horseshoe needs to be removed immediately—if a shoe is loose, for example. A shoe that is half off can seriously injure a horse. Ask your farrier to teach you how to pull a shoe, and practice under supervision. You should buy a clinch cutter, hammer, pull-offs, and a nail puller for this purpose.

How To Tell Whether a Horse Needs Re-shoeing

- The shoe is loose or cast, that is, fallen off.
- The shoe has worn thin.
- The clinches have risen and are no longer close to the wall.
- The foot is overlong and out of shape.

Horses' hooves grow at a steady rate and feet will need to be trimmed and the shoes replaced by a farrier every four to six weeks.

Common Types of Shoe

Traditional front

Traditional hind

Hunter front

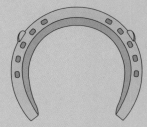

Hunter hind

Full grip

Aluminum

Egg bar

Heart bar

" Horses and poets should be fed, not overfed. "

CHARLES IX , *KING OF FRANCE (1550–1574)*

Did You Know?

Water makes up approximately 50 percent of a horse's total body weight.

Feeding

The natural diet for a horse is grasses and herbs such as alfalfa and yarrow. Horses in the wild can live adequately on this alone; the working horse expends more energy and needs supplementary feeding to compensate.

There are two main types of food— bulk and concentrates, also called "hard feed." The main bulk food is hay or chaff—chopped hay—but bran and sugar beet may also be included to add roughage to the diet. Hay should make up between 50 and 70 percent of the horse's total diet. It should be of a good quality, and should smell sweet and be light green to light brown in color. There are two main types

All horses should be provided with a salt lick in their stall.

Clean, fresh water should always be available, for the stabled horse and the horse at pasture.

of hay, legume hay—alfalfa is the most common of these—and grass hay—timothy is the most common—and these two types are often mixed together. Legume hay has more protein but is not suitable for all horses.

Concentrates include oats, barley, corn, bran, and linseed. They are often fed in compound form as a complete horse pellet. Minerals in powder or pellet form are sometimes added to the hard feed. Salt should be available as a lick in every stall.

Guidelines to Feeding

- Feed little and often. The horse has a relatively small stomach, and the most natural and healthy way for a horse to eat is to have the stomach nearly always two-thirds full.
- Feed plenty of bulk to keep the digestive process in good working order. Although the horse has a small stomach, it has a large intestine.
- Try to feed at the same time each day.
- Dietary changes should be introduced gradually, over several days.

- Feed good-quality food, especially hay. Moldy or dusty hay can cause illnesses, such as colic (*see p. 304*).
- Feed according to age, size, general condition, and the type of work the horse is doing. As an approximate guide, feed two and a half pounds (1.1 kilograms) per 100 pounds (45 kilograms) body weight to maintain current weight.
- Feed a treat every day—for example, an apple or carrot.
- Leave at least one hour between feeding and exercising the horse.
- Remove uneaten food from the stall.
- Feeding utensils must be kept clean. Scrub all feed-buckets and mangers daily.

Watering

An adult horse drinks between ten and 15 gallons (38 and 57 liters) of water a day, and a horse should always have access to fresh, clean water. Water is essential for all bodily processes, and a horse cannot survive for long without it. Only withhold water from a horse when it is overheated; offer a small amount of slightly warmed water until the horse has cooled down sufficiently. It can then have free access to water.

There are two main ways to give water to the stabled horse: in a bucket or by automatic drinking bowls. Buckets can be placed on the stall floor or secured to the wall with a ring. (For the horse that likes to play with its water bucket, try placing it in the center of a tire.) Automatic water systems provide the horse with a constant supply of water, but they do not allow the horse owner to monitor whether the horse is drinking enough.

The Horse at Grass

All horses enjoy being out at pasture; it is relaxing and offers a horse the opportunity to play and socialize with other horses. Some horses are fed off grass alone, and these horses need at least one and a half, preferably more, acres of good pasture to sustain them. Even the stabled horse should have access to pasture on occasion, either on its nonworking day or for a week or fortnight's "vacation." However long a horse spends at grass, the field must provide it with a safe environment.

Clean, fresh water must be available at all times, and any stagnant water should be fenced off. The field must be fenced securely and strongly, as horses are notoriously "hard" on fencing. Suitable fencing includes post-and-rail, post-and-wire, and electric fencing. Never put a horse in a field with barbed wire; it can cause permanent injury and can even be fatal.

Gates must be wide enough for the horse and handler to pass through safely, and should have horse-proof latches.

There must be some kind of shelter in the field. Trees or hedges provide some degree of protection against sun, wind, and rain, but a field shelter is preferable. This should be a three-sided roofed construction.

All fields should be checked regularly for potential hazards, such as poisonous plants (*see opposite*), rabbit holes, and sharp objects.

All horse droppings should be removed regularly—ideally on a daily basis—to prevent worm infestation.

Time spent at pasture gives the stabled horse the opportunity to relax and socialize in a herd situation.

Red maple   Yew   Ragwort

Keeping Fields in Good Condition

Grassland that is continuously grazed will eventually become "horse sick." Over time the horses will selectively eat all the best grass and will avoid the weeds, areas where manure has accumulated, and patches of poorer grass. Consequently, the less edible species will thrive, taking over more of the field until there is virtually no good-quality grazing. Careful management is needed if the field is to remain healthy and nutritionally valuable.

Before this point is reached, a field needs to be rested. If it is possible to bring in cattle and then sheep to graze the whole field and level the grass, so much the better. Any weeds should be removed, and if there are areas of standing water then drainage should be improved.

An analysis of the soil will reveal whether any nutrients—such as nitrogen, lime, phosphates, or potash—are lacking, and any deficiencies should be made good. Harrowing and rolling the field in spring will aerate the soil and remove dead grass, allowing new growth to flourish.

Common Poisonous Plants

If there is an abundant food supply, most horses will avoid ingesting poisonous plants, simply because most of them aren't very palatable. However, the hungry or greedy horse, or one that is on overgrazed pasture, may well be tempted—with fatal results. It is always best, therefore, to learn to recognize problem plants and remove them by pulling up or by using a registered herbicide. Hay, too, should be examined for any trace of poisonous plants.

Common poisonous plants in North America include: black walnut, bracken fern, buttercups, castor bean, cherry, cocklebur, crotalaria, death camas, fireweed, horsetail, lantana, locoweed, nightshade, oleander, poison hemlock, rayless goldenrod, red maple, Russian knapweed, tansy ragwort, St. John's wort, senecio, sorghum grass, tall fescue grass, white snakeroot, yellow star thistle, and yew.

Types of Trailer

There are two main types of horse trailers in North America: the straight-haul trailer and the gooseneck trailer. Straight-haul trailers are smaller, less expensive, and will carry up to two horses. They attach to a trailer hitch on the towing vehicle. There is also a variation on this design, the angle-haul, in which horses travel at an angle, which is considered safer in the event of an accident or braking too rapidly. The gooseneck trailer attaches to a fitting in an open-bed truck. Goosenecks are more expensive, but have more carrying capacity, both in terms of horses and storage. Most have separate tack rooms and many have sleeping and/or cooking facilities. Whatever type of trailer you buy, always make sure that it is in sound condition, particularly the flooring.

Preparing for the Journey

The horse should be in good health before any journey, as transportation will only exacerbate any illness (*see* Shipping Fever, *opposite*). Depending on the climate and season, the horse may need a cotton sheet or blanket. Take care, however, not to overheat a horse, as it will get quite hot in such a confined space. Shipping boots or bandages should be worn to protect

The straight-haul trailer (right) is cheaper than the gooseneck (below), but has less carrying capacity and storage space. Competitors who frequently stay overnight at horse shows often prefer a gooseneck trailer with built-in sleeping accommodation.

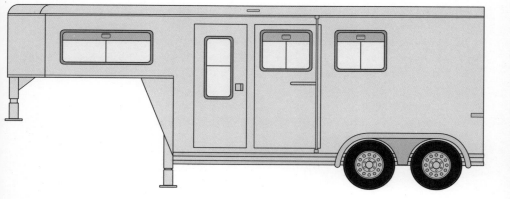

the legs, and a nervous or head-shy horse should wear a head bumper. Bandage the tail to prevent injury or rubbing (see p. 284). The horse should wear a halter and should be tied securely during travel. Give your horse a haynet. Make sure that you have sufficient hay, feed, and water with you, as well as a good first-aid kit.

Loading a Horse

It is very important to get your horse used to traveling in a trailer. Some horses will happily hop into a trailer with the minimum of fuss. Others, though, may take more persuasion. Let a reluctant horse sniff the trailer first before trying to load. A nervous horse may be encouraged to load if a stable companion is already in the trailer. The sight of a haynet, too, may prove tempting. For a really difficult horse, ask two helpers to hold a lunge line either side of the horse's quarters. The lunge line should be pulled gradually from the sides to encourage the horse to move forward.

When the horse is loaded, initially, go for short rides only—this will teach it that the trailer is nothing to fear.

Shipping Fever

Symptoms

Shipping fever, or pleuropneumonia, is a serious and potentially life-threatening bacterial disease that affects both the lungs and the pleural space surrounding the lungs. It is often contracted by a horse during or after long-distance travel. Dehydration, poor ventilation, reluctance to urinate in the trailer, and not being able to lower the head all impair the clearance of foreign and infectious material from the airways. Stress is also an important consideration, as it produces the hormone cortisol, which decreases immunity, making the horse more susceptible to infection.

Symptoms

- Lethargy, depression, and loss of appetite
- Cough
- Nasal discharge
- Fever
- Shallow breathing

Good ventilation, low-dust bedding, and regular rest breaks will all help to prevent problems. On long journeys, stop every two or three hours to check the horse for any sign of distress and to offer water. It is also essential to make sure that the horse is fully fit before traveling, and that it has no signs of fever or infection.

Tack and Accessories

Saddlery has come a long way since the first rudimentary rope bridles and stirrupless cloth saddles of ancient times, and tack shops are now stuffed with a wealth of sophisticated equipment. To the novice owner or rider the choice is bewildering. This chapter is intended as a gentle introduction to basic English tack and its accessories. You need to understand the terminology used in saddlery before you can discuss equipment intelligently. Knowing how to fit tack correctly, too, is vital. Finally, once you have invested in your tack, you need to know how to care for it.

The Bridle

The bridle fits around the horse's head and is used to control pace, speed, and direction. It is generally used in conjunction with a bit. The snaffle bridle is the most basic and common bridle seen in English riding, and it can be used with almost any type of bit.

Parts of the Snaffle Bridle

Headpiece The headpiece includes the throat latch and the straps to which the cheekpieces fasten. It should lie flat, just behind the ears, and hang down behind the projecting cheekbones. The throat lash fits under the throat of the horse, and prevents the headpiece from slipping over the horse's ears. It should never be done up too tightly—there should be enough room to allow the width of an adult hand between it and the cheekbones.

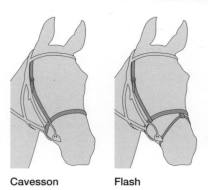

Cavesson   Flash

The cavesson is the simplest and most common noseband. The flash noseband prevents the horse from opening its mouth.

Cheekpieces The cheekpieces are attached to the bit and fit to straps on the headpiece. They must be equal in length to ensure that the bit is level.

Browband The browband connects to the headpiece. It fits around the forehead and should fit just below the

Did You Know?

Despite the name, the scold's bridle has nothing to do with horses. Used in medieval times, the scold's bridle was used to punish a troublesome, brawling woman. It consisted of a metal cage for the head, with an inbuilt "gag." In particularly gruesome examples, this gag took the form of a tongue spike.

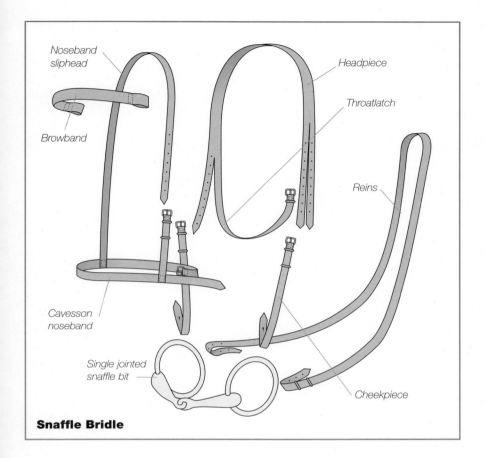

Noseband
sliphead

Headpiece

Throatlatch

Browband

Reins

Cavesson
noseband

Single jointed
snaffle bit

Cheekpiece

Snaffle Bridle

ears, not touch them. The browband should be tight enough to prevent the headpiece from slipping backward, but loose enough to prevent chafing. Browbands can be plain or decorated with studs or ribbons.

Noseband The noseband should sit two fingers' width below the projecting cheek bone. It should not be adjusted too tightly—there should be enough room to get two fingers between the noseband and the horse's nose.

Reins Reins are attached to the bit. English reins are joined together by a central buckle. They are usually made of leather and can be plain, braided, or laced, although they can also be covered with rubber or made with nylon. Smooth leather reins can be slippery in wet weather.

Bits

The bit is a mouthpiece that helps a rider to communicate with and control the horse. It regulates pace and direction, and influences the position in which the horse holds its head. Bits are made from a variety of materials, including stainless steel, nickel, vulcanite, and rubber. The bit rests on the gums in the interdental space between the incisors and the molars. This space is called the "bar" of the mouth.

Finding the Correct-sized Bit

An incorrectly sized bit will work inefficiently and, more importantly, will rub and cut your horse's tongue or lips. As a rule of thumb, when your horse is fitted with a bit, you should see two wrinkles in the corners of his mouth. Also, check tongue size. A horse with a large tongue may benefit from a thinner mouthpiece or one that has a groove or hinge in the center. To find the correct size, measure your horse's mouth from one corner to the another—going through the mouth not round the outside—and buy a bit that is half an inch larger than this measurement.

Types of Bit

Although there are hundreds of different designs of bit available, they can be divided into three basic types: snaffle, curb, and combination—or pelham—bits.

The snaffle may be jointed or unjointed, and it applies pressure to the corners of the mouth, the bars, and the lips. It is the mildest bit, and is recommended for novice riders and green horses.

The curb bit consists of a mouthpiece with a shank on either side and a curb chain or strap that passes under the horse's jaw. When pressure is applied to the reins, the bit is levered down on the tongue and bars of the horse's mouth. At the same time, the curb chain or strap applies pressure to the curb groove under the horse's chin, intensifying the pressure in the mouth. The longer the shank, the greater the leverage applied.

The combination or **pelham bit** is a combination of the snaffle and curb, and requires two reins. Applying pressure with the top rein applies pressure in the same way as a snaffle, while pressure on the lower rein creates the levering action of the curb bit.

Different Types of Bit

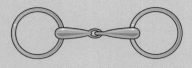

Single-jointed snaffle

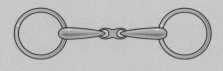

French link

Straight bar

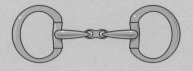

Eggbutt

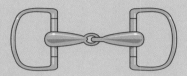

D-ring

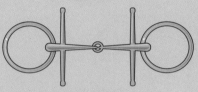

Loose-ringed fulmar

Fixed mouth curb

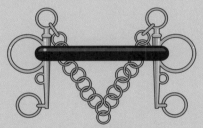

Vulcanite pelham

Standard pelham

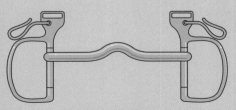

Kimblewick pelham

English General-purpose Saddle

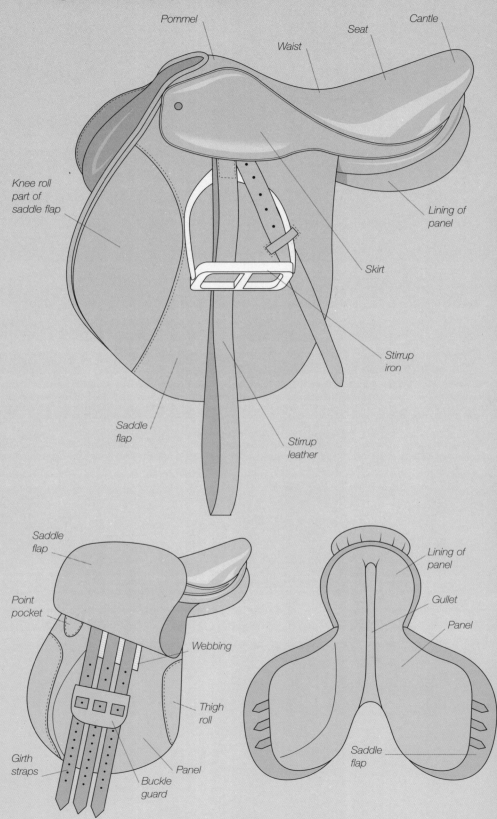

Pommel

Waist

Seat

Cantle

Knee roll part of saddle flap

Lining of panel

Skirt

Stirrup iron

Saddle flap

Stirrup leather

Saddle flap

Lining of panel

Point pocket

Gullet

Panel

Webbing

Thigh roll

Girth straps

Panel

Buckle guard

Saddle flap

Types of Saddle

There are many types of saddle, including the English general purpose, dressage (*see p. 154*), racing (*see p. 201*), Western (*see p. 128*) and side-saddle (*see p. 250*). However, the main purpose of all these saddles is essentially the same, that is, to make riding comfortable for both horse and rider. The saddle helps to keep the rider balanced, and distributes his or her weight evenly over the horse's back.

General Purpose Saddle

As its name suggests, this saddle can be used in a variety of disciplines, from hacking to schooling to jumping. This type of saddle has a medium-cut flap and a deep seat. The design falls midway between the "close-contact" jumping saddle, with the forward flap, and the deep-seated dressage saddle, with the long, straight flap.

Structure of the Saddle

Saddles are typically made of leather, although synthetic materials are also used. The heart of the saddle is the "tree," traditionally made from beechwood, but now more often from laminated wood or fiberglass. The shape of the tree prevents the saddle from touching the horse's spine. Bands of webbing are attached to the tree, and this framework is then stuffed and covered with leather or a synthetic material. The stirrup bars are attached to the tree and covered with a skirt. The panels are the part of the saddle that touches the horse, and the part in

> **Did You Know?**
>
> *The modern English saddle developed out of the eighteenth century hunting saddle. Before that time, riders of all disciplines used saddles that had both a high pommel and a high cantle. Keeping up with the fox-hounds, however, required the huntsman to jump ditches, hedges, and banks. The old style of saddle proved burdensome—the high pommel and cantle simply got in the way—so a new type of flat-seated saddle with a low pommel and cantle was developed.*

contact with the horse's back is stuffed with wool or felt. The saddle flaps, against which the rider's legs rest, cover the panels and girth straps.

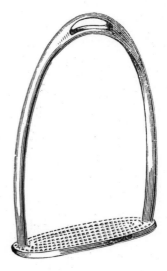

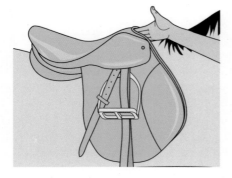

A correctly fitting saddle should have four finger width's clearance between the pommel and the horse's withers.

Fitting a Saddle

Because of the proximity of the spine, an ill-fitting saddle can cause untold damage to a horse. Pressure points may occur, resulting in soreness, bruising, spinal misalignment, and a "cold back." As a result of pain, behavioral problems such as being "nappy," bucking, rearing, or refusing at jumps may develop.

The weight of a saddle should be evenly distributed on the horse's back muscles. There should not be any weight on the loins or pressure on the spine.

Checking for Fit

To check for fit, a saddle should always be placed directly onto the horse's back, never with a saddle pad. The saddle should first be checked for fit without the rider. Look at the front arch of the saddle. It must rise high enough above the horse's withers to avoid any pinching. You should be able to get a hand's width between the pommel and the horse's spine with the rider mounted. If there is less space than this without a rider, the saddle

will not fit. Check around the shoulder area—the saddle should fit snugly but should not pinch—the shoulder blades must be able to move freely. Always pay attention to the condition of the saddle flocking, that is, the stuffing of the panels. Correct flocking provides a cushioning effect. Uneven or too little flocking can cause pressure points. On the other hand, if there is excessive flocking, the saddle will be hard and will not mold to the horse's back. Flocking should be checked by a saddler once a year.

The cantle should appear slightly higher than the pommel. Try lifting up the cantle; it should only move slightly. If you can lift the cantle up high, the saddle is too wide. This will allow the saddle to bang up and down on the horse's back when it is being ridden, causing bruising and soreness. When viewed from the back of the saddle, you should be able to see straight through the gullet to the other end— the saddle should not be in contact with the spine at any point. Check, too, that the saddle is sitting straight and not to one side.

The saddle should be checked again with a rider mounted. Rising trot is

Glossary

A horse with "cold-back" syndrome displays a negative response to being saddled and/or having the girth tightened.

probably the best pace to assess any excessive movement of the saddle. If in doubt, get a trained professional to help. No horse deserves the pain that can result from a badly fitting saddle.

Saddle Pads

Although it is not strictly necessary to use a saddle pad—or numnah—most riders do, as they provide cushioning and absorb sweat. Saddle pads come in a variety of materials, shapes, and colors. There are also special therapeutic, gel, or foam pads, designed for horses with back problems. The saddle pad is placed under the saddle and is normally attached to the girth straps on either side. The pad should be larger than the saddle; when in place, approximately one inch (2.5 centimeters) of the saddle pad should show all round. To avoid any pressure on the horse's back, the saddle pad should be pulled up into the gullet of the saddle.

Wither Pads

A wither pad can be used to alleviate pressure on withers caused by the front arch of the saddle. However, there is no substitute for a correct-fitting saddle, and wither pads should be used as a short-term remedy only.

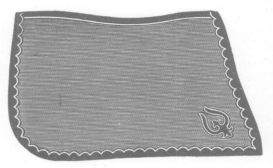

A saddle pad—or numnah— helps to absorb sweat produced by the horse during exercise.

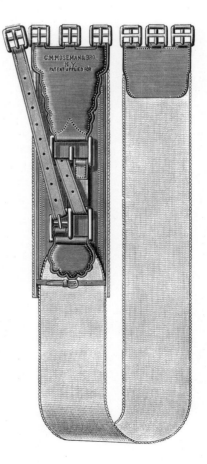

Did You Know?

The word "numnah" comes from the Urdu namda*, which means "carpet."*

Stirrups

The invention of the stirrup by the Chinese (*see pp. 40–41*) totally transformed the way a horse is ridden. Not only does the stirrup give the rider more stability in the saddle it allows more accurate leg positioning, which gives the rider the means to carry out more subtle maneuvers.

The standard English stirrup iron is made of steel and attaches to the saddle with leather straps. There is a tread at the bottom to prevent the foot

Getting the Stirrup Length Right

It's far easier to adjust your stirrups before you are mounted. As a rule of thumb, the stirrup length should match the length of your arm. Place your fingertips at the top of the stirrup leather and stretch the leather out along your arm. The stirrup iron should nestle in your armpit.

from slipping. Rubber stirrup pads can be added to increase traction. Some stirrups are hinged, which helps the rider to get more weight into the heels.

The correct stirrup size is very important. Serious accidents can occur with badly fitting stirrups. If they are too small, there is a risk that the foot could become trapped. Too large, and the foot may slip through. There should be half an inch (one centimeter) either side of your foot.

There are a number of safety stirrups on the market. These are designed to break apart in the event of a fall. The most common design is one that has a thick rubber band on the outside that will unfasten under pressure.

Running up Stirrup Leathers

Stirrups should always be run up to prevent them from banging against the horse or getting caught up, especially when going through doors. This will also keep them out of the way when the saddle is put on or removed. As

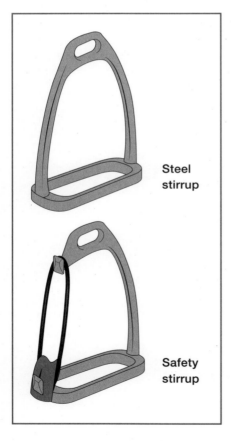

Steel stirrup

Safety stirrup

Regular stirrups are in solid steel but there are safety versions designed to free the foot. This one has a rubber connecting loop or a hinge.

soon as you dismount, run up the stirrups by sliding the iron up to the top of the back stirrup leather, then pull the loop through the iron.

Martingales

A martingale is used to prevent a horse from tossing its head from side to side or raising its head above the point of control. There are two main types of martingale, running and standing.

Standing Martingale Also known as a "tie-down." This is more restrictive than the running martingale. It consists of two straps, one that goes round the horse's neck, and another that runs from the noseband through a slit in the neck strap to the girth. To fit correctly, push the martingale up into the horse's gullet. It should just reach.

Running Martingale A running martingale is also attached to the girth and neck strap. However, the strap divides into two at the neck strap, and there is a metal ring on the end of each strap. One rein passes through each of these rings. Rubber stops on the reins prevent the rings from sliding down to the bit or rein buckles. To fit correctly, when attached to the girth, but not the reins, the rings should reach up to the withers.

Breastplates and Breast Girths

A breastplate or breast girth prevents the saddle from slipping backward. The breastplate consists of a strap that is attached to the D-rings of the saddle on either side of the withers and to the girth between the forelegs. The breast girth consists of a neck strap and

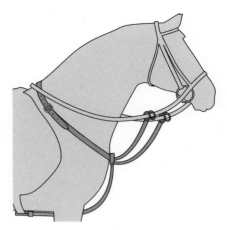

A running martingale is used to prevent a horse from flinging up its head.

a strap that passes round the chest and is then attached to the girth on each side.

Girths

A girth goes around a horse's belly, and is used to secure the saddle. It can be made of leather, synthetic materials, or webbing. It should be fastened to the first and second girth straps on the saddle or the first and third, never the second and third. This is because the second and third girth straps are fixed to the saddle by the same webbing and, should this give way, the girth will become detached and the rider will be unseated.

Did You Know?

The word stirrup comes from the Middle-English stirop, *meaning a "mounting-rope" or a "climbing-rope."*

A halter is basic piece of equipment that gives the horse handler control of the horse when leading or working around the horse.

Halters

Horses are unpredictable creatures, and even the most sensible horse can react suddenly to an external stimulus. So, whenever you are working round the horse, be it grooming, mucking out the stall, or tacking up, you should always put on a halter and tie up the horse securely (*see p. 261*). Better safe than sorry.

Halters can be made of synthetic materials or leather. They come in three sizes: full, cob, and pony. A halter consists of a headpiece, noseband, and throatlatch, and is fastened either with a buckle at the headpiece or a clip fastening on the throatlatch.

Boots

There are various types of boots designed to protect the horse's all important legs while it is being ridden or raced. Boots were traditionally made from leather and fastened with straps and buckles, but most are now made from synthetic materials and have Velcro® fastenings.

Shin boots Horses can easily be hurt when jumping, and shin boots give some protection against blows.

Brushing boots protect the inside of the near fetlock from being knocked by the opposite foot.

Bell—or overreach—boots These are used for horses that have a tendency to step on the heel of the forefoot with the hind foot.

Fetlock and **hock boots** give additional protection to the part of the body after which they are named.

Poultice boot Boots may also be used in the treatment of injuries. This type of boot keeps a poultice dressing in place and protects it from getting dirty.

Traveling and **shipping boots** are long, thick, padded boots that protect the coronary band, heels, knees, and hocks of a horse being transported in a trailer.

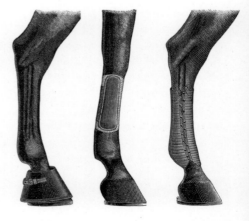

Boots protect the horse's legs from damage during exercise or travel.

Types of Boot

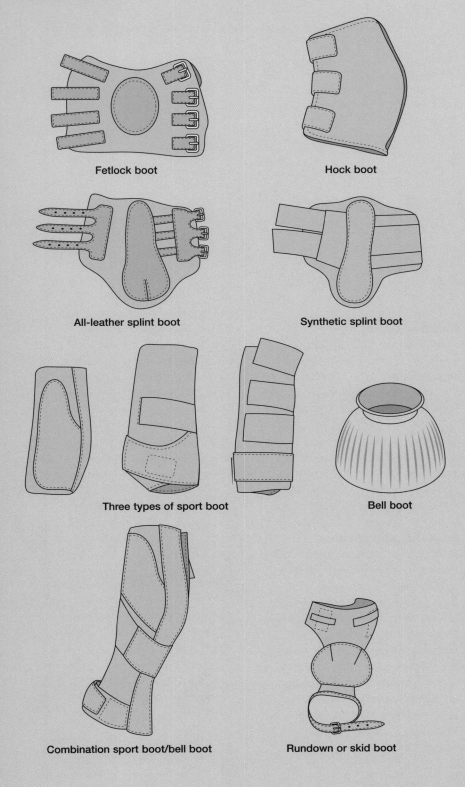

Fetlock boot

Hock boot

All-leather splint boot

Synthetic splint boot

Three types of sport boot

Bell boot

Combination sport boot/bell boot

Rundown or skid boot

Bandages

Bandages are an essential and versatile item and should be found in every tack room. They can be used for support, warmth, or as a cooling or fomenting—meaning heating—treatment.

There are two main types of bandages: stable and exercise bandages. Bandages should never be put on too tightly. Always wind from the front to the back, so that when you pull to tighten a bandage, the pressure will be on the shinbone and not the tendons.

Tail Bandages

A tail bandage is made from a stretchy material, and should be applied to a dampened tail. It is used to protect the tail from rubbing or injury during traveling, to shape the tail after it has been washed, and to protect the tail in wet, muddy conditions. The tail bandage should not be left on more than four hours, and never all night. Use a tail guard if traveling for a long period.

Blankets and Sheets

Blankets come in a variety of thicknesses and materials to suit all seasons and occasions. Horses, especially those who are clipped, should be blanketed in winter. A cold horse will expend a lot of energy on just keeping warm. Blankets should fit correctly or they will rub and cause hair loss and sore patches. Blankets should be washed and reproofed with water repellant regularly. When not in use, store blankets in a trunk to avoid rodent damage.

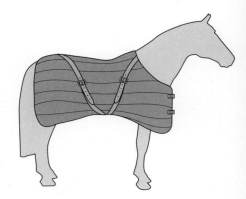

Clipped horses should wear a stable rug during the colder months.

The main blankets that most horse owners will need to buy are:

Stable rug Worn in fall, winter, and early spring by the stabled horse that has been clipped. It may be made of jute, wool, or nylon. Not waterproof.

New Zealand or Turnout blanket A waterproof, lined blanket designed for use in cold weather. An essential winter blanket for the horse owner. Additional blankets can be used underneath in very cold weather.

Did You Know?

In the Middle Ages, the king would present a newly ordained knight with a pair of golden spurs. The expression "to win one's spurs" originates from this medieval tradition.

Rain sheet A lightweight, waterproof blanket, suitable for the horse out at grass in the spring and early fall, when the temperatures are not too cold. Usually made from nylon.

Summer sheet A lightweight sheet used in hot weather as a protection against flies and dust.

Cooler This is put on a sweaty horse after exercise to help it cool down gradually.

Spurs are an artificial aid, which should be used to add refinement to a person's riding, not as a command inducing pain or fear.

Spurs

Spurs are an artificial aid worn on the heel of the rider's boot. Western-style spurs are often quite elaborate. English spurs are short and blunt. They are not generally used, as many people believe, to make a horse go faster, but rather to refine the natural leg aid, especially in the more complicated dressage movements.

Spurs should only be worn by experienced riders who have good lower-leg control, as the inexperienced rider runs the risk of jabbing the horse in the sides, causing pain and fear, and possible "deadening" its response to the leg aids. Spurs should always be worn with the end pointing downward and with the buckle on the outside.

> ### Did You Know?
>
> *Spur derives from the Anglo-Saxon word* sputa, *related to* spornan, *meaning "to kick."*

Whips

Whips are also used to reinforce the leg aids, which should always be used first. If ignored, a short, sharp tap with a whip will usually elicit the desired response. Whips should never be used in anger or to inflict pain.

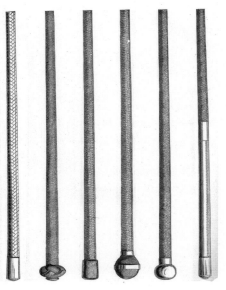

Riding whips were traditionally made using bone, gut, certain types of wood including oak and willow, and mounted elaborately in ivory, gold, or silver handles. The modern equivalents are typically made of fiberglass or cane, covered in leather or fabric.

Tack and Accessories

Looking After Your Tack

Whatever discipline of riding you practice, one thing is for sure, you will have to buy some very expensive items of tack. The saddle and the bridle are the more obvious pieces of equipment, but add to that martingales, boots, blankets, halters, and the rest, and the cost soars. Obviously, once you have made such a large cash outlay, you'll want this equipment to last as long as possible. Take the trouble to store and clean equipment properly and you will prolong its natural life by years.

The Tack Room

A neat, tidy tack room is the sign of a well-run stable or barn. It should be well ventilated, dry, and dust-free. It is important to keep all tack off the floor,

Tack should always be stored away neatly, to preserve its life and prevent rodent damage.

as rodents can wreak havoc in just a single night, leaving your expensive blankets in tatters. Bridles and saddles should be hung on purpose-built racks and hangers. It is helpful to have the name of the horse underneath each item to avoid the incorrect equipment being used. The tack room should also have a trunk or cupboard for every rider, so that they can keep their grooming equipment, boots, bandages, and any other gear neat and tidy.

If you need to store unused leather equipment, make sure that is it clean, oiled, and dry before you put it away. Leather deteriorates fast in storage, so take it out every few months to dust and oil again. Blankets should be stored in trunks. Before putting away winter blankets, have them professionally cleaned and reproofed.

Cleaning Tack

Tack must be cleaned regularly, both for the sake of the equipment and the horse. Dirty, muddy tack is uncomfortable for the horse and can cause sores. After every use, wipe off any mud and give it a quick wipe down. However, tack should be stripped down and cleaned thoroughly at least once a week. Gather together all the tack-cleaning materials that you will need: a bucket of water, two sponges—a large one for washing off mud and grime and a smaller one for applying saddle soap—saddle soap or glycerin cleaner, a soft cloth, and metal polish.

Before cleaning, strip down tack. Take the bridle completely apart. Remove stirrups, leathers, and girth from the saddle. Soak and wash the bit in clean water. All other metal work can be cleaned with metal polish. To clean the leatherwork, first remove any dirt and sweat with a large sponge and

clean water. Try to avoid getting the leather too wet. Next, using a circular movement, apply saddle soap or glycerin with a sponge. Buff dry with a soft cloth. Leather can become very "thirsty," and should be oiled regularly to avoid cracking. Every six to eight weeks is sufficient.

Saddle cloths and saddle pads must also be kept clean, as dried-sweat marks may rub the horse's back. These items can be cleaned in a washing machine. Dry thoroughly before use.

The weekly tack clean also gives an ideal opportunity to check for any signs of wear. Check for rotten stitching, cracked leather, holes, and anything else, and send for repair where necessary. A broken stirrup leather at a full gallop is no joke.

Hanging Up a Bridle

To hang up a bridle neatly, take the central buckle of the reins in one hand and hold it up behind the noseband. Pass the throatlatch across the front of the bridle, round the back and through the reins, round the front again, and then fasten to its end strap. It will have a figure-of-eight appearance. To finish, fasten the noseband around the whole bridle.

Hang specially designed saddle racks in the tack room. Saddle trees can easily be damaged if the saddle is thrown carelessly onto the floor.

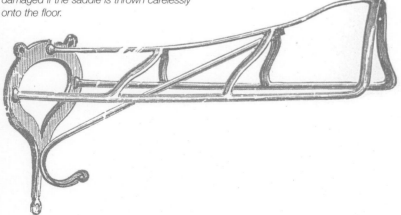

Your Horse's Health

The health of his or her animal should
be the prime concern for anyone who
is responsible for a horse's welfare.
With good care and management, many
ailments can be avoided and minor
health issues can be prevented from
escalating into major problems, so it is
vital that the horse owner or rider learn
to recognize when a horse is feeling well
or when it is sick. This chapter describes
the most common diseases and ailments
that affect the horse and gives advice on
using basic first aid and knowing when
to call the veterinarian.

Knowing your Horse

The starting point for recognizing how your horse is feeling is knowing what is "normal" behavior for it. No two horses are alike, and what is lethargic behavior for one may simply be the "laid-back" nature of another.

Recognizing a Sick Horse

Sometimes it is glaringly obvious when a horse is sick. For example, a horse with a bad case of colic will be in evident discomfort. However, on many occasions the signs of ill health are more subtle. A horse may simply "not be itself." If your horse is acting out of character, check it thoroughly and monitor its behavior.

A horse that is feeling well will take an active interest in what is going on around it.

General Demeanor

If it looks lethargic, droopy, and fails to raise its head when you call its name, this is a sure sign that it is feeling sorry for itself. Do its eyes look dull? Is there any discharge from the eyes or nostrils? Is there any coughing, wheezing, or sneezing? Check its respiration rate (*see p. 292*). Take its temperature (*see p. 292*). Is it sweating or are there visible dried-sweat marks on its body? Is it trembling or shivering? Is its coat "staring," that is, sticking out from its body instead of lying flat? Look at its gums. They should be salmon pink in color and not pale, red, or bluish. Check the gums' capillary refill time (*see p. 293*).

Posture

A horse with abdominal pain will stand "tucked up," with its back arched and tail held high. Chest pain will cause a horse to stand with its elbows away

Signs of the Healthy Horse

It is bright, alert, and taking an interest in its surroundings.

Its coat is flat and glossy.

Its eyes and nostrils are clean and free of discharge.

It is breathing regularly.

Its limbs are cool and free of swellings, lumps, wounds, or sores.

It is bearing its weight on all four legs.

Its hooves should be cool and the foot free of bruising, discoloration, wounds, or stones.

It is eating and drinking normally.

The number of manure piles is normal for it and they are of the correct consistency.

Its urine is light yellow in color and the total quantity is around 1 gallon (5 liters) a day.

from the rib cage. Is its feed uneaten or its water untouched? Is it rolling frequently, lying down for long periods, or turning around to look at its sides? Check its gut sounds (*see p. 293*). Look at its legs. Is it bearing weight on all four legs or is it pointing a foot?

Stable Signs

If your horse is stabled, look at the state of its bedding. It may be "trashed," a sure sign that the horse has had a disturbed night. Look at the stable walls and doors. There may also be signs that your horse has been kicking. It may also have torn or bitten at its blanket. Manure is also a good indication of your horse's health. There may be no manure, or it could be too soft or too hard. Look at your horse's back legs for signs of "scouring," diarrhea. Urine output may be excessive or insufficient and unusual in color. It may be straining as it urinates.

Call your veterinarian immediately if you think your horse is unwell. The sooner the animal receives treatment the better.

How to Keep Your Horse in Good Health

Check your horse thoroughly every day.

Groom your horse daily.

Worm it regularly.

Make sure inoculations are up to date.

Have regular farrier visits.

Feed it correctly.

Ensure your horse has access to clean water.

Keep your stable and equipment in a clean and hygienic state.

Exercise your horse regularly.

Keep your horse away from horses that have infectious or contagious diseases.

The sick horse will appear listless, and may stand with a bowed head, ignoring its surroundings.

Your Horse's Vital Signs

It is important for a horse owner to check the horse's vital signs regularly, ideally once a week, as these are a good indication of an animal's well-being. The horse's usual body temperature, respiratory rate, and resting pulse should be recorded, as they do vary from one horse to another. Any variation from the individual horse's norm may be a sign of sickness.

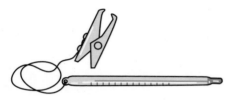

A rectal thermometer should be attached to string to prevent it getting stuck in the rectum.

Taking a Horse's Temperature

The normal body-temperature range for an adult horse is between 99 and 101 degrees Fahrenheit (37 to 38 degrees Centigrade). An elevated temperature may indicate an infection. The reading will be inaccurate if taken immediately after exercise or if the horse is stressed or excited.

Quick Checklist

Temperature	99–101°F (37–38°C)
Pulse rate	30–40 per minute
Respiratory rate	8–16 breaths per minute
Feces (24-hour period)	8–10 piles

A horse's temperature should be taken rectally. You should tie string to the end of the thermometer to prevent it getting lost in the rectum—believe me, this is a common occurrence! Plastic digital thermometers are easier than the older mercury-type, and they beep when they are ready. Lubricate it with petroleum jelly before use.

Ask someone to hold the horse or tie it up securely. Stand to the side of the left flank, lift the tail to one side, and insert the thermometer into the rectum. Most horses do not object to the procedure but position yourself carefully to avoid being kicked. Wash the thermometer and dip it in a cold antiseptic before putting it away to prevent the spread of infection.

Taking a Horse's Pulse

The horse has a resting pulse of between 30 and 40 beats per minute. Its heart rate will increase with fever, pain, excitement, fear, and exercise. No special equipment is necessary to take a horse's pulse, just a watch that indicates seconds. The best place to take a horse's pulse is the facial artery. This can be located on the inside of the left jawbone. Press your forefinger firmly against the artery and count the beats for 30 seconds. Multiply the number of beats you counted by two.

Checking the Respiratory Rate

The respiratory rate per minute in an adult horse averages 12, but ranges from eight to 16. To count a horse's respiratory rate, watch the movements of the chest wall for one minute. Alternatively, watch the horse's nostril. Count the number of times the horse

Capillary Refill Time (CRT) is the time it takes for blood to return to blanched tissues in the gums. It is an indicator of blood circulation.

If you suspect that your horse is unwell, check its mucus membranes. In a healthy horse, the mucus membranes are salmon-pink.

inhales or exhales. Respiratory rate increases with hot or humid weather, exercise, fever, or pain. Consult your veterinarian if there is rapid breathing.

Listening to Gut Sounds

There should always be sounds from your horse's stomach and intestines. This is a good example of when it helps to know what is normal for your horse, as excessive sounds or the absence of sounds may indicate illness.

To listen for gut sounds, use a stethoscope or press your ear against the horse's barrel. You should hear gurgling sounds. The absence of any sounds may be an indication of colic, and you should call your veterinarian.

Checking for Dehydration

Healthy horses drink between five and ten gallons (19 and 38 liters) of water per day, and it is vital for a horse to maintain its fluid intake. To see if your horse is dehydrated, perform the "pinch test." Pinch the skin on its neck. When you let go of the skin, it should flatten

back into place in less than a second. If it takes longer, your horse is dehydrated. Offer plenty of water to drink, and add electrolytes if you think it is seriously dehydrated. If it still won't drink, contact your veterinarian.

Checking Mucus Membranes

The mucus membranes include the lining of a horse's eyelids, its gums, and the inside of its nostrils. They should be salmon-pink in color. If they are very pale, bright red, bluish, or bright yellow, call a veterinarian. Membranes that are bluish in color may be an indication of severe shock. Yellow membranes are associated with liver disease.

Checking Capillary Refill Time

To check a horse's CRT, lift up the upper lip and press your thumb firmly against its gums for two seconds. When you remove your thumb there will be a white mark, but normal color should return within one to two seconds. If it takes longer, the horse may be in shock.

Wounds

Wounds to the skin are classified according to size, shape, and depth.

Puncture wound A small hole, often hard to see. A nail in the foot is one of the most common causes. The puncture track may penetrate deep into underlying tissue, trapping infection. A horse with this wound that has not had a tetanus injection within the last three months should have a booster.

Lacerated wounds These are large with ragged edges, which increases the risk of contamination and makes it difficult to remove any debris. Underlying tissue may be damaged and torn, and permanent scarring is common.

Incised wounds These may be superficial or deep, but are characterized by their straight, clean-cut edges. These wounds often need to be sutured—or stitched—although wounds sutured over joints are liable to burst apart with movement.

Basic Equine First-Aid Kit

All horse owners should possess a basic first-aid kit for use in routine and emergency situations. A well-stocked medicine cabinet should contain:

- Stethoscope
- Rectal thermometer
- Scrub brush
- Saline solution
- Large dosing syringe
- Stainless-steel bowl
- Surgical gloves
- Electrolytes
- Petroleum jelly
- Commercial poultice or chemical cold pack
- Antiseptic—iodine or hibitane
- Blunt-ended bandage scissors
- Wound spray and ointment
- Eye drops or topical eye ointment
- Cotton padding
- Roll of nonsterile cotton
- Gauze, sponges, and bandages
- Vet-Rap®
- Roll of plastic tape
- Leg wraps

Every stable should possess a basic first-aid kit—no horse, unfortunately, goes through life without requiring treatment at some time. Make sure you store the kit in an easy-to-reach position.

Bruises These occur when the small blood vessels under the skin break and leak their contents into the soft tissue. They are often caused by kicks from another horse. Swelling is also common with this type of injury. Apply an ice pack or hose the injury with cold water to limit the damage.

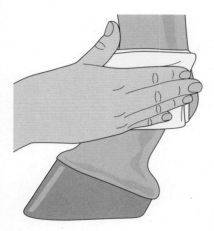

Stopping bleeding is an important first step in treating a wound.

Stopping Bleeding

A horse with a wound may bleed profusely— a frightening experience for its owner. However, bear in mind that a horse has about ten gallons (38 liters) of blood, and a little blood does go a long way, so compose yourself and then try to calm the injured horse. Keep it as still as possible to avoid disrupting the blood-clotting process, and then try to stop the bleeding. Bleeding may occur in a steady flow from a vein or it may spurt from an artery.

If the accident has occurred at home and you have access to a first-aid kit, hold a sterile gauze pad over the injury and apply direct pressure. If the blood

soaks through, add another layer. If sterile material is not available, use any item of clothing. The wound can be cleaned later.

Cleaning and Dressing a Wound

If the wound is contaminated with foreign material such as glass or wood slivers, make sure that you do not push this debris deeper into the tissue. Use a large dosing syringe rather than a hose for cleaning such wounds. Wounds should be thoroughly cleaned with a mild antiseptic solution before any dressing is applied. Soak a gauze swab or piece of absorbent cotton in the solution and then carefully clean the injured area. Once the area is clean, apply a nonadhesive dressing to the wound. If the wound is on a limb, cover the dressing with padding and use a bandage to secure.

Your veterinarian may ask you to take an injured horse's pulse. Normal heart rate is between 30 and 40 in an adult horse, up to 100 in a very young foal, and around 70 in an older foal. The best place to find the pulse is under the side of the jaw or behind the elbow.

Moon Blindness

More correctly known as "equine recurrent uveitis," moon blindness is the most common cause of blindness in the horse. It can be caused by a virus, bacteria, parasites, or by trauma to the eye. Symptoms include redness, swelling, pus, pupil constriction in the dark, cloudiness, squinting, and aversion to light. Horses that have had one attack of the disease will almost certainly have another. Unfortunately, each attack leaves residual damage and may eventually lead to permanent blindness. Aggressive treatment in the early states will, however, slow the progression of the disease. Usual treatment includes atropine to dilate the eye and either steroid or antibiotic medication. The Appaloosa breed seems to be more susceptible to the disease than others.

Did You Know?

Equine recurrent uveitis can recur every few weeks, and was once thought to be linked to the cycle of the moon, hence the synonym "moon blindness."

Eye Injuries

Eyes should be checked daily for any signs of injury or discharge.

Conjunctivitis is an irritation of the lining of the eyelid, and is the most common eye problem in the horse. It is caused by an infection or an irritant, such as pollen or dust. Clean the affected eye with a sterile eye wash. If there is infection, your veterinarian will treat the horse with an antibiotic ointment.

Torn eyelids are commonly caused when a horse rubs its face against a sharp object, a protruding nail, for example. Any such injury should be treated by a veterinarian.

Tumors

There are two main types of tumor that affect the eyelids of a horse. Carcinomas occur on the eyelid or on the third eyelid, and there is usually increased tearing or discharge in the eye. Carcinomas should be removed surgically. Sarcoids are a cauliflower-like growth, and are usually located above and to the side of the eye. They are often difficult to remove and may ulcerate.

Moon blindness occurs more commonly in the Appaloosa horse population than in most other breeds.

"No foot, no horse."

The Lame Horse

Lameness in the horse is a common problem and one that makes it unfit for work of any kind, for, as the saying goes, "No foot, no horse." Lameness is the term that applies to anything that impedes the movement of the horse, and may be caused by an injury or condition of the foot or the leg.

If you suspect that your horse is lame, examine it thoroughly. Run your hands down the leg to feel for any signs of heat, swelling, or tenderness. Compare each leg with the corresponding one on the other side. If your horse suddenly becomes lame while you are riding, dismount and examine its foot carefully, as the most likely cause is a stone or other foreign object. Removing the object may result in immediate soundness.

How to Tell Whether Your Horse is Lame

Ask someone to trot your horse up. Watch its action carefully. If the lameness is in a foreleg, the horse will bob its head more than usual as the sound foreleg strikes the ground. If the

If your horse is showing signs of lameness and you do not know the cause, ask someone to trot him up. This should give a good indication as to the whereabouts of the problem.

hind leg is affected, its stride will be uneven, and there will be a "stutter" in motion before the painful leg is put on the ground.

Ringbone

Ringbone is a bony growth most usually found on the pastern. It is classified as high ringbone when it affects the long pastern bone, and as low ringbone when it affects the short pastern bone. It usually only causes lameness if a joint is affected. Ringbone may be caused by conformation factors: horses with upright or overlong pasterns are more vulnerable. Concussion—impact on hard ground—overwork, and blows are also possible causes. Long periods of rest and immobilization of the foot are often advisable. Corrective shoeing may also help (see pp. 262–263).

Splints

A splint is caused when there is ossification—bone formation—of the tissue between the cannon and splint bones. Splints most commonly form on the inside of the forelegs, but may also occur on the outside. Splints are caused by concussion and generally form in young horses that have been worked too hard, too early. They rarely form in horses over the age of six years old. Weak conformation may also make a horse more prone to splints.

While the splint is forming, there may be lameness that increases with work. The horse requires complete rest. Once formed, splints on the lower part of the leg cause little problem, although they will be visible. However, high splints may affect the action of the knee, and splints that are positioned far back will affect the movement of the tendons.

Bone Spavin

A bone spavin is a bony enlargement on the inside of the hock caused by overexertion and concussion, particularly if the horse is immature.

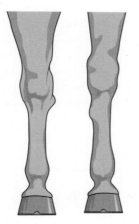

Splint

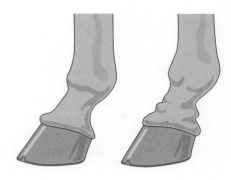

Bone spavin

Those horses with weak hocks are more prone to bone spavins.

Your veterinarian should decide what treatment is best for your horse. Initially, hot fomentations should be applied until the inflammation has subsided. This can then be followed by cold irrigation, that is, hosing with cold water. Surgery may also be an option.

Bog Spavin

A bog spavin is a swelling on the inside, lower part of the hock. The swelling is usually cold and painless. Bog spavin is most commonly seen in horses with straight hocks.

Sidebone

Sidebone is the ossification of the cartilages under the coronary band and the wall of the hoof. Lameness is uncommon except in the initial inflammatory stage.

Bowed Tendon

A bowed tendon involves an injury to one or both flexor tendons in the cannon region. With this type of injury, the cannon area resembles an archer's bow when seen from the side. A horse with a tendon injury will be in a great deal of pain and will attempt to keep its weight off the injured leg. The back of the leg will be hot, swollen, and very tender. Tendon injuries occur when too much stress is placed on the tendon, such as too much galloping or landing incorrectly after a jump.

Tendon injuries require immediate veterinary treatment. The leg should be firmly bandaged, with cotton padding underneath to spread pressure evenly. The horse must have complete rest, and exercise should recommence only on the advice on the veterinarian. Tendon injuries take a long time to heal and can leave an inherent weakness.

Curb

Curb is an enlargement of the ligament at the back of the hock, about four inches (ten centimeters) below the point of the hock. It is commonly caused by concussion. Horses with sickle-hocks are more prone to the injury. The horse may be lame, and there is usually heat and pain.

Thoroughpin

Thoroughpin is the swelling of the tendon sheath above and in front of the point of the hock. It is typically associated with poor conformation of the hocks. It does not usually cause lameness.

Windgalls

A windgall is a swelling around the fetlock joint. It is normally painless and does not cause lameness. Many horses have windgalls and they are not considered a problem.

Diseases and Ailments of the Foot

The delicate structures in a horse's foot can easily become damaged. Something as simple as a stone or thorn in the foot can cause considerable pain, since the foot takes all the weight of the horse. Too much roadwork or jumping on hard ground can cause severe jarring and inflammation.

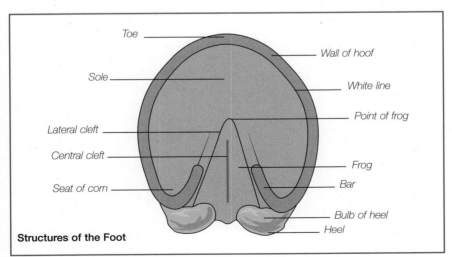

Structures of the Foot

Toe — Wall of hoof — Sole — White line — Point of frog — Lateral cleft — Central cleft — Frog — Seat of corn — Bar — Bulb of heel — Heel

Common Ailments of the Foot

The conformation of some horses' feet also make them particularly susceptible to injury. For example, horses with flat feet are more likely to get a bruised foot or suffer from corns. A horse with a foot injury will normally react to the site of pain when hoof testers are applied.

Bruised Sole

Bruises can be caused by stepping on a sharp object, such as a stone. Keeping a horse's shoes on for too long or excessive trimming of the feet can also cause bruising. There will usually be heat in the sole, and often the bruise will appear in the sole as a dark stain.

Abscesses

An abscess is a collection of pus within a horse's hoof. It can be caused by a puncture to the sole of the foot, an infected bruise (*see above*), or by an injury received in shoeing—a pricked foot or nail bind, for example. Once the area of infection has been found, a hole should be pared out to release the pus and allow free drainage. A hot antiseptic poultice will relieve pain and encourage drainage.

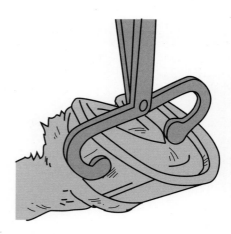

Hoof testers can be used to determine the site of pain in the sole or wall of the foot.

Navicular Disease

Navicular disease is a chronic, degenerative process in the navicular bone, a tiny bone in the foot located behind the coffin bone. It causes intermittent lameness in one or both front feet. Navicular disease is often mistaken for shoulder lameness because it causes a similar change in gait—a horse with navicular disease typically has a shortened, choppy stride.

Causes of Navicular Disease

Horses that engage in strenuous work, such as show jumpers or barrel racers, are prone to the disease. So, too, are horses that are exercised on hard surfaces. Conformation also plays a part, and horses with proportionately small feet and those with straight, upright pasterns are more likely to develop the disease. Incorrect trimming of the hoof may also be a cause. Navicular disease is more common in American Quarter Horses, Warmbloods, and Thoroughbreds; it is seldom seen in Arabian horses.

Did You Know?

A horse's hoof grows at the rate of approximately ½ inch (1 cm) a month.

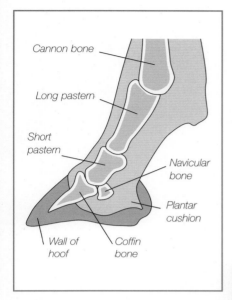

Cannon bone

Long pastern

Short pastern

Navicular bone

Plantar cushion

Wall of hoof

Coffin bone

Quarter horses are anatomically predisposed to navicular disease. Their naturally upright pastern results in the hoof wall being at a much lower angle than the pastern. A confined or stall-kept horse can also develop this problem.

There is no cure for navicular disease, but good management may alleviate the symptoms. Treatment usually includes anti-inflammatory medication and corrective shoeing. Surgery—neurectomy—may be performed as a last resort. Neurectomy involves cutting the heel nerves.

Seedy Toe

Seedy toe is a separation of the hoof wall from the white line in the toe region. This results in a cavity between the hoof wall and the sensitive laminae. Dirt, broken-down horn, and other debris accumulates in this hole, and it can become infected. It does not usually cause lameness unless there is infection.

Seedy toe is often the result of poor hoof care, especially when the toe is allowed to grow too long. It may also occur in cases of chronic laminitis (*see p. 301*).

Seedy toe is usually discovered when a farrier removes the horse's shoe. The diseased part of the horn should be removed by a farrier or veterinarian with a hoof knife. The cavity should be regularly cleaned and treated with an antiseptic until the tissues heal. The horse may need special shoes to take weight off the toe until the hoof grows again.

Your farrier will discover any incidence of seedy toe when removing the horse's shoes.

Ailments of the Foot contd
Cracked Hoof or Sandcrack

A sandcrack is a vertical split in the hoof wall, and is common in horses with weak, brittle feet. The crack may be deep or superficial. Deep cracks may need remedial shoeing.

Thrush

Thrush is an infection of the frog. There will be an offensive odor and discharge in the cleft of the frog. Thrush is generally caused by poor hygiene. A horse that is left to stand on wet, dirty bedding is most susceptible. Insufficient exercise may also contribute to the problem, because the frog needs movement to cleanse itself. The frog and cleft must be thoroughly cleaned and the foot soaked in hot water and Epsom salts. Once dry, the frog should be treated with a foot antiseptic.

Laminitis and Founder

Laminitis is inflammation of the sensitive laminae, the inner tissues of the foot. It is caused by a reduction in blood flow to the feet. In severe cases, there is permanent damage to the laminae, and the coffin bone

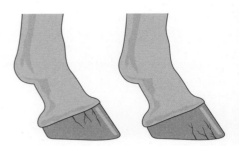

Sandcracks (left) are less serious than grasscracks (right), which require treatment.

can become detached from the hoof wall and rotate downward. This is technically known as "founder," although laminitis and founder are often used interchangeably.

The Symptoms of Laminitis

If the front feet alone are affected, as is most common and first apparent, the horse will stand with its hind legs well under its body to take as much of its weight as possible, and the front

Causes of Laminitis

Carbohydrate overload: grazing on lush pasture, particularly early spring grass, or too much grain.

Drinking large amounts of cold water when overheated.

Standing too long on a hard surface.

Mare retaining the placenta.

Concussion: hard or fast work on a hard surface.

Heredity or malconformation: wide, flat feet, and weak horn.

Debilitating disease—colic, for example.

Laminitis affecting the front feet only causes this backward stance in the horse.

legs extended forward with the weight on the heels. The horse may appear "footy" on stony, rough, or uneven ground, and be reluctant to walk. When it can be persuaded to walk, it may place the heels on the ground first. If all four feet are affected, the horse may constantly shift its weight from one foot to another or it may lie down to get relief from the pain.

The feet may also feel hot, and there is usually an obvious digital pulse, which is located over the fetlock joint. Other signs may include fever, sweating or shivering, rapid breathing, and diarrhea.

Each attack of acute laminitis may leave a ring formation on the hoof, and a horse with chronic laminitis will have multiple rings or ridges on its hooves.

Treatment and Prevention

If your horse shows signs of laminitis, call your veterinarian. Treatment will be administered to relieve pain and reduce swelling. Chronic cases will require corrective trimming by a farrier at frequent intervals. Corrective shoeing may also be necessary. The horse must also be put on a carefully monitored feeding program, and will probably have to be kept off pasture.

Most cases of laminitis can be avoided with good management. Some types of horse are more likely to founder than others. Be particularly vigilant with horses that have thick, cresty necks. Ponies are also more liable to the disease. Do not overfeed your horse, and keep grain in a secure bin to avoid accidental ingestion of large amounts. Limit the amount of

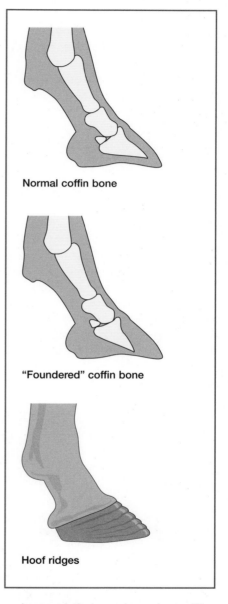

Normal coffin bone

"Foundered" coffin bone

Hoof ridges

spring grass that your horse has—45 minutes should be the maximum at first, gradually increasing the amount of time over a period of weeks. Do not give your horse too much water after exercise, particularly if it is very hot.

Colic

The most common digestive ailment in horses is colic, a term used for any acute abdominal pain in the horse. There are many causes for such pain, ranging from mild to life-threatening. In the early stages of colic, it is difficult to distinguish a mild attack from a more serious, potentially fatal one. For this reason, you should always call your veterinarian immediately if your horse is showing any symptoms of colic.

Signs of Colic

Horses with mild colic may have less obvious symptoms. In cases of severe colic, a horse may become quite violent. The following list includes the most common signs of colic:
- Depression
- Lying down more than usual
- Getting up and down frequently
- Standing stretched out
- Pawing at the ground
- High pulse rate and sweating
- Reduced gut sounds
- Passing feces infrequently or not at all
- Repeatedly curling the upper lip
- Looking or biting at the flanks
- Kicking the abdomen or kicking out
- Not eating
- Rolling

Frequent and agitated rolling may be an indication of colic.

The Major Types of Colic

Impaction colic occurs when the gut—usually the large intestine—becomes blocked by undigested food. Impactions may occur when the horse eats poor-quality, indigestible forage. Young and starving animals that eat foreign, non-edible material are also at risk, as are animals with dental problems that prevent them from grinding up their food adequately.

Gas colic is caused by the accumulation of excess gas in the digestive tract. The gas causes the intestine to stretch, resulting in pain.

Spasmodic colic is caused by violent intestinal contractions.

It may stop as quickly as it starts and usually responds to treatment.

Torsion or "twisted gut"

A "torsion" occurs when part of the intestine twists. The horse's physiology predisposes it to such intestinal displacements. Its large intestine is between nine and 12 feet (three and four meters) long and has a capacity of over 13 gallons (50 liters). However, despite its great size, the large intestine is only attached to the abdominal wall at two points, at the beginning and the end, rendering it susceptible to twisting. When this occurs, immediate surgery is the only option.

Enteritis and colitis

Some cases of colic are caused by inflammation of the small (enteritis) or large (colitis) intestines. Both are serious, and require immediate veterinary attention.

Peritonitis

Peritonitis is an acute bacterial inflammation of the abdominal cavity lining, and can be caused by the rupture of any part of the digestive tract. A rupture may occur if the horse has gorged itself on grain or, more commonly, a substance that expands in the digestive tract—dried beet pulp, for example. A horse with peritonitis will almost certainly die within a few hours.

Preventing Colic

Colic is a common problem in the horse and often has no obvious cause. However, there are a number of good stable-management practices that may help to reduce incidences:

If your horse keeps turning to and biting at its flanks, suspect a case of colic.

- Avoid a sudden change in diet
- Do not feed moldy hay or grain
- Ensure constant access to clean water
- Do not feed on sand
- Provide access to forage for as much of the day as possible
- Do not exercise a horse too soon after feeding
- Do not give a large amount of food or cold water to a hot or tired horse
- Maintain a regular exercise program
- Maintain a worming program

Choke

Choke is caused when a horse tries to swallow food it hasn't sufficiently chewed. Material becomes lodged in the esophagus, and food and water cannot pass through to the stomach. A horse that suddenly stops eating after a few mouthfuls, or one that is found straining, with its head and neck extended, is probably suffering from choke. There will commonly be a discharge coming out of the animal's nose that may well contain particles of the material that is causing the problem. Call your veterinarian immediately if your horse has choke.

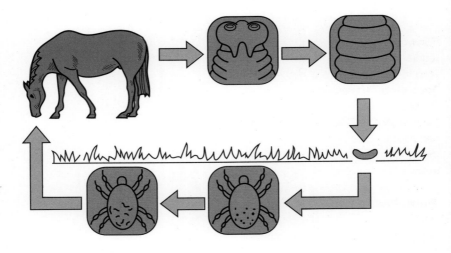

Types of Parasite

Various types of parasite affect the health of the horse. These include:

Strongylids—large and small strongyles (redworms and bloodworms) These are the most dangerous parasites to the horse. They are blood-sucking worms that may cause damage to the arteries, liver, and pancreas.

Ascarids (roundworms) Ascarids are the largest internal parasites found in the horse, and adult worms can be up to 20 inches (50 centimeters) in length and half an inch (1.3 centimeters) in diameter. They are most commonly seen in young horses. The migrating larvae can cause liver and lung damage. Adult roundworms can cluster in the small intestine, causing colic, impaction, and even ruptured gut.

Tapeworms The life cycle of the tapeworm requires an intermediate host, the oribatid free-living mite, which eats the eggs of the tapeworm. For a horse to become infected, it must eat these mites. Tapeworms can cause a

Tapeworm eggs are passed in the horse's feces, hatch inside orbatid mites, and are eaten with the grass.

blockage where the small intestine and caecum meet, the ileocaecal junction, and horses with tapeworm infestation often show signs of recurrent colic. Deworm in late summer with a double dose of pyrantel.

Bots Bot flies lay their eggs on a horse's hair, generally on the legs, shoulders, and abdomen, during the late summer and fall. They hatch into larvae and are then ingested by the horse as it self-grooms. They remain in the mouth for some weeks before migrating to the stomach, where they attach themselves to the stomach lining. If untreated, bots can cause irritation to the stomach, ulceration, and colic.

Lungworms Lungworms live in the air passages in the lungs. Horses with lungworm infestation develop parasitic bronchitis, a chronic persistent cough. Adult horses normally develop a resistance to lungworms, but foals are susceptible to infection.

Pinworms (whipworms) Pinworms occur in the large intestine, colon, and rectum. They are annoying rather than seriously harmful to the horse. They cause intense itching around the anal region, as this is where the adult females lay their eggs. An infected horse will rub its tail in an attempt to relieve the discomfort.

Parasites and Deworming

Internal parasites are a fact of life when it comes to horses. All horses harbor worms in their gastrointestinal tract to some extent. The degree of damage caused by these parasites depends on the species and numbers involved, the regularity and efficiency of your deworming program, and the measures taken to reduce reinfestation.

Deworming Program

Ask your veterinarian to recommend a deworming program best suited to your region. Deworming should be carried out every two to three months to coincide with the lifecycle of the particular parasite being treated. Treat all horses on the property at the same time. Foals should be dewormed monthly from the age of two months up to a year. Brood mares should be dewormed prior to and after foaling. If you have a new horse and are unsure of its worming history, your veterinarian can take a fecal sample for laboratory analysis.

Control of Parasites

Good management will help with parasite control. Remove droppings regularly from pasture, preferably daily. Rotate the pastures and keep

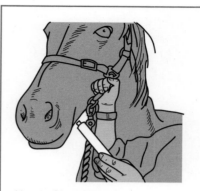

How to Give a Wormer
1 *Make sure that there is no feed in the horse's mouth.*
2 *Remove the cap from the end of the syringe and adjust the dose setting.*
3 *Place the tip of the syringe inside the horse's mouth where the bit rests and gently push the plunger until it stops, depositing the gel on the back of the tongue.*
4 *Remove the syringe from the animal's mouth and raise the animal's head slightly to make sure it swallows the gel.*

Signs of Worm Damage
Anemia • Dull coat • Decreased stamina • Tail rubbing • Depression • Colic • Weight loss • Coughing • Pot-bellied appearance • Diarrhea • Loss of appetite

the number of horses per acre to a minimum. Mow or plow pastures to expose eggs and larvae. If using horse manure to fertilize your fields, make sure that it is well rotted before use and keep horses off the field for six months.

If feeding horses outside, use a feeder for grain or hay rather than putting it directly on the ground. Remove bot eggs from the horse's hair. Rotate dewormers to ensure maximum efficiency.

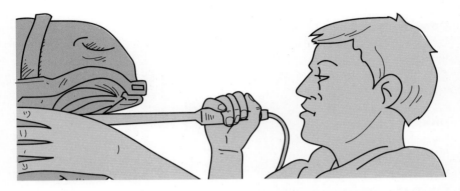

A horse's teeth should be floated annually by a veterinarian or equine dentist.

Teeth

Equine teeth continue to grow and wear down until the horse is around 25 or 30 years old. Horses need regular dental care throughout their lives so that any dental problems can be quickly treated before they cause long-term harm, either to health or performance. Dental problems can make it difficult for a horse to eat properly and get the necessary nutrition from its food. A painful mouth will also make the bit feel uncomfortable, affecting a horse's performance.

Floating Teeth

In the wild, a horse forages on tough plant materials that wear down the outer edges of the molar teeth. The diet of the domestic horse, however, involves less chewing, and the teeth are not worn down in the same way. Sharp points may develop on the outer surfaces of the teeth, which can cause pain to the inside of the cheeks or the tongue. Floating the teeth—rasping the points down—removes them. It should be carried out annually.

Equine Dental Program

Foals
- Check that teeth are developing normally.
- Correct problems such as over- or underbite.

2–6 year olds
- Check for, and remove, retained caps (baby teeth).
- Remove wolf teeth, the premolars that erupt along the upper jaw.
- Check for impacted teeth.

Adults
- Check teeth annually to monitor and correct wear problems and/or disease.

Geriatric
- Teeth need checking more frequently—three-month intervals are advisable—as the older animal may lose teeth or wear them down to the gums.

Signs of Dental Problems
Difficulty in chewing
Loss of condition • Slow eating
- Loss of appetite • Drooling
- Dropping food while eating
- Bad breath • Facial swelling
- Nasal discharge • Head tossing
- Tooth bump on lower jaw

Common Skin Conditions

The horse is susceptible to many of the same skin conditions as humans, including allergies, dermatitis, fungal infections, and ringworm.

Hives

Hives are round swellings that appear under the skin. These lumps appear very suddenly and may spread rapidly all over the body. They often develop as an allergic reaction to a change in diet. An antihistamine may help. Fortunately, an outbreak of hives disappears as quickly as it appears.

Sweet Itch

Sweet itch, or recurring seasonal dermatitis, is an extremely uncomfortable skin irritation. It mainly affects the mane and tail region but may also occur on the ears, poll, face, chest, and abdomen. It is caused by a hypersensitive reaction to midge bites, and is therefore more common in the summer months. A horse with sweet itch will often rub and bite itself so forcefully that the sores run and bleed. The skin often becomes thickened and scaly, and there is hair loss in the affected areas.

Susceptible horses should be stabled during daylight hours to reduce their exposure to midges. Apply fly repellant regularly to prevent the midges from biting.

Rainrot and Mud Fever

Rainrot and mud fever are both caused by the organism *Dermatophilus congolensis*, which is best described as a cross between a fungus and a bacterium. This organism lives on a horse's skin and thrives in wet and muddy conditions. Rainrot—also known as rain scald—causes lesions to appear on the neck, shoulders, back, and rump. The skin will be covered in scabs and the hair will be matted into clumps. Mud fever occurs on the legs, especially the back of the pastern. The limbs are often hot, swollen, and tender. Keeping your horse clean and dry will help avoid both rainrot and mud fever. Stable if possible during periods of wet weather.

Ringworm

Ringworm is a highly contagious fungal infection. Initial symptoms appear as circular patches of raised hair. These patches increase in size and the hair falls out. The disease is mainly transmitted by direct contact with an infected animal or contaminated equipment. An infected animal should be isolated and treated with a topical medication. Ask your veterinarian for advice. Disinfect all grooming equipment and tack.

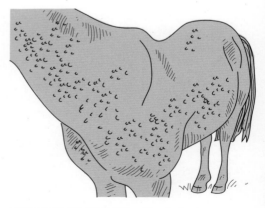

Hives are an allergic reaction either to food or medicine. Their treatment is straightforward.

Common Respiratory Diseases

Respiratory diseases are common in the horse and may be caused by a virus (equine influenza, for example, *see below*), a bacterial infection (pneumonia is a common cause), parasites such as lungworm (*see p. 306*), or an allergy.

Equine Influenza

Equine influenza is a highly infectious viral disease that affects the horse's upper respiratory tract. Secondary infections, such as pneumonia, are common. The disease can spread rapidly through a stable yard, through horse-to-horse contact or via infected rugs, grooming brushes, etc. For this reason, isolate an infected horse to prevent further transmission of the disease and be scrupulous in your stable hygiene.

The horse should be given complete rest, and it should be kept warm in a well-ventilated stable. A good, nourishing diet will help. Secondary infections may be treated with antibiotics.

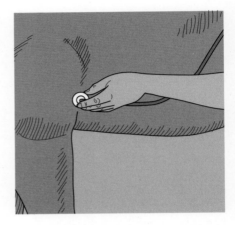

Your veterinarian will listen to your horse's chest for sounds of respiratory distress.

Horses can, and should, be vaccinated against this serious respiratory disease. After the initial vaccination, boosters are generally given at six-monthly intervals. Performance horses may be vaccinated more frequently.

Heaves

Heaves is also known as chronic obstructive pulmonary disease (COPD) or broken wind. It is similar to asthma in human beings and is caused by an allergic reaction to inhaled particles (allergens) such as pollen, dust, or mold. It is rare in warm, dry climates and in Australia and New Zealand where horses spend little time in stables. Heaves causes inflammation and constriction in the airways—the trachea, bronchi, and bronchioles.

A horse with heaves will show labored breathing that gets worse with exercise. Watch a horse's flanks as it breathes out: it will appear to lift its abdomen and "heave" twice—hence the name of the ailment—to

Symptoms of Equine Influenza

Fever—temperature 103–106°F (39.4–41.1°C)

Depression

Exhaustion

Lack of appetite

Nasal discharge

Watery eyes

Coughing

push the air from the lungs through the constricted airways. Other symptoms of heaves include coughing, wheezing, nasal discharge, and intolerance to exercise. Heaves is most commonly seen in horses over the age of six years.

There is no cure for heaves, but good management will minimize symptoms and keep the horse in work. If possible, keep the horse out at pasture. If the animal must be stabled, keep it in a clean and well-ventilated barn. Use shavings not straw for bedding, as straw will exacerbate the ailment. Hay too is a major irritant, so avoid if possible and feed a pelleted alternative, such as alfalfa cubes.

Whistling and Roaring

The terms "whistler" and "roarer" are used to describe horses that can be heard to make an abnormal respiratory noise during exercise. The noise occurs as the horse breathes in, and it varies from a high-pitched whistle to a harsh roar. The noise is generally not heard when the horse is at rest, but is present at faster paces. It is caused by partial or total paralysis of the nerves that move the cartilage on one side—usually the left—of the voice-box, or larynx. The only treatment is surgical, and it involves the removal of pieces of laryngeal tissue. Horses used for light work can usually cope without surgery.

Pneumonia

Pneumonia is a serious, potentially life-threatening disease that requires immediate veterinary attention. It often develops in a horse that has a compromised immune system caused by an ongoing illness, such as influenza or strangles (*see p. 313*). Symptoms include high fever, rapid, shallow breathing, rapid but weak pulse, cough, depression, and loss of appetite. Bacterial infection will generally respond to antibiotics, but viral pneumonia is more difficult to treat. The horse should be kept warm (cover with a blanket unless it is very hot weather) and quiet and be given complete rest.

Contagious Diseases

There are a number of vaccinations that can guard against some of the more serious diseases seen in the horse. Always ask your veterinarian for advice, as a vaccination program will differ according to the number of horses kept together, age, health histories, and the climate and location in which you live. If you intend traveling to other parts of the country or overseas, this must also be taken into account.

Some of the diseases that can be vaccinated against include the following:

Tetanus

Tetanus—also known as lockjaw—is an often fatal disease caused by the *Clostridium tetani* bacterium. The bacterium is present in soil and can gain entry to a horse's bloodstream via puncture wounds, lacerations, and surgical incisions. There will be general body stiffness, and the horse will become highly nervous, reacting to the slightest stimulation. The horse will eventually find it difficult to move its mouth and be unable to eat or swallow, and it is this paralysis that gives the disease the synonym lockjaw. The respiratory muscles also become affected. Treatment is generally unsuccessful, and 80 to 90 percent of clinical cases die. Vaccination against this deadly disease should be given annually, but six-monthly intervals are often recommended. If your horse suffers a wound and it is more than six months after vaccination, give a tetanus booster immediately.

Equine Influenza

Equine influenza is an acute, contagious, respiratory disease (*see p. 310*). The protection offered by the equine flu vaccination deteriorates rapidly, so vaccinate twice to four times a year, depending on the amount of contact your horse has with other horses.

Rhinopneumonitis

Rhinopneumonitis is a respiratory disease caused by the equine herpes virus. It can cause respiratory disease, central nervous disorders, and spontaneous abortion in pregnant mares. Young animals are more at risk, as they have not had time to build up an immunity to the disease. Pregnant mares should be vaccinated at their fifth, seventh, and ninth months of pregnancy with a "killed" virus version of the rhinopneumonitis vaccine. Recommendations for vaccinations are the same as for influenza, and are combined as "flu-rhino."

Potomac Horse Fever

Potomac Horse Fever (PHF) is caused by the bacterium *Neorickettsia risticii* (formerly known as *Ehrlichia risticii*). The disease was first identified in the Potomac River Valley of Maryland, USA, in 1979, although the disease has now spread throughout the USA and to other countries. Outbreaks typically occur in horses that graze near rivers and streams, and it is now thought that horses contract the disease through ingesting infected caddisflies, mayflies, damselflies, dragonflies, and stoneflies. Horses with PHF develop fever and severe diarrhea. Laminitis often follows. There are thought to be at least six strains of PHF. The vaccine has been developed from a single strain, however, and fully vaccinated horses have been known to develop PHF. Check with your veterinarian about the risk factors to your horse. Horses that are traveling a lot, as well as those in the at-risk parts of the USA, should be vaccinated.

Equine Encephalomyelitis

Equine Encephalomyelitis is a mosquito-borne disease that affects the central nervous system. Symptoms include fever, poor appetite, poor muscular coordination, partial or complete blindness, brain swelling, and paralysis. There are numerous strains of the disease, and vaccines are available for three strains: Eastern (EE), Western (WEE), and Venezuelan (VEE). Most horses in the USA are vaccinated against the EE and WEE strains. The vaccine is almost always combined with tetanus vaccine, and these three—two encephalitis strains plus tetanus—make up the commonly used "three-way" vaccine.

West Nile Virus (WNv)

West Nile virus (WNv) is spread by the bite of infectious mosquitoes and causes brain inflammation, encephalitis. Some 40 percent of equine West Nile cases have been fatal, so it is important to protect horses against this virus. After the initial two-shot regimen, an annual booster is the general recommendation. However, in high-exposure areas, some veterinarians recommend booster vaccinations every four to six months during the mosquito season.

> **Did You Know?**
>
> *The incidence of rabies in horses is on the increase in the USA. Cases are 100 percent fatal. There is an inexpensive vaccination available, which should be given annually.*

Equine Viral Arteritis

Equine Viral Arteritis (EVA) causes respiratory-tract symptoms, as well as swelling of the face and limbs. Stallions may have swelling of the sheath and scrotum. EVA can cause abortion, and the disease is transmitted to a mare through the semen of an infected stallion. A live vaccine is available.

Strangles

Strangles is a highly contagious and serious infection, caused by the bacterium *Streptococcus equi*. Strangles is more common in animals under five years of age, especially groups of weanling foals or yearlings. Transmission is through contact with an infected animal or contaminated stable or equipment. Symptoms include apathy, fever, nasal discharge, loss of appetite, and the formation of abscesses around the lymph glands. A live vaccine in the form of an intranasal spray is available, as well as a killed injectable vaccine.

**American Appaloosa Association,
Inc. Worldwide**
P.O. Box 429
Republic, MO 65738
Phone: 417-466-2046
Fax: 417-466-3633
www.amappaloosa.com

**American Association
of Horsemanship Safety**
P.O. Drawer 39
Fentress, TX 78622
Phone: 866-485-6800
Fax: 512-488-2319
www.horsemanshipsafety.com

American Horse Council
1616 H Street NW 7th floor
Washington, DC 20006
Phone: 202-296-4031
Fax: 202-296-1970
www.horsecouncil.org

American Morgan Horse Association
122 Bostwick Road
Shelburne, VT 05482-4417
Phone: 802-985-4944
Fax: 802-985-8897
www.morganhorse.com

American Paint Horse Association
P.O. Box 961023
Fort Worth, TX 76161-0023
Phone: 817-834-APHA (2742)
Fax: 817-834-3152
www.apha.com

American Professional Rodeo Association
P.O. Box 930
Bellefonte, PA 16823-0830
Phone: 814-625-2083
Fax: 814-625-0010
www.apra.com

American Quarter Horse Association (AQHA)
P.O. Box 200
1600 Quarter Horse Drive
Amarillo, TX 79104
Phone: 806-376-4811
www.aqha.com

American Saddlebred Horse Association
4083 Iron Works Parkway
Lexington, KY 40511
Phone: 859-259-2742
Fax: 859-259-1628
www.saddlebred.com

**American Riding Instructors
Association (ARIA)**
28801 Trenton Court
Bonita Springs, FL 34134-3337
Phone: 239-948-3232
Fax: 239-948-5053
www.riding-instructor.com

American Vaulting Association
8205 Santa Monica Blvd. #1-288
West Hollywood, CA 90046
Phone: 323-654 0800 (M-F, 8 a.m. to noon)
Fax: 323-654 4306
www.americanvaulting.org

Appaloosa Horse Club
2720 West Pullman Road
Moscow, ID 83843
Phone: 208-882-5578
www.appaloosa.com

Arabian Horse Association
10805 E. Bethany Drive
Aurora, Colorado 80014
Phone: 303-696-4500
Fax: 303-696-4599
www.arabianhorses.org

Bureau of Land Management
National Wild Horse and Burro Program
Phone: 1-866-4MUSTANGS (toll free)
www.wildhorseandburro.blm.gov

**International Federation
for Equestrian Sports**
Av. Mon-Repos 24
1005 Lausanne
Switzerland
Phone: +41-21-310-47-47
Fax: +41-21-310-47-60
www.fei.ch

The Jockey Club
821 Corporate Drive
Lexington, KY 40503-2794
Phone: 859-224-2700
Fax: 859-224-2710
www.jockeyclub.com

Kentucky Horse Park
International Museum of the Horse
4089 Iron Works Parkway
Lexington, KY 40511
Phone: 859-233-4303
Toll Free: 800-678-8813
Fax: 859-254-0253
www.imh.org

**Missouri Fox Trotting Horse
Breed Association**
P.O. Box 1027
Ava, MO 65608
Phone: 417-683-2468
www.mfthba.com

Pat Parelli
P.O. Box 3729
56 Talisman Dr Suite 6
Pagosa Springs, CO 81147
Phone: 800-642-3335
Fax: 888-731-9722
www.parelli.com

Pinto Horse Association of America, Inc.
7330 NW 23rd Street
Bethany, OK 73008
Phone: 405-491-0111
Fax: 405-787-0773
www.pinto.org

Royal Canadian Mounted Police
www.rcmp-grc.gc.ca

**Tennessee Walking Horse Breeders'
and Exhibitors' Association**
P.O. Box 286
250 N. Ellington Pkwy
Lewisburg, TN 37091
Phone: 931-359-1574
www.twhbea.com

United States Dressage Federation
4051 Iron Works Parkway
Lexington, KY 40511
Phone: 859-971-2277
Fax: 859-971-7722
www.usdf.org

United States Equestrian Federation, Inc.
4047 Iron Works Parkway
Lexington, KY 40511
Phone: 859-258-2472
www.usef.org

United States Pony Clubs, Inc.
4041 Iron Works Parkway
Lexington, KY 40511
Phone: 859-254-7669
Fax: 859-233-4652
www.ponyclub.org

United States Trotting Association
750 Michigan Ave
Columbus, OH 43215
Phone: 877-800-8782 (toll free)
www.ustrotting.com

Index

Index

Index

Index

Index

Acknowledgments

Making horses a part of our lives has opened the doors to innumerable experiences and introduced us to so many good people whom we would like to thank for all the enjoyment and knowledge that they continue to share with us. Gina Karrarigas deserves our special thanks as both a friend and a teacher. Thanks go, too, to all the team that has brought this book to fruition: to Jason, Caroline, and Stephanie at Ivy Press, the illustrators, designer, and picture researcher; to Peter Holmes for his generous advice on hunter-jumper course design; and to Bill Steinkraus for honoring this book with his seal of approval—we even forgive him for knocking Marion and Stroller off the Olympic podium. Last but by no means least, thanks are due to Harry, Blue, Wispa, Rio, and Merrylegs for showing us, through their minor foibles and major strengths, just how different individual horses can be, and for enriching our lives in every sense—except financially.

Color plate credits